THE DISREPUTABLE PLEASURES

Mc-GRAW-HILL RYERSON SERIES IN CANADIAN SOCIOLOGY

General Editor — Lorne Tepperman
Department of Sociology
University of Toronto

Demographic Bases of Canadian Society
Warren Kalbach and Wayne McVey

A Statistical Profile of Canadian Society
Daniel Kubat and David Thornton

Ideological Perspectives on Canada
M. Patricia Marchak

Social Mobility in Canada
Lorne Tepperman

The Canadian Class Structure
Dennis Forcese

Canadian Society in Historical Perspective
S. D. Clark

The Disreputable Pleasures: Crime and Deviance in Canada
John Hagan

FORTHCOMING

Ethnic Group Relations in Canada
Wsevolod Isajiw

Social Change in Canada
Lorna Marsden

Urban Ethnic Communities
Jeffrey G. Reitz

Mass Communication in Canada
Paul Rutherford

Crime in Canada
Lorne Tepperman

Social Psychology as Political Economy
W. P. Archibald

Canadian Families in Comparative Perspective
S. Parvez Wakil

Understanding Data
B. H. Erickson and T. A. Nosanchuk

THE DISREPUTABLE PLEASURES

John Hagan
Department of Sociology
University of Toronto

McGRAW-HILL RYERSON LIMITED

Toronto   Montreal   New York   St. Louis
San Francisco   Auckland   Bogotá   Düsseldorf
Johannesburg   London   Madrid   Mexico
New Delhi   Panama   Paris   São Paulo
Singapore   Sydney   Tokyo

THE DISREPUTABLE PLEASURES:
CRIME AND DEVIANCE IN CANADA

2 3 4 5 6 7 8 9 0 AP 8 9 0 1 2 3 4 5 6 7

Printed and bound in Canada

Canadian Cataloguing in Publication Data

Hagan, John, 1946-
   The disreputable pleasures

ISBN 0-07-082447-9 pa.

1. Deviant behavior.   2. Crime and criminals —
Canada.   3. Social control.   I. Title.

HM291.H14   301.6'2'0971   C76-017099-1

Contents

Contents

Editor's Introduction

The Disreputable Pleasures is a careful, even-handed review of various theories of crime and deviance, written with a facility and good humour that makes it pleasant reading. The book ranges widely over the range of deviant types, of which criminal acts are a subcategory, and it compares Canada to the United States and other countries for which data is available. It thus provides a general framework for considering specific deviant acts in Canada, and for thinking about Canada in relation to its neighbours. No better general introduction to deviance research could be imagined, here or abroad.

Throughout, Professor Hagan shows how the explanation and response to deviance is structured according to one of at least two underlying models of reality: the consensus model and the conflict model. Each model is particularly useful in accounting for some parts of reality and less useful in accounting for others. Thus Hagan's analysis of deviance and crime in Canada becomes a dialogue between these approaches, and no attempt is made here to introduce premature closure. Such a task is left to the reader or to future criminologists. This dialogue does, however, sensitize us to the need to understand deviance and crime in their social context, as acts whose meanings are created in interaction. Very few deviant or criminal acts are unambiguous, in the sense that there is universal agreement as to their "disreputability." This being so, the business of defining, counting, explaining, and responding to deviance is ideologically informed, and because there are many ideologies, so there are many conflicting accounts of deviance, as Hagan shows us.

Looked at from the other side, the business of attaching disrepute to acts which may range, in a "deviate's" mind, from wholly innocuous to intentionally vicious, is an activity needing explanation. Hagan attempts to provide us with some explanation here, although he spends less time on that enterprise than a companion book in this series, *Crime Control: The Urge Toward Authority*. As a result, these two books complement one another for each acknowledges the dual nature of deviant acts while differing in the amount of emphasis given each type of explanation.

I think Professor Hagan's book would deserve a close reading in Canadian universities if only for being the first Canadian textbook in crime and deviance to appear after too many years of collected readings. But *The Disreputable Pleasures* deserves attention for other reasons as well: for its good judgement and common sense, its wit, and its thorough coverage of the sociological literature in the field. Professor Hagan has established a new standard in Canadian writing about deviance and crime, and this book should win justified acclaim.

L.T.

ACKNOWLEDGMENTS

Among my intellectual debts, I would like to acknowledge those most immediate to this book. Many of the lessons I have learned were taught by Gwynn Nettler, James Hackler, Austin Turk, John Clark, and David Bordua. Special thanks go to A. R. Gillis, Rick Linden, Lorne Tepperman, Dan Koenig, Paul Whitehead, Bill Avison, Clifford Shearing, and Charles Hagan for commenting constructively on various parts of the manuscript. Thanks are also due to Lynn McDonald, Jim Giffen, Jim Wilkins, and Richard Ericson for making materials available to me in advance of their publication. Finally, my largest debt is to my wife, Linda, for her patience, good humor, and sound advice.

Thursday, March 27, 1975

PROLOGUE

The title and subtitle of this book require an introduction. The title announces two assumptions we will make in exploring the world of deviance. The first assumption is that in any given society, most behaviors are accorded a socially significant status as either acceptable or unacceptable, reputable or disreputable. A large part of this book is devoted to the causes and consequences of disrepute.

Our second assumption is that most disreputable behaviors involve an element of pleasure, sometimes real and sometimes imagined. Social psychologists remind us that pleasure is experienced in negative as well as positive forms. The positively reinforcing pleasures require no introduction. The negatively reinforcing pleasures range from the "fix" that relieves withdrawal effects, through the defence mechanism that makes "reality" bearable, to the violent act that rejects the unwanted. In other words, the latter pleasures derive primarily from the avoidance of pain.

Some pleasures are experienced by their authors, while others are imagined and attributed by others. In either case, these pleasures become of interest to us when they become the subjects of disrepute. In other words, we are interested in those behaviors that achieve the status of "crime and deviance."

The subtitle of this volume also requires comment. It reflects the fact that this is the first *textbook* to focus on crime and deviance in *Canada*. The first collection of materials on this subject (McGrath, 1965) appeared just over a decade ago. Since then, a variety of materials have become available: several edited books of readings (Boydell, Grindstaff, and Whitehead, 1972, 1975; Mann, 1968, 1971; Haas and Shafir, 1974; and Silverman and Teevan, 1975), a thoughtful commentary on selected aspects of deviance (Vaz, 1976), and an innovative research monograph that takes advantage of some previously untapped Canadian data sources (Tepperman, 1977). However, until recently, the diversity of materials necessary for a textbook discussion has not been available. This is unfortunate.

1

A basic proposition of modern sociology is that deviance varies by social location. Yet, textbook discussions deal predominantly with American materials. Little attention is given to whether American research findings can be applied outside of their national context. We will argue that there are both similarities and differences between the Canadian and American situations. These patterns are explored with the hope of developing a sociology of deviance that is more consistently sensitive to the influence of socially significant— in this case national—boundaries. In this pursuit, it is assumed that a valuable resource of sociology in North America is the possibility of Canadian and American comparisons. To focus on North America is, of course, only a selective first step toward a more fully comparative sociology. Nevertheless, we assume that it is a fundamental first step.

It is important, then, that research is undertaken in Canada, and that the findings of this research are in turn used to expand our understanding of the influence of the social context in which deviance occurs. Our argument is that this undertaking is important not just for Canadians, but for North American sociology more generally. In sum: this book is not intended for Canadian eyes only. It is intended for all who will help to make sense of its subject.

I

DEFINING DEVIANCE:
The Thin Line

Name-calling is a practice of adults, as well as their children. Characteristically, the most interesting of these forms of address are also the least desirable. Our cultural check list is imaginative: we speak, among others, of crooks, gangsters, and hoods; nuts, sluts, and perverts; fiends, fools, and degenerates. All such titles serve a similar purpose: they designate persons and their pleasures as deviant, and therefore as subjects of disrepute.

- But why are some pleasures acceptable, and others disreputable?
- By whom, and how often, are the disreputable pleasures experienced?
- How do we explain deviance and disrepute sociologically?
- What are the pains and pleasures of a disreputable lifestyle?
- How do we, and how should we, respond to deviance and disrepute in Canada?

Answers to these questions help to organize the content of this book. Thus, in succeeding chapters, we will discuss the definition, measurement, explanation, and response to the disreputable pleasures in Canada. In this chapter, we are concerned with the definitions of deviance. Our immediate interest is in determining how individuals and groups draw the line between behaviors considered acceptable, and those considered disreputable. In short, how do we define what is deviant?

Cultural Conceptions of Deviance

Analysts of deviance frequently disagree on the definition of their subject matter. A central factor underlying this disagreement is the variation by culture in what is considered deviant. In this chapter, we will argue that the central themes of a culture are an important

3

influence in determining a society's conceptualization of deviance. It can be noted that contrasting cultural themes are an important part of the Canadian experience, beginning with the fateful meeting of Native Peoples and Euro-Canadian groups, and continuing in a formal national commitment to the goal of multi-culturalism. In particular, the traditions of the Inuit (Eskimo) people of Canada serve as a clear example of the importance of the cultural context in which deviance is defined.

Vivid descriptions of Inuit culture are provided by Cavan (1968), Vallee (1962), and Clairmont (1963). Each of these accounts cites the problem of physical survival in an intemperate environment as a dominant theme in Inuit culture. Cavan notes that there are two types of deviance in Inuit communities, "private wrongs" and "public crimes," with the distinction based on the perceived threat to community survival. Each category reflects striking differences from Euro-Canadian conceptions of deviance.

One of the best known aspects of Inuit culture involved the acceptability of extra-marital sexual relations—so long as the en-counters were authorized by the wife-lending husband. When such liaisons were not so arranged, they became instances of deviance, and therefore a subject of private dispute. Interestingly, in these unauthorized encounters, it was the "other man," rather than the "seduced" wife, who was held accountable. Moreover, the adulterous husband was not considered to have wronged his *own* wife. Revenge, to the point of death, remained the sole prerogative of the offended husband. It is significant to add, however, that an effective restraint on the use of this privilege was that the man who avenged himself by killing the offender was held responsible for the care of the widow and her children.

To this point, we have discussed an example of "non-criminal" deviance in Inuit society. "Private wrongs" became "public crimes" in Inuit culture when the behaviors involved were perceived by the community as constituting a threat to the welfare or survival of the group at large. For example, a person considered guilty of generating conditions of starvation was regarded as a murderer. Pursuing this theme, Cavan (1968) suggests several differences between Inuit and Anglo-Canadian conceptions of criminality.

> Killing another person was not necessarily a crime. The destruction of an old parent or a newborn baby . . . was not a crime. Nor was it a crime to kill the seducer of . . . (one's) wife. But unprovoked killing or a chain of murders that threatened to deplete the supply of men in a community

and therefore endanger the food supply was a serious crime and called for community action (25).*

Thus, many acts held criminal in Euro-Canadian society were not so regarded by the Inuit. Most interesting, however, is a partial reversal in the conceptualization of theft. Hoarding food and possessions beyond one's needs was considered a form of stealing by the Inuit. This was particularly the case during periods of scarcity. However, Vallee (1962) suggests that traditional theft rarely occurred in Inuit communities, and that as a result there were no formal sanctions available when it did occur. Instead, "If someone took something which did not belong to him, it was assumed that he must be in dire need and that he would replace it quietly whenever he could do so." (190.)

A final word should be said about responses to deviance in Inuit society. Sanctions in Inuit communities were predominantly informal. Typical measures included gossip, ridicule, and ostracism (Birket-Smith, 1959). However, in extreme cases threatening the survival of the group, exile or execution were invoked. Such measures followed from a process in which heads of families in the community reached consensus on the threat posed to the group by the offending member. A courtroom description of this process, abstracted from an actual case transcript, is reproduced below.

FIGURE 1-1

The following is abstracted from the court testimony of a prosecution witness in the trial of Shooyook and Aiyaoot, who were tried at Spence Bay in April, 1966, for the "capital murder" of Soosee, the mother of the accused Aiyaoot. Soosee had threatened to kill her husband and everyone else in the band, and had almost killed her child.

CASE TRANSCRIPT

July 6th . . . she started this way. She said there was a hole in her heart. She is the same today on the 7th . . . . Today is the 9th; she's throwing things out of the tent, and she hasn't been sleeping for awhile. She's keeping wandering around and

*Reprinted with permission of J.B. Lippincott Co.

not doing any sleeping . . . . She's throwing rocks, and pulling her hair out. It looks as if she's going to kill her husband, and she's throwing rocks at us all, and blowing her breath. We love her, but we have to tie her up . . . . She gets out of the ropes that she's tied up with. The ropes she was tied up with are all laying outside and we tied her up again. She said she is going to kill us, and we love our children. We are afraid she is going to kill all. We are running away, and have only taken two tents. We are getting ready in a hurry to go to the island. We are sleeping on the island today, today is the 13th. In the morning we saw her outside. We are scared to go to her. She is knocking down the tents, and knocking down the aerial masts . . . . We are going hungry, as we are unable to go hunt meat. Sometimes we manage to get one seal to eat during the day. All this time she is pulling her hair . . . . She also walks in the creek without any boots on. She slaps the ground all around her . . . . She wants to kill us, but we don't want to die now . . . . Why she is doing this we don't know, but she is made to do these things by the devil . . . . God in Heaven is the only one that we can ask to help us . . . . The only thing to do now is for someone to go after her. If she runs away she will not be hurt, and they will not do anything to her. If she comes after them she will be shot, because we are really afraid of her, because she has been saying that she is going to kill everyone, everybody . . . . When she saw them she came towards them. We wanted to look after our children, and we do not want them to get killed. She came after them so she's being shot. She did not die for a long while. She only died after she was shot three times. We knew the police would not like this, but she would have killed a lot of people. That's the reason why we killed her. We all get together and pray . . . .

The jury found Aiyaoot not guilty, and Shooyook, who fired the gun, guilty of manslaughter, "with a strong plea for leniency in sentence." (cited in Schmeiser, 1972:8-9.)*

Of course, cultural traditions are subject to change. This is one reason why the previous paragraphs were written in the past tense. Our attention shifts next, then, to some of the conditions productive of changes in Inuit culture, and consequent changes in definitions of deviance.

Reprinted with permission of Douglas A. Schmeiser.

When Cultures Collide

Cultural differences in conceptions of deviance become dramatically apparent when the cultures themselves come into contact. This process again is seen most clearly in northern Canada. As the Native Peoples of the north followed economic and welfare inducements to settle in the emerging communities of the Northwest Territories (Davis, 1965), they found their cultural traditions weakening under the pressure of an alien lifestyle. For example, Inuit sexual customs, with the absence of even a term for illegitimacy, facilitated the abuse of native women by migrant workers. Under the pressure of the consequences, new sexual mores are emerging (Cavan, 1968:37). Similarly, the Inuit were exposed and engulfed in the problems of alcoholism without a cultural background that either condoned or condemned use of the foreign substance. New norms are emerging here as well (Honingmann, 1965). Finally, previously functional customs involving infanticide, abandonment of the elderly, and the solicitation of community approval for the execution or exile of threatening individuals are largely artifacts of a cultural past.

In all of this, the Canadian courts have played a confusing, and sometimes coercive, role in imposing Anglo-Canadian conceptions of deviance on Inuit communities. One misguided example of this process, involving game and wildlife laws, is cited by Schmeiser (1972):

> ... Matthew Koonungnak ... of Baker Lake, Northwest Territories, was charged with hunting musk-ox contrary to the Game Ordinance. Koonungnak had never before seen a musk-ox, and the animal was approaching his camp. In order to protect the camp, and on the advice of another Eskimo, Koonungnak shot it. He subsequently came to the police department ... to advise the police what had happened, took the police to his camp, and was then charged with the offence. When he appeared before the Justice of the Peace, he readily admitted shooting the animal, and further stated that if he ever saw another musk-ox and it came towards him he would shoot it. The Justice of the Peace interpreted these statements as a plea of guilty, and imposed a fine of $200.00 or four months in jail in default of the payment.*

On appeal, the decision was reversed. One reason given for the reversal involved the acceptance of an invalid guilty plea. The Inuit people apparently have no corresponding word in their language

*Reprinted with permission of Douglas A. Schmeiser.

for the term "guilty." The appellate judge further found that the defendant acted in self-defence, noting that, "It is notorious in the north . . . that an outcast bull musk-ox driven from the herd and wandering in the barrens alone and homeless is a dangerous animal." (Schmeiser, 1972:4.)[1]

The lesson of this episode is that conceptions of deviance are relative to culture and circumstance. Divergent conceptions become particularly problematic when cultures come into close and continued contact. It is extremely doubtful that any enduring solution can be found for such problems. More likely is a continuing pattern of compromise, conflict, and coercion. It is this underlying tension that makes conceptualization of deviance, for purposes of study, as well as day-to-day living, so difficult.

Six Sociological Approaches to the Definition of Deviance

Responses of sociologists to the problems of cultural variation are seen in six approaches to the definition of our subject matter. The six approaches include: (1) a legal-consensus definition, (2) a socio-legal definition, (3) a cross-cultural definition, (4) a statistical definition, (5) a labelling definition, and (6) a utopian-conflict definition. A critical review of the six viewpoints follows. Then, elements of the six viewpoints are combined in a new definition. We will argue that this last approach is best suited to the task of explaining deviance and its control.

The Legal-Consensus Approach. The most articulate advocate of a legalistic definition of deviance was the lawyer-sociologist Paul Tappan (1947). Tappan insisted that we limit our study to criminality as it is legally constructed: "Crime is an intentional act in violation of the criminal law . . . committed without defence or excuse, and penalized by the state . . . . " (100.)[2] He insisted further that persons studied as criminals must be adjudicated (i.e., convicted) as such. Acknowledging that cultures vary in what they call criminal, Tappan argued that governing statutes provide the only clear and definitive indication of what any specific cultural group holds deviant: "Here we find *norms* of conduct, comparable to mores, but considerably more distinct, precise, and detailed . . . . " (100.)[3] In short, Tappan is suggesting that the criminal law provides a reliable guide to what is consensually defined as deviant in any given society.

The salient difficulty with Tappan's approach is that it systematically ignores much of what many analysts of deviance wish to study: the non-criminal but nonetheless disreputable pleasures of various deviant lifestyles. At the same time, the legal-consensus approach neglects the basic issue of why some acts are legislated as criminal, while others remain only informally the subject of disrepute. Further, this approach misinforms us in suggesting that legal definitions clearly reflect societal consensus about what is deviant. This is conspicuously the case in Canada, where the Criminal Code has gone largely unrevised for more than 80 years. Finally, being legally called a criminal depends on getting caught and convicted. This sampling process results in not only a narrowly defined, but also a non-representative, collection of subjects (more correctly called "captives") for study.

The Socio-Legal Approach. Edwin Sutherland (1945) suggested a relaxation of legal criteria that allowed an expansion of attention to various "anti-social behaviors." Retained, however, was an emphasis on criminality, as designated by two explicit criteria: "legal description of acts as socially injurious and legal provision of a penalty for the act." (132.)[4] Sutherland demonstrated with the use of these criteria that it is possible to consider "criminal" many unethical business practices handled in the civil courts. The demonstration consisted of a comparative analysis of the procedures and punishments used in the prosecution of corporate interests in the civil and criminal courts. The conclusion is that, ". . . the criteria which have been used in defining white-collar crimes are not categorically different from the criteria used in defining other crimes. . . ." (135.)[5]

Sutherland's redefinition of the field of study facilitated a new and important emphasis in criminological research on the economic crimes of "upperworld" offenders. However, his reluctance to widen the scope of attention beyond statutory matters leaves his definition open to two earlier criticisms of the legalistic approach: first, non-criminal forms of deviance continue unnoticed; second, like the criminal courts, the civil court dockets probably represent a biased sample of illegal enterprises. Finally, it should be noted that Sutherland's emphasis on white-collar crime neglects undetected occupational indiscretions among workers of lesser social status (Horning, 1970).

A Cross-Cultural Approach. Thorsten Sellin (1938) proposed a definition of deviance that extends attention beyond the realm of law. His argument is that every group has its own standards of behavior called "conduct norms," and that these standards are not necessarily embodied in law. "For every person, then, there is from the point of view of a given group of which he is a member, a normal (right) and an abnormal (wrong) way of reacting, the norm depending upon the social values of the group which formulated it." (30.)[6] Beyond this, however, Sellin argued that there are some conduct norms that are *invariant* across *all* cultural groups. Further, he insisted that these norms were the appropriate focus for research: "Such study would involve the isolation and classification of norms into *universal categories* transcending political and other boundaries, a necessity imposed by the logic of science." (30.)[7]

Unfortunately, Sellin did not specify what the universal conduct norms might be. The weakness of his strategy is the dubious proposition that such norms can be found, either inside or outside of the law. The lesson of a large body of anthropological research is that norms of conduct are remarkably varied, with the universals of human behavior, if any, limited primarily to the trivial necessities of everyday life. Universal *and* non-trivial conduct norms probably cannot be found.

A Statistical Approach. Wilkins (1964) suggests a more plausible approach to our subject matter, while remaining attentive to the problem of cultural variation. He begins with the assumption that, "At some time or another, some form of society . . . has defined almost all forms of behavior that we now call 'criminal' as desirable for the functioning of that form of society." (46.)[8] Wilkins then takes as his criterion of deviance the frequency with which various forms of behavior occur in any particular society. Said simply, high frequency behaviors are considered normal, and low frequency behaviors deviant. The resulting definition of deviance is thus pictured in the form of a normal bell-shaped curve presented in Figure 1-2: "It may be supposed that the model given by the normal frequency distribution shown in this chart represents the distribution of ethical content of human action." (47.)[9] Serious crimes and saintly acts form the two extremes in this definition. The range of additional acts to be considered deviant remains at the discretion of the researchers.

One weakness of this approach lies in its simplicity. While infrequency of behavior is one measure of deviance, the statistical approach neglects the role of societal groups in selecting from infrequent acts those considered undesirable. Obviously, all infrequent

FIGURE 1-2

CONTINUUM OF GOOD AND BAD ACTS

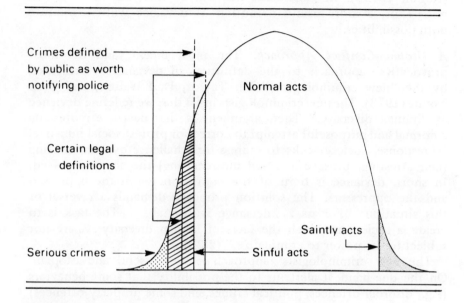

Crimes defined by public as worth notifying police

Normal acts

Certain legal definitions

Saintly acts

Serious crimes

Sinful acts

Reprinted with permission of Associated Book Publishers, Ltd.
Source: Wilkins (1964:47)

occurrences are not designated as deviant or criminal. Beyond this, "saintly acts" are seldom of interest to analysts of deviance, unless the acts become problematic for those who observe them. What is required, then, is an addition of analytical content to the quantitative framework provided.

The Labelling Approach. If the statistical approach minimizes the importance of the societal response, the labelling approach clearly does not. Howard Becker (1963) provides a concise statement of this viewpoint: "The deviant is one to whom that label has successfully been applied; deviant behavior is behavior that people so label." (9.) Becker's point is that behaviors are not recognized as deviant unless others, as members of cultural groups, react to them as such. This approach is important in making us aware of the significance of the ways in which we respond to deviance. However, as a definition of deviance, the labelling approach also creates problems.

Bordua (1969) observes that the labelling definition tends to make deviance "all societal response, and no deviant stimulus." His point is that the labelling approach characteristically assumes a passive subject who plays little or no part in eliciting a response (Hagan, 1973b). In some cases this will be true, but often it will not. Thus, a more useful definition of deviance will incorporate both possibilities.

A Utopian-Conflict Approach. The most recent, and the most provocative, approach to the definition of deviance is presented by the "new criminologists," Ian Taylor, Paul Walton, and Jock Young (1973). The new criminologists insist that we redefine deviance as "human diversity." Their argument is that deviance represents a normal and purposeful attempt to correct or protest social injustice. In response, society seeks to repress this challenge by criminalizing (i.e., arresting, prosecuting, and incarcerating) the actors involved. In short, deviance is born of the conflict between the oppressed and the oppressors. The solution proposed demands a reversal of this situation: "For us, . . . deviance is normal . . . . The task is to create a society in which the facts of human diversity . . . are not subject to the power to criminalize." (282.)

The new criminologists' approach is both useful and utopian. On the one hand, it alerts us to the possibility that some behaviors (e.g., disorder offences, political crimes, and some property offences) may be called deviant or criminal because they are offensive or threatening to privileged segments of society. On the other hand, to assume all acts of deviance, particularly the most serious (e.g., murder, rape, and child abuse), are justifiable artifacts of a politically meaningful lifestyle is utopian. As students *and* potential victims of deviance, the issue is one of how far we can go, while still wishing to live in the society of our design. In short, there is a crucial difference between ranting and raping, and it is essential that our definition of deviance, however imperfectly, make this type of distinction.

What, then, is the appropriate definition of deviance? Our approach follows.

Defining Deviance as a Continuous Variable

Our basic definition is simple: deviance consists of variation from a social norm. Our further argument is that the many varieties of deviance can be divided and sub-divided into several categories, and that these categories in turn can be conceived theoretically as ranging from those considered least to most serious in any given society. This can be said more concretely. There is an obvious difference in our society between multiple murder and adolescent marijuana use. We are saying further that most deviant acts can be located empirically on a continuum of seriousness between these two extremes. It is true that not all persons or groups, in any given society, will agree, or have strong feelings about, the wrongfulness of each act. For example, most persons will have no strong feelings about whether it is "right" or "wrong" to dress in "erotic clothing," or, even more to the point, about what "erotic clothing" is. However, this in itself is our first measure of seriousness: the degree of agreement about the wrongfulness of an act. This assessment can vary from confusion and apathy, through high levels of disagreement, to conditions of general agreement. We will regard this as an index of agreement about the norm.

Our second measure of seriousness is the severity of the social response elicited by the act. Social penalties vary from public execution to polite avoidance, with a range of responses in between. The more severe the penalty prescribed, and the more extensive the support for this sanction, the more serious is the societal evaluation of the act.

Our third measure of seriousness involves a societal evaluation of the harm inflicted by the act. Some possibly harmful acts, for example drug abuse, seem largely personal in their consequences, and therefore are increasingly regarded as "victimless." Other acts, like gambling, are "victimless" in the sense that the persons involved frequently are willing and anxious participants. Finally, some acts, for example most crimes of violence, are more clearly interpersonal, or social, in their consequences. Here there is also a more definite sense of victimization, although the issue is sometimes resolved by nothing more than who first had access to the most effective weapon. Thus, much of the debate that goes into an evaluation of harmfulness is concerned with the degree of victimization and the personal or social harm that a set of acts may involve.

Our argument is that in most modern societies the three measures of seriousness are closely correlated. In other words, the more serious acts of deviance are likely to involve (a) broad agreement about the wrongfulness of such acts, (b) a severe social response, and (c) an evaluation as being very harmful. This situation can be visualized (see Figure 1-3) in the form of a pyramid, with the less serious forms of deviance at the base, the more serious forms of deviance at the peak, and each vertical axis representing one of our measures of seriousness. The form of this pyramid suggests that the most serious acts of deviance in a society tend also to be less frequent, while less serious acts may be considerably more common. Acts included in the pyramid include two general categories (criminal and non-criminal forms of deviance) and four subdivisions (consensual crimes and conflict crimes; social deviations and social diversions). Although the division between these categories is imprecise, each can be discussed individually.

FIGURE 1-3

THE VARIETIES OF DEVIANCE

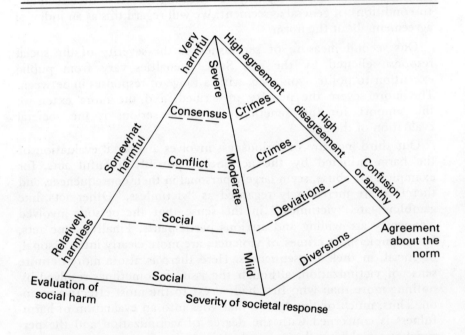

The Varieties of Deviance

Our discussion proceeds generally from the most to the least serious forms of deviance. It needs to be emphasized, however, that this designation of seriousness is empirically, rather than ethically, determined. Many students of deviance point out that unethical, but non-criminal, business practices are often morally more serious than the rapes, robberies, or even murders of individuals. They argue, for example, that unethical multi-national business arrangements can create conditions of poverty, inhumanity, degradation, and famine. From an ethical viewpoint, these arguments are important.

However, our interest is not in creating a universal scale of immorality. Our goal is to describe and explain the institutionalization and the violations of the norms of an existing social order, specifically as it is represented in Canada. Our results will likely be relevant to, but not sufficient for, the formation of moral judgments.

Criminal Forms of Deviance

The most serious forms of deviance are defined by law as criminal. The first Criminal Code of Canada was enacted by Parliament in 1892 and has remained largely unchanged for nearly 80 years. The Code was based largely on Sir James Stephen's English Draft Code, which, ironically, was never adopted in the United Kingdom.

The administration of criminal law in Canada is governed by the British North America Act. This act assigns to the federal government the power to make criminal laws, and allots administrative responsibilities to the provinces (Hogarth, 1971). Ideally, this would mean that the federal government creates law, while the provinces apply it. However, as we will discover later in this chapter, there are instances where applying the law involves a process of *re*creation. Nonetheless, it can probably be said that the criminal law in Canada is more consistent across local boundaries than it is in the United States, where most powers to enact criminal law reside with the individual states.

The Consensus Crimes. Our attention is directed first to the crimes that concern most of us, the more visible, predatory crimes. Legal philosophers at one time characterized such acts of deviance as *mala en se*—"wrong in themselves." However, modern sociologists emphasize that few, if any, human behaviors are universal or timeless in their criminal character. Nonetheless, for several centuries most Western societies have shown considerable consensus in designating as criminal a select group of behaviors. Among the most easily listed of these offences are premeditated murder, violent rape, incest, and kidnapping. Not surprisingly, research by Akman, Normandeau, and Turner (1967) reveals that American, English Canadian, and French Canadian populations rank the relative seriousness of such offences similarly (see also Rossi *et al.*, 1974).

It is essential to note that this group of behaviors, called by Toby (1974) the "consensual crimes," is neither immutably nor permanently criminal. Nonetheless, the fact that such behaviors have been consensually defined as crimes for successive generations makes them of primary interest to some sociologists. These sociologists ask the same question posed by an outraged and scared public: why do persons dare to defy the social rules that so many of us feel so strongly about? In the following chapters, we will argue that the consensus theories answer this question best. Meanwhile, we turn our attention next to a second·variety of deviance.

The Conflict Crimes. Continuing controversy surrounds the presence of many offences in our Criminal Code. These crimes are sometimes referred to as *mala prohibita,* or "wrong by prohibition," for example, as proscribed and punished by statute. As one moves away from the statutes, however, it becomes clear that public opinion is divided about the appropriate status of such offences. Most importantly, social class and interest groups are the frequently cited roots of such conflict. The sociological concern is that the criminal law may be used by one class or interest group to the disadvantage of another.

Included in a non-exhaustive list of the conflict crimes are the public disorder offences (malicious mischief, vagrancy, and creating a public disturbance), chemical offences (alcohol and narcotics offences), political crimes (treason, sedition, sabotage, espionage, subversion, and conspiracy), minor property offences (petty theft, shoplifting, and vandalism), and the "right-to-life" offences (abortion and euthanasia). The feature that unites these offences is the public debate that surrounds them. This is a different way of saying that we lack societal consensus on the dimensions of public disorder, the use of comforting chemicals, permissible politics, the protection of private property, and the limits of life. Lacking this consensus, many of us, given the opportunity or need, may feel free to deviate.

The important feature of conflict crimes, then, is that the persons involved are less likely than those who commit consensual crimes to differ in significant ways from the general population. For example, Turk (1977) notes that, ". . . political criminals are extremely diverse in regard to their origins, motivations, character traits, activities, sophistication, and effectiveness."[10] He concludes " . . . that there is probably nothing distinctive about political criminals apart from the fact that they happen to have been identified as current or potential political threats."[11]

It is not surprising, then, that sociologists are less interested in asking why individuals are involved in conflict crimes, and more concerned with the reasons why such persons are considered criminals by law. We will argue in following chapters that this second type of question is best answered by the conflict theories of deviance. Further we will argue that these theories are also of assistance in explaining the status of the non-criminal forms of deviance.

Non-Criminal Forms of Deviance

The non-criminal forms of deviance depend for their definition on the informal processes of social control. In other words, it is the family, peers, and other community groups that guide our impressions of the normal and the abnormal, the good life and the bad. Violations of the resulting norms can be considered in two groups: the social deviations and the social diversions.

Social Deviations. The most frequent forms of social deviation are of three types: adolescent (juvenile delinquency), interpersonal (psycho-social disturbances), and vocational (non-criminal violations of public and financial trust). The theme uniting these experiences is that although they are not considered criminal, they are nonetheless disreputable. Of particular interest is the stigma that may follow contact with the non-criminal agencies of social control: the juvenile courts, psychiatric agencies, and the civil courts. Each of these institutions formally attempts to minimize its stigmatizing effects. Juvenile courts "treat" rather than convict "delinquents"; psychiatric agencies protect the identities of their patients; and the civil courts forego criminal procedures in processing "technical violators." These efforts vary in their effectiveness, and sociologists are particularly interested in determining how access to personal resources affects these outcomes. The concern, for example, is that while doctors can be found in malpractice without experiencing a loss of income, "common criminals" may encounter a stigma that makes earning their future livelihoods more difficult (Schwartz and Skolnick, 1964).

A second sociological concern is that the boundaries of social deviation are remarkably vague. For example, Tappan (1960) finds typical definitions of delinquency so uncertain that, " . . . to a great extent delinquency is what the particular court says it is." (393.) A similar situation exists in relation to mental illness. For example, in Ontario, New Brunswick, and Newfoundland, mental illness is defined simply as " . . . any disease or disability of the mind." Marshall and Hughes (1974:163) note the similarity between these Canadian criteria of mental illness and those offered in Shakespeare's *Hamlet*: " . . . what is it but to be nothing else but mad." The trouble with such definitions, of course, is that they are circular, offering only vague guidance for those who must distinguish the sane from the insane, the delinquent from the non-delinquent.

Doubting the accuracy with which psychiatrists distinguish the sane from the insane, Rosenhan (1973) designed a unique study to test these skills. Rosenhan and eight other individuals with histories free from mental disorder sought admission to twelve different psychiatric hospitals. Each person complained of fictional symptoms (hearing voices saying "empty, hollow, thud") resembling no known form of mental illness. Despite the fictitious symptoms, all of the pseudo-patients were diagnosed as schizophrenics. Immediately following admission, the pseudo-patients ceased to report symptoms and resumed what they regarded as a normal pattern of behavior. After an average period of more than two weeks, all of the pseudo-patients were released as "schizophrenics in remission." None of the individuals, in other words, was discovered *sane*.

Nettler (1974b) properly notes that these results do not indicate that there *are* no differences between the sane and the insane, but rather that mental hospital personnel may often *overlook* them. One source of such errors of omission may be the quality of our operating definitions; another source may be the incapacity of patients to demand their caretakers' attention. Meanwhile, Nettler offers some parting advice: "Never let yourself fall into the hands of the 'official helper.' You won't like it." (1974a:31.)

Social Diversions. The social diversions are frequent and faddish, ranging from harmless acts (e.g., talking to plants and animals) to dangerous feats (e.g., "the Alka-Seltzer Screw," *"Playboy* Advisor," 1975:35). Two types of diversions are of particular interest, the sexual (the homo-, hetero-, and autosexual pleasures) and the symbolic (clothing, speech, and mannerisms).

The motivations for diversion are universal: the search for personal stimulation and social reinforcement. However, our thresholds of boredom and isolation vary. Thus, Evel Knievel, an acknowledged taste-setter in the world of dangerous diversions, summarizes an independent thinker's appetite for the diverse: "My life is exciting, but my death will be glorious." (Toronto *Star,* 1974:A7.) Most of us are more sociable in our search for stimulation.

Among the more sociable diversions are the sexual. Foreshadowing a new and bold approach to the study of such deviance, Kinsey revolutionalized our conceptions of sexuality by asking (personally!) more than 7 000 respondents how often they did what to whom. The resulting sexual statistics demonstrated that the erotic pleasures are socially conditioned. For example, Kinsey showed that males of different social, educational, and economic levels, as well as of different generations and religious beliefs, varied in their sexual behavior patterns. In addition, Kinsey established the near universal incidence of masturbation among adolescents, and developed a continuum approach to the measurement of homo- and heterosexual behavior. These findings not only informed, but probably also altered, norms of sexual behavior (Boorstein, 1973).

Studies of the symbolic diversions, including styles of dress, speech, and mannerism, are less common. Among the most interesting of these, however, are the studies of slang and its use in various groups. Linguists typically distinguish two types of slang: argot and cant. Argot refers to slang used for technical purposes and the encouragement of group solidarity by non-criminal groups. Cant, on the other hand, is the slang presumably used by a criminal group to conceal its purposes and activities from outsiders. Polsky (1969:100) points out, however, that the use of slang for the latter purpose—secrecy—is not common in North America. Instead, the slang of criminals and conformists alike probably best serves a more common social purpose: the separation of "us" from "them." For example, in the manner of most professional groups, Letkemann (1973) reports that the more experienced and highly skilled offenders in Canadian prisons refer to themselves as "rounders," thus distinguishing themselves from their less esteemed associates.

Much argot enhances group solidarity at the expense of potential victims. For example, con artists refer to their customers as "marks," prostitutes market their wares to "tricks," and pool hustlers label their victims "suckers"—unless they return repeatedly, for which they earn the special status of "fish." (Polsky, 1969:105.) The common use of these and related terms in the socially acceptable professions is a reminder of the frequently thin line between the "legitimate" and "illegitimate" vocations. In both instances, the presumed result of using these terms of reference is to increase the sense of social solidarity. For the sociologist of deviance, the interest is in understanding how related modes of diversion, including dress and demeanor, similarly contribute to social, group-related needs.

We have considered a wide range of deviant acts, from the less frequent consensual crimes, to the very common social diversions. We have argued that among the varieties of deviance, the criminal forms are the more serious, and the non-criminal forms less so. This conclusion was not founded on a moral evaluation of the acts involved, but rather it was based on an index measuring the perception of harm, agreement about the norm, and the severity of societal response to infractions. The placement of persons and acts within sub-categories of this scale will necessarily vary by time, place, and circumstance. An example will help to clarify this point.

In Canada, during and immediately following the kidnapings and murder that provoked the October Crisis of 1970, active involvement in the *Front de Libération du Québec (F.L.Q.)* nearly achieved the status of a consensual crime. During this period, the Quebec government utilized powers of the War Measures Act to arrest 453 citizens on suspicion of seditious conspiracy to overthrow the government. In November of 1970, the Canadian Institute of Public Opinion conducted a cross-country poll revealing that 86.6 per cent of those interviewed approved of the government's implementation of the War Meaures Act for the purpose of suppressing the F.L.Q. (Crysdale and Beattie, 1973:187.) With the advantage of retrospection, many Canadians would today probably express a less supportive view. Thus, categorizing most F.L.Q. activities of this period as conflict or consensual crimes will depend on what level of agreement we designate as consensus and the time period we consider.

The lesson of this example is that our conceptualization of deviance is dependent for its validity on the context in which it is applied. In addition, the categories imposed on our continuum of deviance are defined by flexible boundaries, indicating the shifting nature of the designations involved. Thus, to speak of one act as a social diversion and another as a social deviation is a matter of convenience, indicating the approximate location of an act on the larger continuum. The purpose of this strategy is to acknowledge the changeable character of deviance, without losing sight of the seriousness of a specific act, within its particular context.

In all of this, probably the most important change that can occur in the societal evaluation of an act involves the movement from criminal to non-criminal status. An important question to ask, then, is why some deviant acts elicit a criminal response, while others do not. In short, what are the social conditions that move deviant acts back and forth between criminal and non-criminal status?

The Social Construction of Criminality

Societies vary in what they call criminal. This variation is linked to the themes that dominate a society. Thus, we noted that in Inuit society, acts became criminal when they threatened the physical survival of the community. We noted also that in almost all modern societies some serious violations of person and property are held criminal. Beyond the most serious consensual crimes, however, there are marked variations in the acts legislated as punishable. In the following discussion, we demonstrate that self-interested groups are frequently active in the law-making process. It is noted further that as groups act on their interests, they commonly mobilize central societal themes on their behalf (cf., Hopkins, 1975). This process is discussed in terms of legislation defining juvenile delinquency, vagrancy, and narcotics abuse.

Juvenile Delinquency. In Canada, the first Juvenile Delinquents Act was passed in 1908. Although this act followed by several years similar legislation in the United States, the origin of the actual institutions involved is subject to historical debate. Hagan and Leon (1976) note that in a 1933 *Mail and Empire* article (see Figure 1-4),

FIGURE 1-4

JUVENILE COURT HAD TORONTO ORIGIN

By Fred Williams

DO YOU KNOW that while Chicago is credited with establishing the first juvenile court and Judge Ben Lindsay of Denver, who entered the field a year later, is regarded as the great apostle of the movement it was really a Canadian enterprise, appropriated by social workers of the big American city?

The actual fact is that Toronto was the first city on the continent to establish a children's court. It was inaugurated here in 1894 as a juvenile branch of the adult court presided over by Colonel Denison, but later Alderman John Baxter was appointed by the Government as commissioner to deal with youthful offenders.

The beginning of the juvenile court law is to be found in an Ontario Statute passed by the Legislature in February, 1888, the section reading as follows: "The Lieutenant-Governor may, upon the request of any municipal council, appoint a commissioner or commissioners, each with the powers of a police magistrate, to hear and determine complaints against juvenile offenders, apparently under the age of sixteen years."

The plan to remove children entirely from the adult courts was amplified in the Children's Protection Act passed by the Ontario Legislature in 1893. As the province could not legislate on criminal matters a supplementary Dominion act was passed in 1894, promoted in the Senate by the Hon. G.W. Allan. This legislation applied only to Ontario, and in view of the general desire for better methods of saving delinquent children from criminal pursuits the Dominion Parliament in July, 1908, placed on the statute books a juvenile court law applicable to all Canada.

The various world-wide conferences held during the World's Fair had an important bearing on the Juvenile Court movement. On October 11, 1893, in the Hall of Washington at the Memorial Art Palace, Michigan Avenue, Chicago, J.J. Kelso, Superintendent of Neglected and Dependent Children of Ontario, was invited to give an address before the Waif-Saving Association of America. The president of this conference was General Russel A. Alger of Detroit; the treasurer, L.D. Drake of Boonville, Mo.; secretary, T.E. Daniels, and recording secretary, J.A. Fraser of Chicago. Mr. Kelso explained the Children's Aid work as carried on in Ontario and in the course of his address said:

"The Ontario Children's law also provides for a Children's Court which is in every sense of the word a private court. This court is presided over by a judge of a court of record, and every time the child is brought in its parents or guardians must be there also. In case any person has reason to believe that a child is being ill used all he has to do is to report his suspicions to any person competent to sit as a judge in the Children's Court who thereupon issues a warrant upon which the officer of the Children's Aid Society may investigate the matter and summon the parents or guardians to court."

This extract is taken from the printed report of the Waif-Saving Association. The following day the Chicago Tribune gave a report in which it said: "J.J. Kelso of Toronto, who is the official guardian of dependent children in the Province of Ontario, gave the Waif-Saving Congress an interesting account of the provincial law for the protection of children. This law provides for every contingency possible to anticipate in the life of an unfortunate child. The province has a superintendent or guardian and a children's court is provided where boys and girls under 14 are tried in private for alleged offences. No begging or selling of small articles by children is permitted. Girls are not allowed to sell papers or any other article under any circumstances."

There was considerable discussion and advocacy in Chicago in the following two or three years until finally a committee was appointed under the guidance of Hon. Harvey B. Hurd to formulate a suitable Juvenile Court law for Illinois. This was passed in 1897 and soon after the Chicago Court was opened. Inspired by this good example, Ben Lindsay, a young lawyer in Denver, just elected Judge of the Probate Court, threw himself into the movement with such enthusiasm that he soon made it widely known. He has always given due credit to J.J. Kelso of Toronto.

Source: Mail and Empire, *Oct. 4, 1933:6. By permission of the* Globe and Mail, *Toronto.*

the juvenile court was labelled a "Canadian enterprise" that had been "appropriated by American social workers." The argument is that a Canadian journalist, J.J. Kelso, addressed the Waif-Saving Association of America in 1893, focusing on the development of the Children's Court in Toronto. An extract from this speech appeared in the *Chicago Tribune* on the following day and is said to have formed the basis of discussions that led over a several year period to the first Chicago Juvenile Court. The truth or falsity of this claim is difficult to determine. However, Hagan and Leon note that more important than the issue of origin is the more general indication of a close connection between the development of American and Canadian juvenile justice systems.

Anthony Platt (1969) links the background of juvenile justice legislation in the United States to the activities of the American "child saving movement." The initial participants in this movement were primarily middle and upper class feminist reformers who were concerned with the care and fate of lower class youth. Arguing in a manner that parodies today's "chauvinist," feminists of the period insisted that, " . . . even if a woman's place was in the home, she was certainly entitled to give her opinion on garbage disposal, cleanliness of the streets, and the care and education of children" (Platt, 1969).12 Platt appropriately notes that feminists of this period were not challenging to any great extent basic assumptions about the woman's role in society. Nonetheless, the movement was successful in creating a new set of careers for women—juvenile court work, counselling, and social work—while reinforcing dominant societal themes stressing motherhood and the care of children.

In Canada, Hagan and Leon (1977) note that three periods preceded the passage of delinquency legislation: an initial period in which lengthy stays in reformatories replaced sentences spent in common gaols; a second period during which treatment-focused industrial schools began to replace reformatories; and a third period when probation emerged as a new treatment strategy influential in the development of delinquency legislation. Advocates of probation, as members of a growing treatment bureaucracy, formed an interest group that worked energetically for a juvenile court system that they would later help to operate. However, they were opposed by a second interest group, the police, who to this point had predominated in the handling of juveniles. A report prepared by members of the Toronto force charged that the new proposals:

> . . . work upon the sympathies of philanthropic men and women for the purpose of introducing a jellyfish and abortive system of law enforcement, whereby the judge or magistrate is expected to come down to the level of the incorrigible

street arab and assume an attitude absolutely repulsive to British subjects. The idea seems to be that by profuse use of slang phraseology he should place himself in a position to kiss and coddle a class of perverts and delinquents who require the most rigid disciplinary and corrective methods to ensure the possibility of their reformation (Archibald, 1907:5).

Nonetheless, the reformers prevailed in passing the Juvenile Delinquents Act of 1908. Under the current version of this act, children are considered in a "state of delinquency" if they violate a provision of the Criminal Code, or any other statute or by-law, if they are guilty of sexual immorality, or any similar form of vice, or if they are liable by reason of any other illegal act under the provisions of any provincial statutes. In short, much of the fun of adolescence is made illegal and punishable by this act!

Cousineau and Veevers (1972b) have provided a description of recent Canadian efforts to replace the Juvenile Delinquents Act with a Young Offenders Act. In essence, the Young Offenders Act was an effort to introduce legal safeguards into the processing of juveniles in the courts. Advocates of the act in the House of Commons described it as a "bill of rights for young people." However, in the protracted debate that followed, the Canadian Mental Health Association seemed to assume the role previously filled by the American child saving movement. Representing various treatment groups, the association argued that the pressing psychological needs of young people should take precedence over the delays involved in following formal legal procedures. In the view of this group, the new act would have wasted valuable treatment time with unnecessary court hearings. Critics will note that this position is protective of the interests of persons employed in court-related treatment roles. Meanwhile, it is significant to note that the traditional treatment view has prevailed; the Juvenile Delinquents Act remains in effect.[13] This is so in spite of the fact (see Chapter Six) that there is no clear evidence that the "treatment" advocated actually works.

Vagrancy. Many of our legal conceptions of crime originated in the common law of England. One means of demonstrating the significance of this historical background is to consider, as an example, the emergence of early vagrancy laws in England, and their later development in Canada. William Chambliss (1964) provides the material necessary for the first part of this account.

The original vagrancy statute was passed in England in 1349. Prior to this, religious houses provided assistance to the poor, sick, and feeble. Passage of the statute made offering and receiving this aid illegal. The temper and purpose of the statute is suggested in its original wording: "Because . . . many beggars . . . refuse to labor, giving themselves to idleness and vice, . . . it is ordained, that none . . . shall . . . give anything to such which may labor, . . . so that thereby they may be compelled to labor for their necessary living." (cited by Chambliss, 1964:68.)

Chambliss suggests several factors that contributed to this legislative change of events. First, the church was no longer anxious to assume the financial costs of supporting growing numbers of the poor. Second, a desperate labor situation was facing the feudal land owners. The Black Plague had ravaged England, taking in its death toll nearly 50 per cent of the labor force. This problem was aggravated by the land owners' selling many of their serfs into freedom to raise money in support of the crusades. Thus, religious and feudal interests were combined in support of vagrancy legislation that forced laborers to accept employment at low wages.

In time, feudalism died and the vagrancy statutes lapsed into a period of dormancy. However, in 1530, the laws were reactivated to fulfill a new function. England was now experiencing rapid growth in commerce and industry. As patterns of trade developed, business interests perceived a need to protect their goods during the periods of their transportation between sellers and buyers. In this context, the vagrancy statutes found new purpose as a flexible means of controlling persons in the countryside who seemed to threaten safe transportation of goods and materials. Thus, the vagrancy laws were revived and refocused to include " . . . any ruffians . . . (who) shall wander, loiter, or idle use themselves and play the vagabonds." (cited in Chambliss, 1964:72.)

The English common law conception of vagrancy was transmitted into Canadian law in the Criminal Code of 1892. The vague and inclusive character of this law is revealed in the original section of the Criminal Code reproduced in Figure 1-5. Criminalizing references to "loose, idle, or disorderly persons," and persons "living without employment," remained part of the law in Canada for more than 50 years.

Objections to the Canadian vagrancy laws were finally officially recognized in 1954. These objections noted that the law contained inappropriate references to persons being in particular (often unavoidable) *conditions* (e.g., being unemployed), rather than their having committed specifiable *acts* (see Martin *et al.*, 1955:272). Thus, comparison of the 1974 version of the vagrancy law with its predecessor (see Figure 1-5) reveals that most of the offending sections are now repealed. One can speculate that such repeals became possible because of the endemic surplus of unskilled labor in modern Canadian society. This explanation carries through the earlier point that the development of the vagrancy laws was influenced by the economic interests of the various groups involved. This discussion, then, reveals the manner in which deviant acts can move back and forth between criminal and non-criminal status, and the relatedness of this movement to changing social conditions.

Narcotics Legislation. Canada's first federal narcotics law, the Opium Act of 1908, preceded its American counterpart, An Act to Prohibit the Importation and Use of Opium for other than Medical Purposes, passed in 1909. In addition, Hamilton Wright, a doctor educated in Canada, drafted the early American narcotic legislation, and Charles Brent, an Episcopal Bishop born and raised in Canada, organized the Shanghai Opium Convention of 1908, the first of a series of important international conferences. In a detailed social history of American drug legislation, Charles Reasons (1974) has indicated the importance of each of these figures in a successful international movement that eventually criminalized the non-medical use of narcotics in most Western Nations.

A social history of Canadian drug legislation is provided by Shirley Cook (1969; 1970). The origin of this legislation is traced to the early activities of Mackenzie King, then Deputy Minister of Labor. King's involvement began when he was sent to supervise the payment of compensation to Chinese and Japanese victims of the Vancouver Anti-Asiatic riots of 1907. Among the claims King received were two from Chinese opium-manufacturing merchants. In investigating these claims, King found that opium could easily be purchased in an over-the-counter manner. His reactions to this situation resulted in a government *Report on the Need for the Suppression of Opium in Canada,* and, in turn, to the Opium Act of 1908. Shortly thereafter, King was appointed to a British delegation of five that attended the Shanghai conference of 1909. By 1911, King was ready to propose more punitive legislation, the passage of which was linked to "a worldwide movement which has for its object the suppression of this kind of evil in all countries." (cited in Cook, 1970:13.)

Cook argues that King's legislative success was contingent on the social context in which it occurred. In particular, a set of cultural beliefs surrounding drug use, and the presence of intensely hostile attitudes toward Asian-Canadians, assisted this process.

A cultural stereotype of the drug user as "dope fiend" was developed most prominently in a series of books and articles by an Alberta provincial court judge, Emily Murphy (known also by her pen name—Janey Canuk!). Murphy linked three kinds of activities in her writings: drug use, sexual promiscuity, and race-mixing. Thus, a typical illustration from Murphy's (1922) best known book, *The Black Candle,* features a white woman and a black man lying on

FIGURE 1-5

DEFINITIONS OF VAGRANCY IN THE CRIMINAL CODE OF CANADA, 1892 AND 1974

1892*

207. Vagrant Defined—Every one is a loose, idle of disorderly person or vagrant who—

(a.) not having any visible means of subsistence, is found wandering abroad or lodging in any barn or outhouse, or in any deserted or unoccupied building, or in any cart or wagon, or in any railway carriage or freight car, or in any railway building, and not giving a good account of himself, or who, not having any visible means of maintaining himself, lives without employment;

(b.) being able to work and thereby or by other means to maintain himself and family wilfully refuses or neglects to do so;

(c.) openly exposes or exhibits in any street, road, highway or public place, any indecent exhibition;

(d.) without a certificate signed, within six months, by a priest, clergyman or minister of the Gospel, or two justices of the peace, residing in the municipality where the alms are being asked, that he or she is a deserving object of charity, wanders about and begs, or goes about from door to door, or places himself or herself in any street, highway, passage or public place to beg or receive alms;

(e.) loiters on any street, road, highway or public place, and obstructs passengers by standing across the footpath, or by using insulting language, or in any other way;

(f.) causes a disturbance in or near any street, road, highway or public place, by screaming, swearing or singing, or by being drunk, or by impeding or incommoding peaceable passengers;

(g.) by discharging firearms, or by riotous or disorderly conduct in any street or highway, wantonly disturbs the peace and quiet of the inmates of any dwelling-house near such street or highway;

(h.) tears down or defaces signs, breaks windows, or doors or door plates, or the walls of houses, roads or gardens, or destroys fences;

(i.) being a common prostitute or night walker, wanders in the fields, public streets or highways, lanes or places of public meeting or gathering of people, and does not give a satisfactory account of herself;

(j.) is a keeper or inmate of a disorderly house, bawdy-house or house of ill-fame, or house for the resort of prostitutes;

(k.) is in the habit of frequenting such houses and does not give a satisfactory account of himself or herself; or

(l.) having no peaceable profession or calling to maintain himself by, for the most part supports himself by gaming or crime, or by the avails of prostitution.

*Source: Snow (1901)

1974*

Vagrancy— Punishment—Aged or infirm persons.
175. (1) Every one commits vagrancy who
(a) [Repealed. 1972, c. 13, s. 12(1).]
(b) [Repealed. 1972, c. 13, s. 12(1).]
(c) [Repealed. 1972, c. 13, s. 12(1).]
(d) supports himself in whole or in part by gaming or crime and has no lawful profession or calling by which to maintain himself; or
(e) having at any time been convicted of an offence under a provision mentioned in paragraph 689 (1) (a) or (b), is found loitering or wandering in or near a school ground, playground, public park or bathing area.**

**Section 689 defines sexual offences.

Source: Martin (1974)

MacLean's Magazine

THE GRAVE DRUG MENACE

By EMILY F. MURPHY
Magistrate of the Province of Alberta

He dreams more often of tremendous glooms and fatal slopes.

Foreword

MY OBJECT in writing for MacLean's Magazine four articles on the subject of Drug Addiction has been to show: (1) How widespread this evil has become in Canada. What the Federal Government has done to check it; and what further steps should be taken by them to this end.

(2) To discuss its relation to insanity, crime, social deterioration and social wastage.

(3) To consider whether prohibitory laws tend to the increase of drug consumption.

(4) To throw some light on "the gradual reduction" or "ambulatory method" as practised by the medical profession, and to show how it has failed to cure.

(5) To tell how the habit is most frequently acquired, and how the illicit traffic in drugs is carried on.

(6) To show what the police-arm of the Government is doing to grapple with the evil, and how the cases are usually dealt with in our Courts of Summary Jurisdiction.

(7) To consider whether drug addiction is a crime, or a disease, or both.

While facing the drug evil without flinkers, I shall endeavor to discuss it without offending the sensibilities of the readers. The only excuse any writer or worker can have for acquainting the public with the particulars of this or other social evils, is that the public may be warned of their dangers, and aroused to strike them down before they gain the strangle-hold.

All honest and orderly persons should rightly know that there are men and women who batten and fatten on the agony of the unfortunate drug-habit — palmer-worms and human cater-pillars, who should be trodden under foot like the despicable grubs that they are.

And all folks of gentle and open hearts should know that among us there are pale and glorious lads who, without any obliquity in themselves, have become victims to the thrall of opiates. 'Till they perish and they suffer. Some 'lie whispered down in hell.' It is fitting then, that both as readers and writers, we should approach this urgent matter with tenderable spirits, with tolerance for each other's opinions; and with with realty to act in conjunction where duty seems to direct.

iN OPIUM smoker has questioned. "If I should gain heaven for a pic (coin), why should you be envious?"

His question is based on two lies. The smoker does not gain heaven, and we are not envious.

Certain slack-twisted persons of both sexes, in search of possible adventures, or desirous of surcease from the pain of their own inefficiency, may be led to think there is something felicitous in the smoker's "heaven" as we here set forth, but they think amiss.

One has but to come closely in touch with the smoker to know that his vaunted "pipe dreams" are not invariable visions of moon-haunted nights, flower-starred islands, and the hushing of velvet wings.

On the country, he dreams more often of tremendous glooms and fatal shapes, so that he cries aloud for help with a voiceless throat.

Instead of a heaven, his open-eyed dream ultimately becomes a terrible hell, "a dwelling deadly cold, full of bloody eagles and pale adders."

Opium addicts, especially if they be poetic, throw a lure over their vice and write of it as "a song that sleeps in the blood," but few write of their tears that are bitter as ink, and how they get to know all the untold sorrows of the world.

Of course, they do not tell these things, for every drug-fiend is a liar. The dream in their blood is only a morbid and clamorous appetite — yes, and a vulgar one.

Besides, an inveterate user of drugs has no more blood in his body than a shrimp. Indeed, because of their pallor and extreme emaciation the Chinese denominate the advanced addicts as "opium ghosts." And the name is apt, being descriptive above all others of these ashly-faced half-witted drunkers; these unfortunate ring-ing creatures who are so properly castigated by the whips and scorpions they have made for themselves.

"Why then do they smoke?" you ask. Again I reply, for forgetfulness. Maybe, they smoke too for the excitation of the senses, an effect which the new smoker gets on five grains but which, it is said, requires as high as 270 grains for an old smoker.

Leads to Broken Homes

SOMETIMES, a man will come to the magistrate to tell of his domestic infidelity and how his wife has deteriorated both mentally and physically. She has become careless of her appearance, and indolent; neglects her home, and remains away all night or even for days. He has thought of every reason but opiates, and is staggered when the idea is first suggested to him. Then, he begins to understand why she stole money from him; why she has become so ill-looking and her face so fretted with wrinkles. He begins to comprehend the cause of her continuous despondence and her desire to commit suicide, and why she is "grey ill to live wit."

A man or woman who becomes an addict seeks the company of those who use the drug, and avoids those of his own social status. This explains the amazing phenomenon of an educated gentlewoman, reared in a refined atmosphere, consorting with the lowest classes of yellow and black men. It explains, too, why sometimes a white woman deserts or "farms out" a half-blood infant, or on rare occasions brings it to the juvenile court for adoption.

Under the influence of the drug, the woman loses control of herself; her moral senses are blunted, and she becomes "a victim" in more senses than one. When she acquires the habit, she does not know what lies before her; later, she does not care. She is a young woman who is years upon years old.

Realizing that no woman may become or remain degraded without all women suffering, you may attempt something in the way of salvage, only to find that to reform her would be about as difficult as making Eve from the original rib. Unrestrained by decorum, void of delicacy of soul, moulded by vice, the companion of debauchees and drabs, she seems to be one of those desperately "down-and-out" women who, for her life dictum, has taken the words "Evil be thou my good."

Sometimes, her husband takes her to another city, or the police may gather her in for a term in jail. Sometimes, she goes to the asylum, and sometimes she dies, but more often she just lives on, a burden and heartscald at home and abroad.

Figure 1-6

Maclean's. Vol. 33, No. 3. February 15, 1920. Reprinted with permission. Reproduced by Metropolitan Toronto Library Board.

a bed with opium smoking equipment between them. The caption reads, "When she acquires the habit, she does not know what lies before her; later she does not care." (cited in Cook, 1970:22.)

More than blacks, however, the Chinese and Japanese were the groups receiving attention (see Figure 1-6). In the period preceding passage of the original Opium Act, the House of Commons was busy with the debate of a proposed trade treaty that would have opened doors to additional Japanese immigration. In this context, the evils of drug-traffic became an easy tool to arouse anti-Asiatic sentiment. The two issues were gradually fused in a combined moral crusade. Remarks of the Secretary of the "Anti-Asiatic Exclusion League," read into the House record, suggest the temper of the effort:

> Here we have a disease, one of many traceable to the Asiatic. Do away with the Asiatic and you have more than saved the souls and bodies of thousands of young men and women who are yearly being sent to a living hell and to the grave through their presence in Canada (cited in Cook, 1970:25).

It was in this background of racial conflict and cultural stereotypes that Canada's narcotics legislation emerged. Mackenzie King represented a political interest group that was able to arouse nascent cultural concerns for the purpose of criminalizing narcotic drug use. The resulting legislation formed the nation's emerging drug policy.

We have reviewed the social history of three pieces of Canadian legislation. In each instance, we called attention to the group interests and cultural themes that influenced the laws involved. The purpose of this discussion is to illustrate how factors other than the behavior of concern can significantly influence whether an act is considered legal or illegal, deviant or criminal. This discussion does not deny that some attacks on persons and property are held criminal in most modern societies. It simply asserts that beyond this basic consensus, one society's deviance may be considered part of another society's "crime problem."

The Thin Line: A Summary

Conceptions of deviance vary by culture. For example, many of the acts Euro-Canadians hold criminal, Native Peoples did not. In addition, the historical collision of indigenous and invading cultures in northern Canada provides an example of how cultural conceptions of deviance may be coerced into new forms. The lessons of these experiences include an awareness that the meaning of deviance is often relative to culture and circumstance.

Sociological definitions of deviance attempt to accommodate this variability. Although several definitions are available, we have suggested that deviance is best conceptualized on a continuous scale that ranges from the most to the least serious acts in any given society. According to this definition, the more serious acts of deviance are likely to involve high agreement about what the norm is, a widespread perception of harmfulness, and a severe social response. The continuum envisioned includes two general categories of deviance (criminal and non-criminal forms of deviance) and four sub-divisions (consensual crimes and conflict crimes; social deviations and social diversions). A major sociological concern is to determine in any given society why some of these acts are considered criminal, while others are not.

Consideration of Canadian laws dealing with vagrancy, narcotics, and juvenile delinquency reveals that interest groups mobilize cultural themes for the purpose of designating acts legal and illegal, criminal and non-criminal. This does not mean that the societal evaluation of *all* behaviors is influenced by interest group activity. Among the most serious forms of deviance, the consensual crimes, the influence of interest group activity may be minimized. In later chapters, we will want to consider the theoretical implications of this conclusion.

Having decided on a definition of deviance, our attention turns next to the measurement of our subject matter. How much deviance is there? Who is involved? Are Canadians as deviant as their American neighbors? These issues help to organize the next phase of our discussion.

1. From Douglas A. Schmeiser, "Indians, Eskimos and the Law." Unpublished manuscript, Saskatoon: University of Saskatoon, University of Saskatchewan. 1972. Reprinted with permission of Douglas A. Schmeiser.

2. From Paul Tappan, "Who Is the Criminal?" *American Sociological Review, Vol. 12,* February, 1947:96-102. Reprinted with permission of the *American Sociological Review.*

3. Ibid.

4. From Edwin Sutherland, "Is 'White Collar Crime' Crime?" *American Sociological Review, Vol. 10,* 1945:132-139. Reprinted with permission of the *American Sociological Review.*

5. Ibid.

6. From Thorsten Sellin, *Culture Conflict and Crime.* 1938 Social Science Research Council. Reprinted with permission of Social Science Research Council.

7. Ibid.

8. From Leslie Wilkins, *Social Deviance,* 1964 Tavistock. Reprinted with permission of Associated Book Publishers, Ltd.

9. Ibid.

10. From Austin Turk, *Political Criminality and Political Policing.* 1974 MSS Information Corporation. Reprinted with permission of MSS Information Corporation.

11. Ibid.

12. From Anthony Platt, *The Child Savers: The Invention of Delinquency.* © 1969 University of Chicago Press. Reprinted with permission of the University of Chicago Press.

13. As this book goes to press, the latest efforts have focused on yet another bill titled "Young Persons in Conflict with the Law." The final form and fate of this legislation are at the date of this writing uncertain.

II

COUNTING DEVIANCE:
The Measures of Disrepute

Who, what, when, and, for good measure, how often? These are the perennial questions about deviance. Yet, the answers given to these questions seldom fully satisfy the curious. Dissatisfaction follows from widespread agreement that our measures of deviance are imperfect. Still, students of sinful statistics, like voyeurs, are optimists: they are stubbornly hopeful that however imperfectly, they will see something. This optimism is grounded in the assumption that practice makes (more nearly) perfect, and that a good imagination is (some) substitute for obscured vision. In short, statisticians of deviance are pragmatists, making the best of their faulty resources. The assumption is that some inadequacies can be corrected, and that even imperfect measures can tell us many things that we otherwise would not know.

In this chapter, we will adopt the pragmatist's assumption to investigate some of the most frequently asked questions about the occurrence of deviance.

HOLDING THE ACCOUNTANTS ACCOUNTABLE

We begin our discussion with three bothersome questions: who's counting? Who's counting what? And, who's counting whom? The purpose of these questions is to emphasize that the measurement of deviance is a socially organized activity, with correlated social purposes. For example, the official counting of crime is done by the police, courts, and correctional institutions—all organizations whose budgets may be affected by the counts delivered. This, in turn, may influence what and whom get counted. Thus, Giffen (1966) suggests in a Toronto study that one latent function of processing skid row alcoholics in a "revolving door" fashion is that it makes the criminal justice system look both busy and efficient. In addition, skid row alcoholics are unlikely to dispute their fate. In short, the "skidder" is a rewarding target for crime control. Some statistics, then, say as much about who is collecting them, as about the persons and events collected (Kitsuse and Cicourel, 1963). The challenge is to make these statistics interpretable.

The first step in interpreting the statistics of deviance is to recognize that all such data consist of two components. The first component is made up of actual behaviors and the authors of these behaviors. The second component is an error term, representing either the over- or under-reporting of acts and persons in the particular statistic involved. Both components can be studied, and as sociologists we are as interested in the error term as we are in the behavioral component. For example, we have suggested the advantages to the criminal justice system of counting skid row alcoholics. The error component of this "court measure of alcoholism" consists in part of the many white collar alcoholics who never find their way into such statistics. Fortunately, behavior and error terms of this type often can be estimated through the use of alternative (or multiple) measures (cf., Campbell and Fiske, 1959; see also Henshel and Silverman, 1975:Chapter 1). In the case of alcoholism, we will see later in this discussion that one comparison measure is based on the number of persons who die of cirrhosis of the liver. More generally, to the extent that different measures agree, we will be encouraged as to the validity of their results; to the extent that the different measures may disagree, we will be directed to possible sources of error.

Data suitable for the purposes we have described come from five sources: (1) official agencies of social control; (2) non-official agencies; (3) first-person accounts; (4) victimization surveys; and (5) observational reports. Data from one or more of these sources can be used to evaluate the answers commonly given to several important questions:

How much deviant behavior is there?

Are Canadians as deviant as Americans?

Are rates of deviance increasing?

Do some social groups experience more deviant behavior than others?

Responses to these questions will depend, of course, on what *types* of deviance we are discussing. Here we are clearly captive to our measures: the most frequent counts of deviance seem to involve crime, delinquency, mental illness, and alcoholism and other forms of drug abuse. Our discussion must therefore focus on these forms of deviant behavior. This is not to deny the significance of other forms of deviance, but rather to indicate that if answers are to be given at all, then we must begin with data available. Before turning to our list of specific questions, however, we will first introduce in some additional detail each of the different sources of our data.

OFFICIAL AGENCY DATA

Official data on deviance are readily available from various public agencies of social control, including the police, criminal and civil courts, correctional institutions, mental health centres, and various agencies dealing with alcohol and drug abuse. Unfortunately, although the data available from these public agencies are the most easily obtained, they are also the least happily received. Speaking for many criminologists, Giffen (1965) notes that, "Apparently nobody is happy about the state of criminal statistics, but no serious student of criminology can get along without them." (59.) This ambivalent attitude reflects the knowledge that the official data tell us only part of the story, but nonetheless a part that is very important. Said simply, the official data on deviance fulfill one very important function: they indicate the extent to which, and the method whereby, the public agencies of social control are dealing with the deviance they define (Zay, 1963).

Notwithstanding this important function, the common deficiencies of official data on deviance should be indicated:

(1) An indeterminable amount of deviant behavior goes undetected, is handled by private means, or otherwise remains beyond public knowledge (e.g., crime against bureaucracies [Smigel and Ross, 1970], including much white collar crime).

(2) Some deviant behavior that is reported to public agencies is not recorded (e.g., American studies indicate that up to 26 per cent of the incidents reported to the police go unrecorded [see Hood and Sparks, 1970:35]).

(3) Categories of deviant behavior are vaguely defined and variously recorded (e.g., mental illness, see Chapter 1).

(4) Bases used in computing rates vary, and are frequently inappropriate (e.g., using the number of females *and* males as the base for computing rape rates [see also Engstad, 1975]).

One of the challenges of working with official data is to identify the sources of these deficiencies, and to correct or compensate for them. In this spirit, Hindelang (1974) argues that, " . . . researchers who refuse to examine even a blurred reflection of the phenomenon may be discarding an opportunity to reduce ignorance about the phenomenon in question; further, by refusing to explore ways in which prior indicators of a phenomenon may be improved, lack of progress toward more satisfactory measurement is more likely to be ensured." (2.)[1] In short, official data are both errorful and essential, leaving as our only good "option" earnest efforts to understand and reduce these errors.[2]

NON-OFFICIAL AGENCY DATA

Non-official sources of data provide a variety of checks on the information gathered from public agencies of social control. For example, one non-official measure of variations in property crimes is provided in the premium rates charged by insurance companies offering coverage against criminal property losses (Price, 1966). These rates are calculated on the basis of past losses, and they can be considered valid to the extent that insurance companies use such knowledge, independent of other means, to make a profit. In short, insurance companies have a financial interest in achieving factual accuracy.

A second source of non-official data is the mortality records of public and private hospitals. These records are used most effectively in estimating the prevalence of alcoholism, with the predictions based on deaths designated as resulting from alcoholism, liver cirrhosis, and suicide (Brenner, 1967; Lipscomb, 1959; Schmidt and de Lint, 1969). A limitation of these estimates, of course, is the accuracy of the coroner's records themselves (Leon, 1975).

Some of the most interesting non-official data is gathered from the security forces of large department stores (Cameron, 1964; Sellin, 1937; Hindelang, 1974) and various private policing organizations (Becker, 1974; Shallo, 1933). Private policing is a growth industry in Canada (Jefferies, 1973), with nearly every large commercial enterprise having either an internal security division, or contracted coverage from an outside policing agency. The importance of the records kept by such organizations is that much of the deviant behavior they monitor is never brought to the attention of the public agencies.

Other less frequently tapped sources of non-official data include private physicians, public health agencies, and business accountant and consultant firms. The records of physicians and public health agencies have provided useful information on such diverse problems as mental illness (Williams, Kopinak, and Moynagh, 1972) and homicide (Hindelang, 1974). Business accountants and consultants possess similarly useful information on patterns of internal theft (Jaspan, 1960). However, in both the profit-making and health-keeping professions, there are serious concerns about the confidentiality of the records kept. These concerns have limited the use made to date of this type of information.

More generally, although non-official sources of data seldom provide a sufficient basis for the calculation of generalized deviance rates, they are nonetheless an important resource for confirming or expanding knowledge of various areas of deviance.

FIRST PERSON ACCOUNTS

An obvious objection to the measures we have considered thus far is that they are usually several steps removed from the source. Said differently, they offer third person records of the behaviors under study. We have noted that there are serious possibilities of bias involved in the transmission of data from source to record. In an effort to reduce the error-producing distance to the source, some sociologists have developed strategies for collecting first person accounts. The two most significant of these strategies are (1) self-report questionnaires, and (2) field encounters.

Self-report questionnaries are paper and pencil instruments that ask (usually anonymous) respondents to confess, in Kinsey-like fashion, the quality and quantity of their symptoms (in the case of mental illness) and/or indiscretions (in the case of crime and delinquency, alcohol and drug abuse). Such surveys are used extensively with students in the classroom (Nye and Short, 1957), as well as with adults (Wallerstein and Wyle, 1947). The weaknesses of the self-report approach include memory lapses and deceit among subjects, as well as vaguely stated test items and indefinite periods of coverage. Nonetheless, self-report data are suggestive of the volume and social location of various forms of deviance, and, if appropriate questions and sampling procedures are used, the findings can be generalized and compared with official data sources. In the absence of representative sampling procedures, comparisons can still be drawn between the subjects who acknowledge deviant acts, and the proportion of these persons who find their way into official files.

Moving one step closer to the source, field encounters provide the opportunity of meeting the deviant in his or her own setting. This first hand approach to the collection of data is uncommon in the study of deviance. One obvious reason such studies are so infrequent is the presumed problem of getting subjects to talk to. Yet, Ned Polsky (1969), the most forceful advocate of this approach, indicates that, " . . . from students, faculty, and others I have had more offers of introductions to career criminals—in and out of organized crime—than I could begin to follow up." (124.)[3] From this starting point, Polsky suggests that "the most feasible technique for building one's sample is 'snowballing': get an introduction to one criminal who will vouch for you with others, who in turn will vouch for you with still others." (124.)[4] Polsky stops short of urging researchers to participate in, or even witness, their subjects' acts. The emphasis instead is on first person recollections, developed through in-depth interviews and group discussions. One example of this type of field research in Canada is found in John Klein's and Arthur Montague's (1975) research among cheque forgers.[5]

VICTIMIZATION SURVEYS

Many criminal acts of deviance involve both a perpetrator and a victim. The victim too, then, is a source of information about deviance. This resource is tapped through victimization surveys. Such surveys began in the United States in the mid-1960s (Biderman *et al.*, 1967; Ennis, 1967). Recognizing the significance of such research, the American government has since inaugurated a regular surveying programme on a national scale, as well as several local and state-level investigations (e.g., *Crime in Eight American Cities*, 1974). Canada has lagged behind in developing similar efforts; however, an exploratory survey is available for Toronto (Courtis, 1970; Section 2), and a mail-back survey has been conducted in British Columbia (Koenig, 1976).

The initial victimization surveys were conducted on a house-to-house basis, with one respondent used to represent all members of the household. Questions asked of the respondents included the following: (1) whether they personally had been victims of specific crimes in the past year; (2) whether any member of the household had been victimized; (3) the "very worst crime" that had ever happened to the respondents; and (4) the "very worst crime" that had ever happened to anyone currently living in the household (Biderman *et al.*, 1967; Ennis, 1967).

Victimization surveys are limited, of course, in their subject matter. They are concerned explicitly with *crimes*, committed by *individuals*, against *persons*, and their *property*. They are *not* concerned with the "victimless crimes": gambling, prostitution, public disorder offences, and alcohol and drug abuse. Similarly ignored are crimes by, and against, corporations. Added to this, there are also several deficiencies of method.

- Some respondents are unwilling or unavailable to participate (e.g., commuters are less frequently available than housewives and old people).
- Problems of memory, deception, and the reluctance to recall some types of events (e.g., family quarrels or sexual attacks; for a description of the "model victim," see Figure 2-1).

FIGURE 2-1

THE "MODEL VICTIM"

WOMAN, 94,
FAILS TO CATCH A THIEF IN 3-BLOCK CHASE

A 94-year-old Etobicoke woman who says she has read crime magazines for nearly half her life chased a purse snatcher yesterday and apologized to police for not catching him.

"I must be getting old . . . I couldn't run like a boy any more," spinster Stella Wingart said after she chased the thief, about 14, for three blocks on Bloor St. W. before he disappeared.

Miss Wingart, of Grenview Blvd., gave police a description of the youngster who grabbed her purse while she was returning from her daily one-mile walk to attend mass at Our Lady of Sorrows Church.

"Reading about detective work has taught me that getting a good description is very important," she said in an interview.

"I ran after him, but I couldn't keep up, and I lost him," added Miss Wingart, a retired dental nurse who said she can still thread the needle in her mother's 100-year-old sewing machine.

The thief escaped with $1.37, but Miss Wingart was more concerned about the Latin prayer book in her purse. "They don't make prayer books in Latin any more. I still prefer the Latin and the old ways."

Reprinted with permission of the Toronto Star
Source: Friday, May 10, 1974, Toronto Star

- Varying interpretations of survey categories and the events included within them.
- "Foreward telescoping," or the process of remembering events as more recent than they are, thus invalidating the intended time coverage of the survey (Skogan, 1975).

The existence of these deficiencies must be weighed against the unique findings victimization surveys provide, and the short history of the techniques involved. Development of this survey method holds the promise of providing a reliable, census-like measure of the predatory deviant behaviors.[6]

OBSERVATIONAL DATA

An attractive step beyond first-hand accounts and victim reports is direct observation. Although observational studies are not frequent in sociology, the methods involved are receiving increased attention (see McCall and Simmons, 1969; Reiss, 1971a, 1971b). Examples of this approach in the field of deviance vary from studies where the observers are overt or covert participants in the situations observed ("participant observation studies"), to arrangements where the participants are less aware of the observers' presence ("field observation studies").

A provocative example of a participant observation study in the field of deviance is Laud Humphreys' (1970) research on homosexual encounters in public washrooms. Humphreys' initial problem was the obvious: how " . . . to take a 'natural part' in the action without actual involvement of a sexual nature." (26-27.)[7] The "solution" was found in an organizational role crucial to the behaviors to be explained:

> The very fear and suspicion encountered in the restrooms produces a participant role, the sexuality of which is optional. This is the role of the lookout ('watchqueen' in the argot), a man who is situated at the door or windows from which he may observe the means of access to the restroom (27).*

Not unexpectedly, the use of these and other techniques resulted in a set of findings that is dramatically different from other research on homosexuality. Among the more important results is the finding that adult homosexuals seeking sex in public washrooms avoid, rather than approach, young persons under the age of consent. Notwithstanding the significance of such findings to a concerned and ill-informed public, some of the more vivid passages in the account led one reviewer, Barry Krisberg (1972), to call the research "sociological pornography" (to be explicit, a "blow-by-blow account.") A more modest observation study of homosexual activity in the gay bars of Montreal is found in Sawchuk's (1974) account of "Becoming a Homosexual." This study, when compared with earlier work done in Montreal by Leznoff and Westley (1956), reveals that the decriminalization of homosexuality in Canada has not been a sufficient basis for public lifting of the stigma on the lifestyle involved.

Albert Reiss' (1971b) research on police behavior provides an example of a study where systematic observation is combined with a reduced participatory role. Reiss utilized thirty-six trained observers

Reprinted with permission of Aldine Publishing Company, Chicago, and Gerald Duckworth and Company, Ltd., London.

in this study to record observations in three of North America's largest cities. The observers rode in patrol cars and walked with police on their beats on all shifts, each day of the week, for seven consecutive weeks, in each of the three cities. One important concern of this research was that the simple presence of the observer not distort the encounters under study. To help minimize police concern, observers indicated to the officers that they primarily were interested in the behavior of suspects. Beyond this, all observers were instructed to avoid any involvement in the encounters. However, the following report of an observer illustrates the truism that all rules are made to be broken:

> Both officers were very grateful to have this observer along in an on-view incident. A fight ensued in No. 3 incident where both officers lost control of the offender and this observer had to restrain him. . . . I might add that in the process of the fight either I was bitten by the offender or my hand scraped against his mouth, because I have two lovely abrasions on my hand (Reiss, 1971a:20).*

In addition to problems of participation, and the resulting bias that may be introduced into the collection of data, there are also ethical and legal concerns. In both the examples of observation research that we have described, no effort could be made to obtain the informed consent of persons observed. In Humphreys' research on homosexuality, the situation was further complicated by a follow-up interview. These interviews were made possible by Humphreys' carefully noting the licence numbers of his subjects' cars as they departed from the public washrooms. He then used these licence numbers to organize follow-up interviews. The issue is that these interviews were disguised as social health surveys. Predictably, these research techniques are a topic of considerable debate (e.g., see Horowitz and Rainwater, 1970; Von Hoffman, 1970). Many sociologists regard such deceit as an intolerable invasion of privacy (Sagarin, 1973). More pragmatic researchers argue that if you do not "exploit" the subjects, reveal or otherwise demean them, that no harm is done in assuming a "false front." Beyond this, some observers offer to guarantee the confidentiality of their findings. A problematic feature of this approach, however, is that observers of deviance are subject to court subpoenas and other legal devices to stimulate disclosure. Reiss (1971a) correctly notes that, "One cannot be certain that one's observers will fulfill the guarantees given, and lacking the professional privilege of confidentiality of information, one cannot protect one's employees against legal sanction." (16.)[8] Candor aside, Reiss

Reprinted with permission of Jossey-Bass, Inc.

concludes that, "This is not to say that one must simply inform organizations that no such guarantees can be given." (16.)[9]

None of the legal and ethical questions surrounding the use of observational techniques can minimize the "quality of closeness" that the methodology allows. For the moment, then, we will leave these difficult issues with the authors involved. For our purposes, we can take advantage of the fact that the data are already "in" on the studies we have described. We are ready, then, to move on to our original questions.

HOW MUCH DEVIANT BEHAVIOR IS THERE?

The only safe answer to the question "how much?" is "more than most of us imagine." Discrepancies between popular conceptions of deviance and "actual" levels of behavior are in part a function of the selection processes of official agencies. Most agencies of social control operate with a funnel-like effect, constantly selecting and rejecting candidates for further processing.

An example of this funnelling effect is available in the criminal justice system in Canada. Figure 2-2 provides a sequential model of the passage of cases through the judicial system. An indication of the shrinkage of cases is provided first by comparing the number of offences known to the police with those cleared by charge; second, we can contrast the number of persons initially charged with those actually convicted; finally, we can compare the number of adults convicted with those ultimately incarcerated. 72 per cent of the offences known to the police are cleared by charge.[10] Beyond this, 64 per cent of the adults charged are convicted, and only 3 per cent of those convicted are finally sentenced to prison. In short, the shrinkage between these measures of input and output is striking.

A second revealing picture of the funnelling process is found in a longitudinal study by Hogarth (1974) of 500 juveniles processed over a 6 month period in North Toronto. The first finding of this study was that 43 per cent of the cases involved behavior for which the juvenile could not be prosecuted for delinquency. Among those cases qualifying for prosecution, discretionary or non-charging dispositions were imposed approximately 50 per cent of the time. Summarizing, roughly 25 per cent of all cases led to a final charge and adjudication. Hogarth notes that this is actually a rather *high* prosecution rate, a conclusion that is confirmed by Bordua's (1969) description of departments with release rates of over 90 per cent. In explanation, Hogarth notes that in North Toronto, court referrals proved the most effective means of linking juvenile offenders to

FIGURE 2-2

CANADIAN CRIMINAL JUSTICE SYSTEM

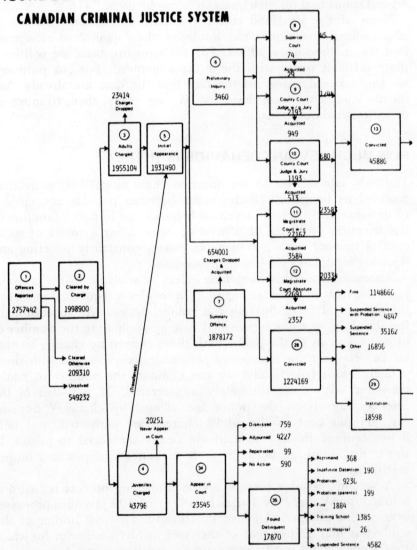

Source: Silverman and Teevan (1975:71), from Information and Statistics on the Canadian Criminal Justice System, *by R. Gordon Cassidy and G. Hopkinson, Ministry of the Solicitor General, Government of Canada and Queen's University, Kingston, Ontario. Reprinted with permission.*

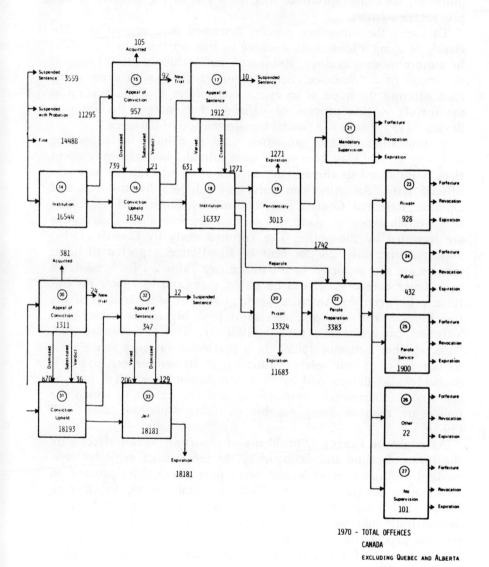

1970 - TOTAL OFFENCES
CANADA
EXCLUDING QUEBEC AND ALBERTA

service resources specifically suited to their needs. For our current purposes, we can simply note that the social sifting involved in this process is extensive.

To some, the funnelling process described may suggest the efficiency of using a loose knit stocking to transfer liquid into a bottle. In a more modest analogy, Rubington and Weinberg (1973) suggest the image of a "deviance corridor"—or a hallway with many exits, each offering the hope of an escape route from final designation as deviant. It is this process of officially becoming a deviant that Buckner (1970) calls the "social transformation of deviance."

Victimization reports are often used as a basis for suggesting in a very general way how *much* more criminal behavior may occur than is indicated in the social transformation of criminal acts into official data. An American survey, conducted by the National Opinion Research Center, and reported by Ennis (1967), reveals that overall, twice as many offences are reported during surveys as are recorded by the police. The Toronto study by Courtis (1970) indicates that only 20 per cent of all offences reported to interviewers are also reported to the police (see Table 2-1 for breakdown by offence category). It can be noted that Courtis regards the difference between the American findings and his as an artifact of the test items: "The reason ... lies most probably in the rather wide 'offence' categories ... used." (1970:31.)[11] He concludes that, "... whether behavior falling in a particular category is reported to the police is not solely a function of its seriousness ... but is probably also determined by both the degree to which it may, if reported, embarrass the respondent, and the extent to which the police are seen as being capable of doing something about it." (30.)[12]

As might be expected, problems of reporting do not affect only the areas of crime and delinquency. In the area of mental illness, medical insurance records and self-report check lists provide an informative comparison with official hospital figures. In Ontario, Hanly (1970) used provincial medical insurance data for 1967 to demonstrate that while as much as 5 per cent of the population receives psychiatric treatment by physicians over a 1 year period, less that 0.50 of 1 per cent of the population is actually institutionalized. In turn, when self-report check lists are used, as much as 25 per cent of the Canadian public is indicated as experiencing psychological impairment (Leighton *et al.*, 1963; Urban Social Redevelopment Project, 1966; Coates *et al.*, 1969). Analogous techniques in the areas of alcohol use (Schmidt, 1971) and drug use (Smart and Fejer, 1971) similarly suggest that actual rates of abuse are considerably higher than official figures indicate.

Table 2-1

REPORTED LEVELS OF VICTIMIZATION BY RESPONDENTS OVER
A TWELVE MONTH PERIOD PRIOR TO TIME OF INTERVIEW

Response Category	*Incidence per 10 000 persons*		*Ratio*
	Gross Level	*Reported to Police*	
Stolen or attempted to steal anything from home	919	413	0.45
Stolen or attempted to steal anything from car	1 400	486	0.35
Stolen or attempted to steal anything from office, work place, restaurant, bar, or other public place	1 012	413	0.41
Stolen or attempted to steal anything from respondent in the street	258	41	0.16
Broken into respondent's home without stealing anything or attacking anyone	434	93	0.21
Deliberately damaged car	1 230	258	0.21
Illegally used car	299	93	0.31
Physically attacked respondent in home	208	20	0.10
Attacked respondent in factory, office building, or some other private work place	226	20	0.09
Attacked respondent in street or park	330	31	0.09
Forged respondent's signature	351	103	0.29
Given respondent counterfeit money	268	51	0.19
Cheated respondent by overcharging	1 116	20	0.02
Cheated respondent by lying about a product or service	1 209	51	0.04
Molested, propositioned, or offended respondent in any way	764	113	0.15
Threatened respondent in any way by phone or letter	1 240	258	0.21
Base: Total number of respondents	967	967	

Reprinted with permission of M.C. Courtis.
Source: Courtis (1970:32)

Summarizing, it seems sufficient to say that actual rates of deviation are far higher than our official measures suggest. In large part, this is as it should be. To deviate is a part of being free, a quality that we value. The societies that monitor deviance most closely are like Orwell's *1984*; in other words, the alternative to the existence of deviation is a totalitarian approach to the control of behavior.

ARE CANADIANS AS DEVIANT AS AMERICANS?

Some Introductory Comments. Having illustrated important deficiencies in the official data on deviance, we will now argue that in spite of these imperfections, the data can still be used in making certain cross-national comparisons. This argument will be grounded in three points: (1) that some measures of deviant behavior may escape these deficiencies; (2) that many of the deficiencies may remain constant across areas, allowing conclusions to be formed on a relative basis; and (3) that the occurrence of systematic biases between areas of comparison is itself a valid topic for study.

There is at least one official measure of deviant behavior, homicide rates, that receives support from various tests of validity. For example, the national victimization survey reported by Ennis (1967) reveals only slightly *fewer* reports of murder than does the official data,[13] while a comparison of data from the Center for Health Statistics (CHS) and Uniform Crime Reports (UCR) over a 36 year period in the United States (see Figure 2-3) yields nearly an identical picture of annual homicide rates (Hindelang, 1974). All of this confirms our suspicion that bodies are difficult to hide, and that official measures of this type deserve some credibility. In short, not *all* official data are biased.

More generally, if it were found that victim surveys and official data produced similar findings regarding the *nature* and *geographic distribution* of criminal offences, one's confidence in the usefulness of the official data would increase. Such findings would suggest that although the official data may substantially underestimate the absolute volume of offences, the relative distribution of offences—for example, in different sections of the country, or between countries—may *not* be substantially biased by failure of victims to report all offences. Said differently, it may be that between and within countries victims have similar patterns of nonreporting. If this is the case, comparisons of areas using official and survey data may result in similar conclusions. To test this set of assumptions, Hindelang (1974) compared overall crime rates as estimated by victim and official reports (UCR's) for four regions of the United States and urban and rural areas. In addition, these comparisons were extended

FIGURE 2-3

RATES OF HOMICIDE IN THE UNITED STATES AS REPORTED BY THE UNIFORM CRIME REPORTS AND THE CENTER FOR HEALTH STATISTICS, 1935-1971

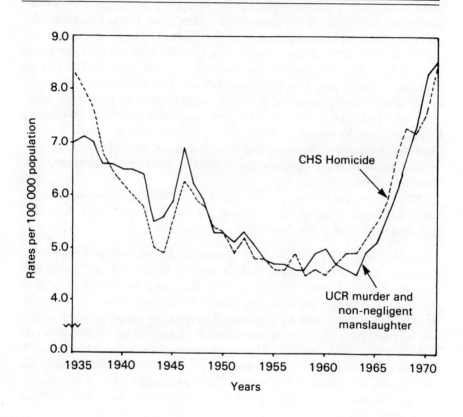

Reprinted with permission of Pergamon Press, Ltd.
Source: Hindelang (1974:4)

into particular offence categories, and to rankings of their relative incidence. Hindelang concludes that, " ... the results are tentative; yet, the essential compatibility of these comparisons ... prohibits summary dismissal of the UCR data as worthless for purposes such as examinations of the relative geographic distribution of offences and time series analyses of at least some offences." (15.)[14] In other words, a cautious argument can be made that official data may in some cases be suitable for *comparisons*, even when such data do not justify estimates of *absolute incidence*.

For those who remain doubtful, there is a third approach to be taken to comparisons of official data. This approach is based on the earlier discussion in this chapter of the error and behavioral components of all measures of deviance. Comparisons of official figures serve as a basis for investigating the relative contribution of error-producing factors in the construction of deviance rates. For example, in 1969, Prince Edward Island had the highest rate of admissions to mental institutions of any province in Canada. However, in the same year, Prince Edward Island also had the highest ratio in Canada of psychiatric beds per 100 000 population. The availability of treatment space, then, seems a probable contaminating factor in comparisons of official rates of mental illness between provinces (Williams, Kopinak, and Moynagh, 1972). Thus, official data not only can be used to investigate the incidence of behavior, but also to explore factors influencing responses taken to the presumed prevalence of these behaviors.

With these preliminary comments recorded, we can turn to a comparative discussion of deviance in the United States, Canada, and other selected countries.

Cross-National Data on Deviant Behavior. By almost any measure, Canada is only a moderately violent nation. Figure 2-4 and Table 2-2 indicate rates of rape, robbery, wounding, and murder in Canada, the United States, England and Wales. In Chapter One, we referred to offences of this sort as consensual crimes, because they represent the infrequent and severely sanctioned violations of widely shared, and strongly held, values. Although some differences clearly exist in the collection and categorization of offences in the countries considered, the consistency of the findings is suggestive of a pattern: Canada occupies a middle position, persistently less violent than the United States.

The conclusion that Canada is a relatively non-violent nation, particularly in comparison with the United States, is echoed in cross-national studies of political violence (Kirkham, Levy, and Crotty, 1970). Such studies demonstrate that despite Canada's experiences with groups like the F.L.Q., the numbers and rates of assassinations, armed attacks, riots, and deaths from political violence have been relatively low. In sum, we seem individually and collectively more violent than some, but nonetheless more peaceful than most.

Surveys of drug use in the United States and Canada suggest another area of American predominance. Berg (1970) has reviewed

FIGURE 2-4

MURDER RATES PER MILLION POPULATION, CANADA, UNITED STATES, AND ENGLAND AND WALES, 1961-1970

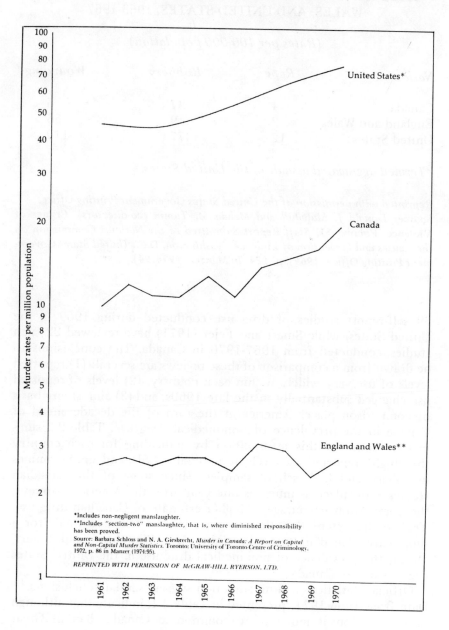

*Includes non-negligent manslaughter.
**Includes "section-two" manslaughter, that is, where diminished responsibility
has been proved.
Source: Barbara Schloss and N. A. Giesbrecht, *Murder in Canada: A Report on Capital
and Non-Capital Murder Statistics*. Toronto: University of Toronto Centre of Criminology.
1972, p. 86 in Manzer (1974:95).

REPRINTED WITH PERMISSION OF McGRAW-HILL RYERSON, LTD.

Table 2-2

AVERAGE RATES OF REPORTED OFFENCES FOR RAPE, ROBBERY, AND WOUNDING IN CANADA, ENGLAND AND WALES, AND UNITED STATES, 1963-1967

(Rates per 100 000 population)

Nation	Rape	Robbery	Wounding*
Canada	4	37	6
England and Wales	2	9	56
United States	12	77	110

*Termed aggravated assault in the United States.

Reprinted with permission of the United States Government Printing Office.
Source: Donald J. Mulvihill and Melvin M. Tumin (co-directors), Crimes of Violence, *Volume 11, Staff Report Submitted to the National Commission on the Causes and Prevention of Violence (Washington, D.C.: United States Government Printing Office, 1969), p. 124. In Manzer (1974:94).*

69 self-report studies of drug use conducted during 1969 in the United States, while Smart and Fejer (1971) have reviewed 22 such studies conducted from 1967-1970 in Canada. The conclusions to be drawn from a comparison of these reviews are several: (1) reported levels of use vary widely within each country, (2) levels of reported use changed substantially in the late 1960s, and (3) almost any basis of comparison places America at the turn of the decade ahead of Canada in the prevalence of non-medical drug use. Table 2-3 summarizes some of this information by indicating for each country the "high" reported use levels of marijuana, LSD, and amphetamines in college and high school samples. Since some of the Canadian studies took place as much as one year after the American surveys, the comparison encourages a higher estimate of Canadian drug use. Yet, to the extent that these reports can be taken as valid (for a supportive Canadian test of validity, see Whitehead and Smart, 1972), the prevalence of non-medical drug use in the United States exceeds that in Canada.

Official statistics on drug addiction suggest similar conclusions.[15] Data from 1966-1971, presented in Table 2-4, indicate that although drug addiction is much more common in Canada than in Great Britain, the American statistics suggest an even more widespread use.

Table 2-3

HIGHEST REPORTED RATES ON NON-MEDICAL USE OF DRUGS IN CANADIAN AND AMERICAN SURVEYS OF COLLEGE AND HIGH SCHOOL STUDENTS

Drug	College Surveys	Per Cent of Drug Use U.S. Canada		High School Surveys	Per Cent of Drug Use U.S. Canada	
Marijuana	University of Michigan	44.0%		San Mateo County, California	36.6%	
	Bishop's University		27.3%	Toronto		23.0%
LSD	*Newsweek* Survey	8.2%		San Mateo County, California	15.1%	
	Bishop's University		3.1%	Toronto		15.0%
Ampheta-mines	University of Michigan	24.7%		San Mateo County, California	20.8%	
	University of Western Ontario		4.1%	Niagara Counties, Ontario		9.0%

Source: Berg (1970:784) and Smart and Fejer (1971:514-517)

Turning to the most frequently abused chemical, alcohol, comparative data are available from a variety of countries. Much of this data is built on the well-known fact that alcoholics contribute a disproportionately large share to mortality from cirrhosis of the liver. This information is built into computing formulas used to estimate the prevalence of alcoholism (Popham, 1956). A resulting ranking of the estimated prevalence of alcoholism in a number of western countries is presented in Table 2-5. This ranking suggests that neither Americans nor Canadians are among the world's heaviest drinkers, but that our southern neighbors may once more exceed us.

Table 2-4

NUMBER OF KNOWN DRUG ADDICTS PER ONE HUNDRED THOUSAND POPULATION 15 YEARS AND OVER[a] FOR THE UNITED KINGDOM,[b] CANADA[c] AND THE UNITED STATES,[d] 1966-1971

Country	1966	1967	1968	1969	1970	1971
United Kingdom	3	4	7	7	6	7
Canada	27	27	27	28	33	44
United States	44	45	45	47	56	54

a Population data for the United States 1968 and 1971 is for the age group 14 years and over, and therefore may be slightly lower than if it were calculated on the population 15 years and over. Problems of data access made these and following approximations necessary.

b Population figures are based on mid-year estimates of the Home Population. The Home Population is defined as "persons actually present in an area."

c Population figures for 1967, 1968, 1969, 1970 are based on mid-year estimates; 1966 and 1971 are based on census figures for the two years.

d Population figures for 1966, 1969, and 1970 are based on mid-year estimates or current data. Figures for 1967, 1968, and 1971 are based on population by age or population by marital status by age statistics.

Sources: Statistics on known drug addicts were obtained from the Home Office, London England; the Department of National Health and Welfare, Government of Canada; and the U.S. Bureau of the Census, Statistical Abstracts of the United States, 1968-1972, Washington D.C.; Population statistics were taken from Annual Abstract of Statistics, 1974, No. 111, London: General Statistical Office; Population Estimates by Marital Status, Age, and Sex, for Canada and Provinces, 1972, Ottawa: Information Canada, June, 1974; and Statistical Abstracts of the United States, as referenced above.

Table 2-5

RANKING OF ESTIMATED PREVALENCE OF ALCOHOLISM IN A
NUMBER OF WESTERN COUNTRIES
(COUNTRIES ARE LISTED ALPHABETICALLY WITHIN CATEGORIES)

Range	*Country*
Extreme High	France
Upper High	Chile
	Portugal
	U.S.A.
Lower High	Australia
	Sweden
	Switzerland
	Union of South Africa
	Yugoslavia
Upper Middle	Canada
	Denmark
	Norway
	Peru
	Scotland
	Uruguay
Lower Middle	Belgium
	Czechoslovakia
	England
	Finland
	Ireland
	Italy
	New Zealand
	Wales
Upper Low	Brazil
	Netherlands
Lower Low	Argentina
	Spain

*Reprinted with permission of The Addiction Research Foundation of Ontario.
Source: Schmidt (1971:502)*

Additional cross-national comparisons, based on consumption patterns, again place the United States somewhat ahead of Canada, but with a reduction in the disparity (de Lint and Schmidt, 1971).

The statistics of mental illness seem the most difficult to interpret. Official data on mental hospital admissions suffer from variations in the definitions of mental illness, varying patterns of discharge and readmission, disparities in available treatment space, and differing policies on voluntary and involuntary admission. A more useful source of data for our purposes, then, involves the use of self-report check lists derived from a variety of standardized psychological tests. Summarizing the results of 9 such surveys completed in the United States and Canada, Williams, Kopinak, and Moynagh (1972) conclude that in both countries approximately 25 per cent of the general population is impaired by psychological disorders. Similarities in American and Canadian patterns of mental health are reported also in John Seeley's (1956) classic community study of *Crestwood Heights.*

More generally, it can be said that the forms of deviance considered most serious by the public (e.g., "violent crime" and "hard drug abuse") are found more commonly in the United States than in Canada. How *much* more deviant behavior occurs in the United States, and whether this disparity will endure, are questions to which we can provide no satisfactory answers. We can, however, comment on how Canadians *perceive* their situation. In a 1969 opinion poll of a representative sample of Toronto households, Courtis (1970) found that 28 per cent of his respondents regarded crime as a very serious problem, 61 per cent as only a moderately serious problem, with the remaining 12 per cent largely unconcerned. This finding can be contrasted with American polls conducted during a similar period by Harris (1968) and Gallup (*Time*, 1968). These polls reveal a consensus that "crime and lawlessness" are America's most serious problems.[16] Data reviewed in this section support these contrasting estimates by Canadians and Americans of current crime problems in their respective countries. Our next task is to compare our current situation with the experiences of our past.

ARE RATES OF DEVIANCE INCREASING?

If Canadians do not see "crime and lawlessness" as a serious problem, they nonetheless see the problem as *increasing.* Courtis (1970:6) reports that nearly 75 per cent of his sample felt that crime was on the increase, while only an extremely small percentage felt (less

FIGURE 2-5

RATES OF CONVICTIONS BY TYPE OF OFFENCE, CANADA, 1901-1969
(RATES PER 100 000 POPULATION AGE 16 YEARS AND OVER)

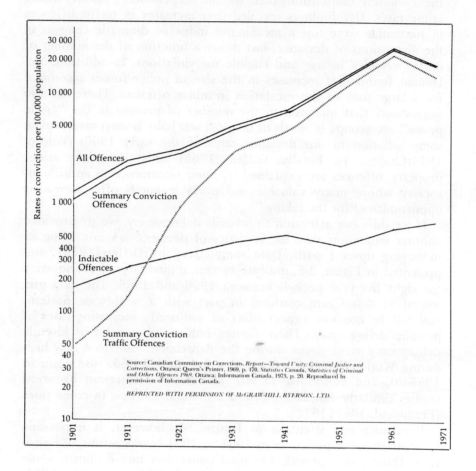

Source: Canadian Committee on Corrections. *Report—Toward Unity: Criminal Justice and Corrections*. Ottawa: Queen's Printer, 1969. p. 170. *Statistics Canada, Statistics of Criminal and Other Offences 1969*. Ottawa: Information Canada, 1973. p. 20. Reproduced by permission of Information Canada.

REPRINTED WITH PERMISSION OF McGRAW-HILL RYERSON, LTD.

than 2 per cent) that it was on the decline. While this perception of our problems may not be in error, it nonetheless requires qualification.

A very general picture of crime in Canada over the past seven decades is provided in Figure 2-5. This figure presents rates of convictions by general offence categories from 1901 to 1971. Convictions for all offences increased steadily from the turn of the century until 1960. However, division of this total rate into its constituent parts reveals that the largest element in this overall increase was the steady ascent in the conviction rates for summary offences, particularly summary traffic offences.

Lynn McDonald (1969b) further analyzed such statistics to test the common contention that we are experiencing *rapidly* rising crime rates. Her findings revealed that increases in traffic offences in particular were not a meaningful index of dramatic changes in the dimensions of deviance, but rather a function of the number of motor vehicles in use. and eligible for violations. In addition, McDonald found that increases in the size of police forces accounted for a large part of the escalation in minor offences. There are also suggestions that increases in the number of persons in the "crime prone" age groups (a result of the post-war baby boom) may explain some inflation in our deviance rates of the early 1960s (Wilson, 1975:Chapter 1). Finally, Giffen (1965) adds that many minor property offences are explained by their occurrence in an affluent society whose many valuable and portable goods offer increasing opportunities "for the taking."

If we shift our attention to juvenile delinquency, we are provided another indication that the statistics of deviance are not all on an unvarying upward path. Data summarized by Giffen (1976), and presented in Figure 2-6, indicate average annual rates of delinquency for eight five-year periods between 1926 and 1965. The data presented in this figure conform in part with a worldwide pattern, and fail to confirm expectations of uniformly increasing rates of juvenile delinquency. These figures indicate that rates of juvenile delinquency went *down* during the depression, *rose* to a new high during World War II, *declined* to a low in 1951-55, *rose again* in 1956-60, and *continued to rise* in 1961-65. American historical studies similarly fail to confirm a unilateral increase in crime rates (Ferdinand, 1967; 1972).

Returning our attention to Figure 2-5, however, it is possible to argue that the period from 1961 to 1971 marks a time of transition. During this period, the total conviction rate declined, while the rate of the more serious indictable convictions increased. This pattern suggests a partial shift of attention away from minor offences, combined with a moderate increase in more serious crimes. This impression gains further support from changes in the rates of crimes of violence recorded in Table 2-6. These data suggest a gradual and consistent upward trend in all categories, with an overall 8 year increase of 118 per cent. Table 2-7 reveals a similar pattern of in-

FIGURE 2-6

RATES OF JUVENILE DELINQUENCY, CANADA, FIVE YEAR AVERAGES, 1926-65

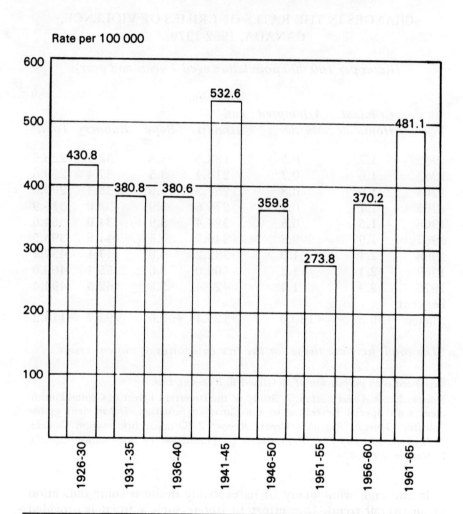

Rate per 100 000

Reprinted with permission of the Macmillan Company of Canada Limited.
Source: Giffen (1976)

crease during this period in rates of juvenile delinquency—with the largest increases in offences against the person and in violent property offences.

Table 2-6

CHANGES IN THE RATES OF CRIMES OF VIOLENCE, CANADA, 1962-1970

(Rates per 100 000 population aged 7 years and over)

Year	Criminal Homicide	Attempted Murder	Wounding and Assaults	Rape	Robbery	Total*
1962	1.7	0.5	188.5	3.8	32.1	226.6
1963	1.6	0.7	216.4	3.5	37.4	259.6
1964	1.6	0.8	257.3	4.6	35.3	299.6
1965	1.7	0.7	276.6	3.9	34.0	316.9
1966	1.5	0.8	324.4	3.9	34.0	364.6
1967	1.9	0.8	346.7	4.5	41.6	395.5
1968	2.1	1.0	382.2	5.0	47.1	437.4
1969	2.1	1.2	405.0	5.6	55.1	469.0
1970	2.3	1.4	424.4	5.8	62.5	494.4
Per cent change	+35.3	+180.0	+125.1	+52.6	+94.7	+118.2

The totals here are those for the five categories of violent crime.

Reprinted with permission of McGraw-Hill Ryerson, Ltd.

Source: *Ezzat Abdel Fattah*, A Study of the Deterrent Effect of Capital Punishment with Special Reference to the Canadian Situation, *Department of the Solicitor General, Research Centre Report 2 (Ottawa: Information Canada, 1972), pp. 94, 108-114. Reproduced by permission of Information Canada. In Manzer (1974:87).*

In the end, what many of us probably desire is some indication of an overall trend. One effort to isolate such a trend is provided in a time series analysis by Bedard and McLaughlin (1970; cited in Giffen, 1976), plotted in Figure 2-7. This graph superimposes a "linear trend line" on the annual 1949 to 1967 conviction rates for indictable offences, using a statistical procedure called the

Table 2-7

JUVENILES

*(Rates per 100 000 population aged 7 to 15 years for 1958-66
and 7 to 17 years for 1967-9)*

Year	Delinquencies Against the Person	Delinquencies Against Property With Violence	Delinquencies Against Property Without Violence	Total
1960	11	92	177	434
1961	11	103	189	477
1962	13	102	204	475
1963	14	108	206	489
1964	14	119	229	528
1965	14	111	207	492
1966	14	115	223	529
1967	17	139	242	579
1968	19	153	238	616
1969	21	160	261	640

Reprinted with permission of McGraw-Hill Ryerson, Ltd.
Sources: Canada, Dominion Bureau of Statistics, Canada Year Book 1963-64 *(Ottawa: Queen's Printer, 1964), pp. 388-9;* Canada Year Book 1966 *(Ottawa: Queen's Printer, 1966), pp. 420-1;* Canada Year Book 1968 *(Ottawa: Queen's Printer, 1968), pp. 439-40;* Canada Year Book 1970-71 *(Ottawa: Information Canada, 1971), pp. 512-3; Statistics Canada,* Canada Year Book 1972 *(Ottawa: Information Canada, 1972), pp. 489-90, 501;* Statistics of Criminal and Other Offences 1969 *(Ottawa: Information Canada, 1973), p. 10. Reproduced by permission of Information Canada. In Manzer (1974:86).*

"method of least squares." The result is a gradual pattern of increase averaging 0.65 per cent per year. The pressing question remains, are these increases "real" or "reported"? In other words, are they a result of changes in criminal behavior or an artifact of changes in public and police response?

No final answer to this question can be given. It is an issue of theoretical debate that we will examine further in latter chapters. Nevertheless, the increase in *recorded* crime *is* real, and we will suggest the following very tentative conclusions[17]: research such as that done by McDonald reveals that in the 1950s and the early 1960s increases in the total crime rate reflected changes in our access to automobiles and increases in police enforcement of minor statutes. The more recent data, however, suggest that current elevations in the crime rate *may* be a function of increases in more serious indictable offences. The contribution of policing activities to these increases is uncertain, but probably less substantial than in previous periods.

FIGURE 2-7

ANNUAL CRIME RATES PER 100 000 OF POPULATION: PERSONS AGED 16 YEARS AND OVER CONVICTED OF INDICTABLE OFFENCES, CANADA, 1949-1967. LINEAR TREND

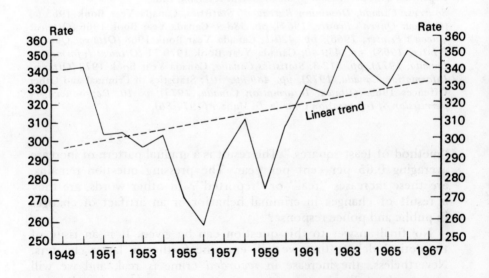

Source: Bedard and McLaughlin (1970). Reprinted with permission.

Comparable findings are reported in other areas of deviance. Drug surveys conducted in Toronto (Smart and Jackson, 1969; Smart *et al.*, 1970) in 1968 and 1970 reveal small increases in the number of high school students who have used marijuana (6.7 per cent to 18.3 per cent) and LSD (2.8 per cent to 8.5 per cent), but small *decreases* in the number who have used glue (5.7 per cent to 3.8 per cent) and stimulants (7.3 per cent to 6.7 per cent). A more recent survey conducted in a community close to Toronto (Oshawa, Ontario) reports use levels quite similar to those found in 1970, with the exception of further increases in marijuana use (Leon, 1974).

Findings in the area of alcohol abuse are less consoling. Two detailed field studies of the alcoholic population of Frontenac County in eastern Ontario, conducted in 1951 and 1961, provide a useful illustration of an increasing alcohol problem in Canada (see Schmidt, 1971:504-507). Information for this study was collected from a variety of sources: from official documents (e.g., police and hospital records) and from strategically located informants (e.g., physicians, public health nurses, social workers, clergy, employers, and selected city and county officials). For the purpose of the survey, alcoholics were defined as individuals whose histories revealed well-established patterns of undisciplined alcohol use which had culminated in damage to their health and/or to their financial and social standing. The results, presented in Table 2-8, reveal a 46 per cent increase in the rate of alcoholism in the county during the 10 year period between surveys. More recently, Leon (1974) reports increasing levels of alcohol abuse among high school populations.

Table 2-8

ALCOHOLICS PER 1000 PERSONS AGED 20 AND OVER IN 1951 AND 1961

Year	Adult Population	Total Alcoholics	Alcoholics per 1000 Adults
1951	43 606	698	16.01
1961	53 138	1 245	23.43
Increase in alcoholism rate			7.42
Percentage increase in alcoholism rate			46.37

Reprinted with permission of the Addiction Research Foundation of Ontario.
Source: Schmidt (1971:505)

FIGURE 2-8

INDICES OF TRENDS IN USAGE OF PSYCHIATRIC HOSPITAL BEDS IN CANADA FOR SELECTED YEARS
(RATES PER 100 000 POPULATION ON A SEMI-LOGARITHMIC SCALE)

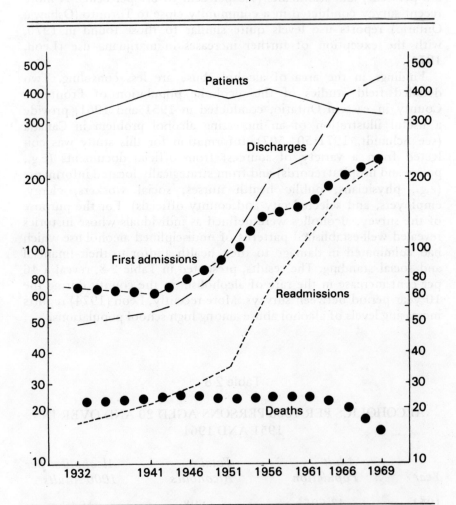

Reprinted from "Mental Health and Illness in Canada" by Williams, Kopinak, and Moynagh in Deviant Behaviour and Societal Reaction *by Boydell, Grindstaff, and Whitehead. © 1972 Holt, Rinehart and Winston of Canada, Ltd. Reprinted with permission of Holt, Rinehart and Winston of Canada, Ltd. Source: Williams, Kopinak, and Moynagh (1972:404)*

Some of the most interesting data in the field of deviance is found in the admission and discharge records of mental institutions. Such records reveal some striking changes in the societal response to mental illness over the past 40 years. For example, in Figure 2-8 we see that the number of patients per 100 000 population in mental hospitals has remained remarkably constant over 4 decades. At the same time, the number of persons per 100 000 population admitted for the first time in their lives has increased rather steadily since 1941. Whether this increase represents an actual increase in mental illness, or an increasing treatment response to its symptoms, is unclear. What is clear, however, is that mental institutions are admitting and releasing patients at a steadily increasing pace. Thus, the rate of discharge shows the largest annual rate of increase in Figure 2-8, with the rate of readmission showing a nearly identical upward trend. Both of these patterns reflect the increasing use of tranquilizers and community treatment programmes in an effort to keep patients functioning in the community for as long a period as possible. This new strategy in the mental health area is discussed more extensively by Gove (1975). For our purposes, it is sufficient to note that this strategy reflects a significant societal trend toward the reintegration of individuals into the community setting. Whether this trend has progressed *far* enough is a continuing issue.

More generally, we can conclude this section by saying that in recent years many measures of deviant behavior show a pattern of increase. There are important exceptions to this statement, particularly in the area of drug abuse. Further, we have seen that during a significant part of this century, increases in the "crime rate" were largely a function of the growing number of cars and increasing levels of police prosecution of minor offences. Finally, we are uncertain whether increasing rates of mental illness reflect changes in actual behaviors, or our treatment responses to them. Nonetheless, among the more serious forms of deviance, the consensual crimes, the recent pattern of increase seems more clear. How this apparent rate of increase is related to the public's perception of it is an important question for further study.

DO SOME SOCIAL GROUPS EXPERIENCE MORE DEVIANT BEHAVIOR THAN OTHERS?

There are few issues in sociology that cause as much controversy as the question of whether deviant behavior is more common in some social groups than in others. This controversy follows in large part from two contrasting assumptions about the occurrence of deviant behavior in society's "underclass." The first assumption is that poverty carries with it many socially injurious experiences, as well as an unequal distribution of opportunities, and that these experiences and pressures lead logically to deviant outcomes. The second assumption is that the poor are victims of prejudice, and that this leads to their more frequent apprehension, prosecution, or "treatment" for deviant behavior. The first assumption implies that the underclass is more deviant, the second that they are differentially processed for being so. Although these assumptions have differing implications, both, of course, can be true. Indeed, we will argue that both assumptions *are* true, and that the more reasonable question is, "*How* true is each?" In this section, we will explore class-linked patterns of deviant behavior. In Chapter Five, we will consider the assumption of prejudice and discrimination in the activities of various agencies of social control.

Official records of crime and delinquency suggest a clear class pattern. Persons officially charged with criminal and delinquent offences are disproportionately of low socio-economic status. The suspicion, however, is that these records under-represent much crime and delinquency that occurs in the middle and upper classes. Self-report surveys are one means of checking on the class distribution of these events. Such surveys have been administered to high school students (Nye and Short, 1957), college students (Porterfield, 1943), and adults (Wallerstein and Wyle, 1947).

Early results from the self-report studies frequently failed to find a relationship between class position and the proportion of respondents admitting criminal or delinquent acts. For example, Edmund Vaz (1966) reports the results of a self-report survey conducted in four Canadian communities. The findings of this survey reveal no higher incidence of delinquency in the lower classes than in the middle and upper classes. This type of study is valuable in suggesting that much middle and upper class delinquency remains "hidden," and that these behaviors too deserve explanation (Vaz, 1967).

Unfortunately, however, it is not always clear that the self-report studies of delinquency are measuring the *same* behaviors as are the official records. Self-report devices vary widely in their content, some containing many items of very minor seriousness, with others tapping more serious infractions. In addition, many self-report surveys do not measure the frequency with which various infractions may take place. Finally, there is a possibility of class bias in recall: middle and upper class offenders may recount many minor infractions in detail, while lower status respondents may less accurately remember more serious acts of deviance. Thus, in spite of the findings reported above, Vaz (1966) concludes his study with the observation that,

"The largest amount and toughest kind of delinquency is found usually in the slum or 'disorganized' areas of large cities." (25.) Vaz bases this estimation on the assumption that his own research " . . . does not include the hard-core nor variety of delinquency found in metropolitan centres." (25.)[18] Evidence consistent with this conclusion includes recent surveys of victims of crimes of violence in 13 large American cities (U.S. Department of Justice, 1975), 12 of which find higher rates of interpersonal violence (i.e., rape, robbery, and assault) in lower, as contrasted with higher, income groups.

One indication that different *types* of behaviors probably *are* class-linked is the derivation by Vaz (1965; 1967) of two uni-dimensional scales for the measurement of middle class delinquency in Canadian communities. Items included in these scales were of the following types: " . . .taken little things that did not belong to you; gambled for money at cards, dice, or other games; driven a car beyond the speed limit; skipped school without a legitimate excuse; been feeling *high* from drinking beer, wine, liquor; bought or tried to buy beer, wine, or liquor from a store or adult; taken a glass of beer, wine, or liquor at a party or elsewhere with your friends; tried to be intimate (go the limit) with a member of the opposite sex." (1967:141.)[19] It can be noted that most of these behaviors do not require, or even encourage, an official response.

Answers to a self-report questionnaire are typically added together to provide a cumulative scale score for each individual. However, an important problem may emerge when, for purposes of analysis, a cutting point is designated as the position above which individuals are considered "delinquent." A mean or median score usually is selected to make this distinction, and the scale results are then correlated with the social class backgrounds of the respondents to determine the presence or absence of a relationship (cf., Chambliss and Nagasawa, 1969). However, Nettler (1974a) notes that, "Since it is not known what score on the questionnaire represents activities equivalent to those for which the same people . . . (would be) *arrested,* the cutting points are arbitrary." (95, emphasis added.) The significance of this observation is that a small change in the cutting point may produce a substantial change in the findings. Put differently, it would be very unlikely that a median cutting point on a scale of trivial items could produce any other finding than that most people are more or less equally deviant. The issue is more meaningfully addressed when a scale of serious items is used.

Two Canadian self-report studies illustrate the points we are discussing. The first study was conducted by Marc Le Blanc (1969; 1975) in Montreal, using the self-report instrument originally developed by Nye and Short (1957). The second study was conducted by Stephen Tribble (1972), in Fredericton, New Brunswick, using an original scale of 15 items. The instruments are presented side by side in Figure 2-9. Some of the items included in the scale used by Tribble represent rather serious offences, while the larger number of items included in the Nye and Short scale give a broader representation to relatively minor indiscretions. Perhaps it is not surprising, then, that Le Blanc's Montreal study reveals a near random class distribution of delinquency, while Tribble's Fredericton study finds delinquency more common among persons of lower socio-economic status.

Our conclusion is that Tribble's study probably more accurately represents the class distribution of serious delinquent acts. However, it must also be noted that the representation of low status offenders in the official records is commonly more extensive than Tribble's study suggests (see Hagan, 1975:544). It is here that Le Blanc's findings become important. Le Blanc reports that 60 per cent of the adolescents with above-average delinquency scores are officially processed as delinquents, while only 32 per cent of the upper-class adolescents experience this fate. In short, the incidence of serious delinquent acts appears to be class-linked (see also McDonald, 1969a), but official records appear to exaggerate the extent of this linkage. Several sources of this over-representation are discussed in Chapter Five.

For the moment, it deserves mention that our conception of what constitutes a serious delinquent or deviant act is subject to change. More interesting still, there is some evidence that as activities become more common in the upper classes, they come to be considered less serious in nature. For example, in the period of one generation, marijuana use moved from a symptom of "reefer madness" to a "radical chic" symbol of status. Thus, although marijuana was once the drug of the ghetto, it is now a social lubricant for those who can afford it. Self-report surveys reflect this change in status: Barter *et al.* (1970) and Suchman (1968) report a higher incidence of marijuana use among persons from high-income families, and a California study (Blum, 1969) comparing patterns of usage in working and middle class high schools reveals higher figures in the latter.

Changes of use in the "hard" drugs are less substantial. Thus, while one American college survey (Francis and Patch, 1969; cited in Berg, 1970) reports that 17 per cent of the students had used some form of opiates 1 or more times, only 1 per cent of those responding had used an opiate often or regularly. In contrast, research by Robins and Murphy (1967) indicates that as much as 13 per cent of a normal male ghetto population may be, or have been, regular users of heroin (see also Chein [1966] and Finestone [1966]).

FIGURE 2-9

SELF-REPORT QUESTIONNAIRES

Within the last twelve months have you ever acted in the following ways?

1. Seriously hurt an animal?
2. Kill an animal without a licence?
3. Purchase liquor?
4. Drive a car or truck without a licence?
5. Drive a car dangerously? *i.e.* above the speed limit, while drunk, etc.
6. Take a car without the owner's permission?
7. Enter somebody's place without his permission?
8. Enter somebody's place and in the process break a lock, door, window, fence, or damage his property in any way?
9. Damage somebody's property?
10. Beat up another person with the intention of really hurting him?
11. "Hung around" the streets in the early hours of the morning?
12. Take something that didn't belong to you under the value of, say, fifty dollars?
13. Forge a cheque?
14. Take something, not belonging to you, and again, without the owner's permission, of a value of more than fifty dollars?
15. Sold, or tried to sell drugs?

Have you ever:

1. Skipped school?
2. Been in a fist fight with another person?
3. Disobeyed your parents?
4. Driven a car without a driver's licence?
5. Left home?
6. Defied openly the authority of your parents?
7. Driven a car dangerously or beyond the speed limit?
8. Taken small objects (less than $2.00) that did not belong to you?
9. Taken objects of an average value (between $2.00 and $50.00) that did not belong to you?
10. Taken objects of greater value ($50.00 or more) that did not belong to you?
11. Taken things, ignoring that they didn't belong to you?
12. Taken part in teenage gang fights?
13. Taken a car for a spin without the permission of the owner?
14. Entered into sexual relations with someone of the same sex?
15. Hit children that haven't done anything to you?
16. Been expelled from school or put on trial?
17. Bought or drunk beer, wine, or other alcoholic drinks?
18. Hurt or inflicted injuries on someone just for kicks?
19. Intentionally damaged or destroyed public or private property that does not belong to you?
20. Used or sold drugs (narcotics, goofballs, etc.)?
21. Entered into sexual relations with someone of the opposite sex?

Reprinted with permission of the Canadian Criminology and Corrections Association.
Source: Tribble (1972:99)

From F. Ivan Nye and James F. Short, "Scaling Delinquent Behavior," American Sociological Review, Vol. 22, June 1957, p. 328. Reprinted with permission of American Sociological Review.
Source: Le Blanc (1969)

Some observations can also be offered on the class distribution of mental illness and alcohol abuse. Official statistics in both of these areas are complicated by the fact that persons of higher socio-economic status are more successful in obtaining various types of treatment. Thus, in the area of alcoholism, Schmidt *et al.* (1968) describe a situation common in Canadian communities, " . . . the Salvation Army facilities cater primarily to the derelict alcoholic; Alcoholics Annonymous serves alcoholics mainly from the middle class of society; and private alcoholism clinics admit the upper classes who can afford the treatment offered." (6.) Similar patterns are found in public and private institutions dealing with mental illness (Gove, 1975). Thus the class composition of particular institutions studied may be dependent on the selection procedures operating. This situation makes the use of official data unsuitable for our current purpose.

Fortunately, alternative sources of data are available in both the areas of alcohol abuse and mental illness. Household surveys asking the following question, "Have you or any member of the household ever had difficulty because of too much drinking?" reveal a higher incidence of such problems in the lower class (e.g., Bailey *et al.*, 1965). The suggestion that these findings simply reflect a class difference in the ability to keep drinking problems hidden is answered in an analysis by Cahalan (1970): " . . . upper-status men also show a markedly lower prevalence of concealable type-of-drinking indicies (frequent intoxication, binge drinking, and symptomatic drinking) as well as in the less concealable interpersonal types of problems." (48.)

Similar types of conclusions are found in the area of mental illness (cf., Roman and Trice, 1967; Murphy, 1969; Clausen, 1971; Dohrenwend and Dohrenwend, 1969; 1974). Thus, Dohrenwend and Dohrenwend (1975) report that "The highest overall rates of psychiatric disorder have been found in the lowest social class in 28 out of the 33 studies that report data according to indicators of social class." (370.) The background of this situation is cogently summarized in a Canadian review of the mental health literature by Williams, Kopinak, and Moynagh (1972:394):

As social status improves, families are more likely to seek better prenatal and postnatal care, to provide better emotional and social childbearing patterns, to protect family members from stress, to afford more opportunities for education and occupational advancement, to have more stable marriages and family life, to recognize emotional problems earlier, and to seek out and utilize better health care facilities. In short, as the social status of a group increases, its members not only are less likely to have mental problems but also are more likely to have the knowledge, motivation, and capabilities to cope with them.*

More generally, the advantages of social class are cumulative, and corresponding disadvantages are reflected in higher rates of alcoholism and mental illness in society's underclass.

There is consistency in our findings. The forms of deviance currently considered serious are unequally distributed through the class structure, with the lower class experiencing more than its equal share of crime and delinquency, hard drug use, problems of alcohol abuse, and mental illness. There is also, inevitably, a footnote to this summation: the more marginal forms of deviance (like marijuana use) are less clearly (if not inversely) class-linked, and the official responses to some forms of deviance (most notably, crime and delinquency) seem to exaggerate actual class differences in the occurrence of these behaviors. Finally, as some behaviors once thought serious become more apparent in the upper classes, the evaluation of their seriousness may change. Acknowledging the latter patterns, however, should not obscure the importance of our more general conclusion that the disadvantages of social class are reflected in a higher incidence in the underclass of those forms of deviance now considered most serious, and dealt with as such.

CONCLUSIONS

The statistics of deviance are problematic, and therefore subject to interpretation. We suggested that all such data contain two components. The first component is made up of actual behaviors and their authors, while the second component is an error term, representing either the over- or under-reporting of the events and persons involved. The best statistics on deviance are informed by comparisons of alternative measures, drawn from a variety of sources, including: (1) official agencies of social control, (2) non-official agencies, (3) first person accounts, (4) victimization surveys, and (5) observational studies. When estimates based on several of these measures agree, we are encouraged as to the validity of our results; to the extent that different measures may disagree, we are alerted to possible sources of error.

Using a variety of measures, and focusing on problems of crime and delinquency, mental illness, alcoholism, and other forms of drug abuse, our discussion of the statistics of deviance suggested several necessarily tentative conclusions.

• Actual levels of deviation appear far higher than many of our official measures indicate. Just how high these "actual" levels might be is unknown, and probably unknowable. Further, it is one of the measures of the freeness of a society that only the more serious forms of deviance are closely monitored. Unfortunately, a troublesome moral issue is that of deciding which forms of deviance should be considered serious.

• Those forms of deviance widely seen as most serious by the public (violent crime and "hard" drug abuse) are found more commonly in the United States than in Canada. At present, we cannot say how great this difference between the United States and Canada is, nor whether this disparity will persist.

• In recent years, several measures of deviance have shown some increase in Canada. It is in the area of the more serious forms of deviance, the consensual crimes, that the recent patterns seem most apparent. Balanced against this statement are the observations that some patterns of drug abuse seem to have stabilized, and that some prior impressions of *rapidly* rising crime rates were a function of increasing levels of police prosecution of minor offences.

•Official records frequently over-represent the link between social class and rates of deviant behavior. Nonetheless, evidence reviewed indicates that forms of deviance currently considered serious and treated as such are unequally distributed through the class structure, with the lower class experiencing more than its fair share of crime and delinquency, hard drug use, problems of alcohol abuse, and mental illness.

Differing types of explanations are offered for the patterns of deviance we have described. We will argue in the two chapters that follow that these explanations are of two fundamental types: (1) the consensual theories of deviance, and (2) the conflict theories of disrepute. It is to the task of explanation, then, that we turn next.

1. From Michael Hindelang, "The Uniform Crime Reports Revisited," *Journal of Criminal Justice*, 2(1):1-17. Reprinted with permission of Pergamon Press, Ltd.

2. For a discussion of attempts to improve the quality of the official data on crime in Canada, see Cassidy and Hopkinson (1974).

3. From Ned Polsky, *Hustlers, Beats, and Others.* © 1969 Aldine Publishing Company. Reprinted with permission of Aldine Publishing Company.

4. Ibid.

5. These authors note that, "several of these subjects augmented interv data with demonstrations of some basic methods of passing cheques. T demonstrations were carried through to the point of certainty but not criminality, i.e., the next step in the process would have broken the law . . . ." (276n.)

6. Whether or not this promise is fulfilled, self-reported criminal victimization can at least provide a useful perceptual measure of an individual's sense of well-being with respect to crime.

7. From Laud Humphreys, *Tearoom Trade.* © 1970 Aldine Publishing Company. Reprinted with permission of Aldine Publishing Company, Chicago, and Gerald Duckworth and Company, Ltd., London.

8. From Albert Reiss, "Systematic Observation of Natural Social Phenomena," in Hebert Costner (Ed.), *Sociological Methodology 1971*. 1971 Jossey-Bass, Inc.

9. Ibid.

10. This figure would be much lower were it not for the large number of "self-clearing" offences where the apprehension of the suspect is effectively synonymous with the official discovery of the crime (e.g., impaired driving and public drunkenness). For offences like theft, the clearance rates are often between 10 and 20 per cent.

11. From M.C. Courtis, *Attitudes to Crime and the Police in Toronto*, 1970 Centre of Criminology, University of Toronto.

12. Ibid.

13. This disparity is, presumably, a comment on "how soon we forget," and the inability of the victims themselves to provide a reminder!

14. From Michael Hindelang, "The Uniform Crime Reports Revisited," *Journal of Criminal Justice*, 2(1):1-17. Reprinted with permission of Pergamon Press, Ltd.

15. One indication that the official data in this area may be better than is frequently assumed is found in a field study by McAuliffe (1975) of addict "copping sites." McAuliffe found that local police identified and recorded the names of 90 per cent of the addicts sampled. He concludes that, " . . . being 'pulled up' by the narcotics squad is an important part of feeling one is a 'sure-enough junkie' and of claiming to be one among addict peers." (209-210.)

16. Surveys conducted in the summer of 1975 find 4 per cent of an Ontario sample ranking "law and order" as their province's most important problems, while 19 per cent of a national American sample ranked "crime and drugs" as their nation's most important problems (Toronto *Star*, Sept. 2, 1975; Houston *Post* July 27, 1975).

17. Since these conclusions *are tentative*, the critical reader is encouraged to regard them as opinions.

18. It is of interest to note that in devising the type of scale used in the self-report studies, Nye and Short (1957) issued the following warning that many researchers less careful than Vaz have frequently forgotten: "It is not the suggestion of this paper that the study of delinquency by scales of reported behavior should replace the collection of official data . . . . Some . . . research must remain in the manipulation of officially defined problems and statistics, particularly the study of murder . . . and other very serious offences." (331.)

19. From Edmund Vaz, "Juvenile Delinquency in the Middle Class Youth Culture," *Canadian Review of Sociology and Anthropology* 2(1):52-70. Reprinted from the *Canadian Review of Sociology and Anthropology*, Volume 2, Number 1, by permission of the author and publisher.

III

EXPLAINING DEVIANCE:
The Consensus Theories

"Why would anyone break the rules of life that nearly all of us accept—particularly when observing these rules may be a means of obtaining the things most of us value?" This is the question the consensus theories of deviance try to answer. Before considering the answers provided, however, we should note that the question itself makes a very important assumption. The question posed assumes that most of us *do* agree about the rules we are expected to follow, and the things we hope to obtain. This assumption of consensus is subject to debate, and the conflict theories, considered in the following chapter, voice the alternative side of the argument. For the moment, however, we will accept the assumption of consensus, noting only that it may be truer of some rules of life (e.g., those regulating serious crimes of violence) than others.

There are three types of consensus theories of deviance, and each explains rule-breaking behavior in a different way:

Anomie theory notes that some people find the rules, or norms, of society useless in seeking the good things in life, and that therefore they turn to rule-breaking behavior as an alternative means of obtaining the things they value.

Neutralization theory suggests that although most of us learn the norms and values of society, some of us also learn how to rationalize, or neutralize, their violation.

Control theory argues that some people feel less constrained than others by their experience with the norms and values of society, and that therefore they feel relatively free to deviate.

There is, of course, more to each of these theories than the summary statements just presented. These statements are helpful, however, in making the initial point that each of the consensus theories is concerned with how persons come to violate norms and values that we are assumed to share in common. Our task in this chapter will be to examine each of the consensus theories in more detail.

72

ANOMIE THEORY

Durkheim, Anomie, and Suicide. The concept of anomie emerged in the work of the French sociologist Emile Durkheim (1897). In its initial usage, the term referred to an absence of social regulation, or normlessness. Durkheim introduced his discussion of anomie by noting that physical and social needs are regulated in significantly different ways. For example, when physical hunger is satiated, the body *itself* will resist additional food. But the social needs—including wealth, prestige, and power—are regulated *externally*, through the constraining forces of society. Undisciplined by this guardian social order, Durkheim assumed that our desires are an "insatiable and bottomless abyss." (247.) Further, Durkheim argued that humanity's darkest danger resided in the absence of regulation, or absolute freedom: "It is not true, then, that human activity can be released from all restraint. ... its nature and method of manifestation ... depend not only on itself but on other beings, who consequently restrain and regulate it." (252.) For Durkheim, as for Kris Kristofferson and Bobby McGee, then, "Freedom is just another word for nothing left to lose."

Suicide, the ultimate act of anomie, was the subject of Durkheim's best known research. The assumption that guided this research was that suicide rates vary with two social conditions: social integration and social regulation. Durkheim argued that excessively low *or* high levels of integration and regulation can bring high rates of suicide. Thus, high levels of integration can result in states of *altruism*, exemplified in the human sacrifices of primitive peoples, and the brave but deadly acts of modern soldiers. On the other hand, low levels of integration are said to result in *egoism* and higher rates of suicide among unmarried persons and members of Protestant (as contrasted with Catholic and Jewish) religions. Excessive regulation produces *fatalism* that causes higher suicide rates among childless married women and very young husbands. Finally, low levels of regulation bring *anomie* and higher suicide rates among widows and divorced persons, as well as among business people during economic booms and slumps. For our purposes, anomie, with its attention to economic conditions and its implications for types of deviance other than suicide, is the most important element in Durkheim's discussion.

Durkheim's proposed cure for anomie is found in his suggestion that, "No living being can be happy or even exist unless his needs are sufficiently proportioned to his means." (246.)[1] Rather than social or economic reform, then, Durkheim recommends an attitude of resignation as the solution to the problems of anomie. In particular, Durkheim was stubborn in his belief that economic reforms could not effectively resolve conditions of anomie. He insisted instead

that, "One sort of heredity will always exist, that of natural talent . . . .
A moral discipline will therefore still be required to make those less
favored by nature accept the lesser advantages which they owe to
chances of birth." (251.)[2] Indeed, Durkheim went so far as to find
virtue in poverty, suggesting that, "It is actually the best school for
teaching self-restraint." (254.)[3]

Robert Merton assumed the task of extracting a more liberal
sentiment from this Durkheimian tradition. Merton did this by
reformulating the relationship postulated between goals and means
in anomie theory. Where Durkheim argued that the goals of individuals
are infinitely *variable*, and that stability and conformity depend on
the moderation of unrestricted goals, Merton regarded these goals
as *constant*, and the subject of societal consensus.[4] The attention in
Merton's reformulation, then, shifts to the relationship between
these fixed goals and the *variable means* of achieving them.

Merton, Social Structure, and Anomie. Merton's (1938; 1957;
1959) reformulation of Durkheim's theory of anomie was stimulated
by a basic disagreement with the assumptions underlying the original
discussion. For example, rather than seeing human beings' desires as
"insatiable" and "bottomless," Merton suggested that, "The image of
man as an untamed bundle of impulses begins to look more like a
caricature than a portrait." (1957:31.)[5] Beyond this, Merton was
interested in exploring variations in deviant behavior by social class,
"For whatever the role of impulses, there still remains the further
question of why it is that the frequency of deviant behavior varies
within different social structures . . . . " (131.)[6] Merton's answer to
this question was that some social structures, particularly the class
structure, exert excessive pressure on persons disadvantageously
located in society.

Merton focused on two features of social and cultural structure:
culturally defined *goals*, and the acceptable *means* of achieving
these goals (132). The problem, said Merton, was that in societies
like our own, goals such as financial success often are emphasized
to the neglect of adequate means of achieving them. In Merton's
reformulation, then, anomie does not result simply from the un-
regulated goals that Durkheim discussed, but rather from a faulty
relationship between goals and the legitimate means of access to
them. In sum, the problem is one of shared success goals, and the
limited means for their attainment.

Merton goes on to develop a typology of goals, means, and ways
of adapting to their relationship. This typology is reproduced in
Table 3-1. "Adaptation Type I" in this typology represents what
most theories of deviance leave unexplained: conformity. According

to Merton's theory, conforming behavior occurs where the goals and means of society are accepted, and successfully pursued.

Table 3-1

TYPES OF ADAPTATION TO THE RELATIONSHIP BETWEEN CULTURAL GOALS AND INSTITUTIONALIZED MEANS*

	Culture Goals	Institutionalized Means
I. Conformity	+	+
II. Innovation	+	−
III. Ritualism	−	+
IV. Retreatism	−	−
V. Rebellion	±	±

*(+) signifies acceptance, (−) signifies elimination, and (±) signifies "rejection and substitution of new goals and standards."

From Robert Merton Social Theory and Social Structure. © *1957 Free Press of Glencoe. Reprinted with permission of Macmillan Publishing Co., Inc.*
Source: Merton (1957:140)

Adaptation Type II, innovation, " . . . occurs when the individual has assimilated the cultural emphasis upon the goal without equally internalizing the institutional norms governing ways and means for its attainment." (141.)[7] Foremost in Merton's mind here are the various economic and property crimes of adults and juveniles. His particular concern is that these events may be more common in the lower social and economic classes. The explanation is found in a class-located strain between shared goals and scarce means:

Of those located in the lower reaches of the social structure, the culture makes incompatible demands. On the one hand, they are asked to orient their conduct toward the prospect of large wealth—'Every man a King' said Marden and Carnegie and Long—and on the other, they are largely denied effective opportunities to do so institutionally. The consequence of this structural inconsistency is a high rate of deviant behavior (146).*

Reprinted with permission of Macmillan Publishing Co., Inc.

The victims of this contradiction may not immediately recognize its source. However, if their consciousness is provoked, Merton warns, they may become ready candidates for Adaptation Type V: rebellion. Following Merton, we will consider this possibility last.

If innovation is a common adaptation of the lower class, Merton suggests that it is the lower middle class that is fated to Adaptation Type III: ritualism. The ritualist has foregone all hopes of successfully achieving societal goals, but nonetheless clings compulsively to institutional norms. The ritualist, in other words, is an obsessive follower of rules, without ever wondering why. He is society's "Nowhere Man," "doesn't have a point of view, knows not where he's going to." Ritualists live by a series of cultural cliches: "I'm not sticking *my* neck out," "I'm playing it safe," "I'm satisfied with what I've got," "Don't aim high and you won't be disappointed." In other words, the ritualist has "sold out," "copped out," and, most significantly, "lost out."

The least common of the adaptations is the fourth: retreatism. In this category are located the societal dropouts, including by Merton's enumeration some psychotics, autists, pariahs, outcasts, vagrants, tramps, alcoholics, and drug addicts. Such persons have rejected both the goals and means of our society; they are therefore *in* society, but not *of* it. In other words, the link between such life-styles, and the society surrounding them, is tenuous.

Adaptation Type V brings rebellion. The essence of this adaptation is an organized struggle for change, seeking to "... introduce a social structure in which the cultural standards of success would be sharply modified and provision would be made for a closer correspondence between merit, effort, and reward." (155.)[8] We have noted previously that when Type II Adaptation, innovation, is informed of its class basis, a progression to rebellion can occur. This progression is attested to by the successful "consciousness raising" of the Black Muslims, Black Panthers, and the American Indian Movement in some American and Canadian prisons. Nonetheless, Merton ironically notes that, "... it is typically members of a rising class rather than the most depressed strata who organize the resentful and the rebellious into a revolutionary group." (157.)[9]

The emphasis of Merton's theory of anomie, then, is on socially structured adaptations to failure. The focus in this theory is on problems of access to *legitimate* means of achieving the goals we share collectively. But what of the *il*legitimate means of achieving these goals? Theoretical consideration of the socially structured *deviant* career routes was left to Cloward and Ohlin.

Cloward, Ohlin, and Differential Opportunity.[10] Cloward and Ohlin (1960; see also Cloward, 1959) argue that pressures and motivation toward deviance, no matter how accurately portrayed by Merton, are not enough to explain the *type* of deviant behavior that is pursued. They suggest that the potential thief, like the potential physician, "must have access to a learning environment and, once having been trained, must be allowed to perform his role." (147.) In other words, Cloward and Ohlin assert that we must offer as much attention to deviant as to conforming success routes if we are going to understand the final life styles adopted. To do this, Cloward and Ohlin suggest that we " . . . think of individuals as being located in two opportunity structures—one legitimate, the other illegitimate. Given limited access to success-goals by legitimate means, the nature of the delinquent response . . . will vary according to the availability of various illegitimate means." (152.)

Cloward and Ohlin see the varying illegitimate opportunities of slum life as leading to three types of deviant lifestyles: a stable criminal pattern, a conflict pattern, and a retreatist pattern. The stable criminal career pattern requires that there exist in the community some coordination between persons in legitimate and illegitimate roles (cf., Kobrin, 1951). For example, the delinquent moving toward a stable criminal career pattern must begin to develop contacts with mature criminals, law-enforcement officials, politicians, bail bonders, lawyers, fences, and others. Such experiences are said to expand the potential criminal's knowledge and skills, thus opening up new opportunities for more protected and rewarding activities. Thus, "The criminal, like the occupant of a conventional role, must establish relationships with other categories of persons, all of whom contribute in one way or another to the successful performance of criminal activity." (165.)

Cloward and Ohlin go on to note that violence is disruptive of both criminal and conventional activities, and that therefore where opportunities for either type of career pattern exist, the occurrence of violent conflict will be restricted. However, where neither success route is present, controls on violence are *absent*, and conflict patterns emerge. This, according to Cloward and Ohlin, is the problem of the disorganized slum, populated in part by failures in the conventional world, and also by the outcasts of the criminal world. The result: "As long as conventional and criminal opportunity structures remain closed, violence continues unchecked." (175.)

Finally, there remains the problem of those individuals who fail in their experiences with both the criminal and conflict opportunity structures. Cloward and Ohlin note that competition is intense in both of these spheres, just as it is in the more conventional worlds of opportunity. The resulting "double failures," then, are fated, according to Cloward and Ohlin, to "retreatism," and particularly to drug abuse.

In all of this, Cloward and Ohlin suggest that deviants are likely to be *conscious* participants in the direction of their fate. Unlike Merton, then, these authors see most deviants as being actively aware of the injustices of their class-linked experience (108). Arguing that, ". . . the basic endowments of delinquents are the equal of or greater than those of their nondelinquent peers," Cloward and Ohlin characterize predelinquents as ". . . persons who have been led to expect opportunities because of their potential ability to meet the formal, institutionally established criteria of evaluation." (117.) The suspicion of injustice is awakened, however, as the potential delinquent finds that, ". . . ultimate success is likely to involve such criteria as race, speech, mannerisms, familial ties, and 'connections.' " (118.) Slowly, the predelinquent becomes conscious that the deck is stacked against him, and thus, ". . . he perceives his failure to gain access to opportunities as an injustice in the system rather than as a deficiency in himself." (118.) This view of the situation, according to Cloward and Ohlin, allows the individual ". . . to join with others in a delinquent solution to his problem without great concern about the moral validity of his actions." (118.) Ironically, Cloward and Ohlin add that the efforts of social reformers may unintentionally intensify this process by calling public attention to social injustices. Thus, "The efforts of reformers to expose discriminatory practices actually furnish such persons with further justification for withdrawing sentiments in support of the legitimacy of the established norms. . . ." (122; cf., Banfield, 1968:171; Matza, 1964:95-98.)

Some Critical Comments on Anomie and Opportunity. We can, of course, pick and choose among the thoughts of a theorist, and therefore Cloward and Ohlin's comments on the *conscious* deliberations of the delinquent can be questioned without dismissing the total theory. The root of the problem is suggested in Bordua's comment that, "Each generation does not meet and solve anew the problems of class structured barriers to opportunity, but begins with the solution of its forebears." (1961:134-135.) In other words, Cloward and Ohlin's presentation seems to demand of *each* delinquent that he or she have thought through in conscious terms the contradictions of his or her position in the class structure. A large body of research (Stinchcombe, 1964; Reiss and Rhodes, 1961; Downes, 1966; Hirschi, 1969; Short, Rivera, and Tennyson, 1965) fails to provide evidence of this process. None of this denies that opportunities are unjustly denied to particular groups, but rather suggests that the *historical* background of this situation may blur in most people's minds its connection with current circumstances.

Thus, *in the short range*, the *pleasures* of a deviant lifestyle may provide a more convincing explanation of their occurrence among *individuals* than is found in the picture of the vengeful victim of injustice painted by Cloward and Ohlin. Said differently, Cloward and Ohlin's theory may cite the justifications, rather than the causes, of the individual behaviors they seek to explain. Thus, when the famous bank robber Willie Sutton is asked why he robs banks, his well known answer is *not* that this institution is a particularly noxious symbol of a corporate power structure that has unjustly denied him opportunities, but rather that he has made this particular career choice "because that's where the money is." No sense of injustice is required; this choice is simply a rational selection among the opportunities available.

As an alternative to poverty, it is reasonable to see alcohol and drug abuse, theft, and even violence as pleasurable, satisfying, and, in this context, desirable lifestyles (cf., Nettler, 1974a). As Chief Broom tells us in *One Flew Over the Cuckoo's Nest*, even life in the back wards of a mental institution can be less painful than life in the "underclass." This account will become more comprehensive as it is combined with those theories (considered later in this chapter) focusing on the absence of inducements to conformity in conditions of poverty.

At this point, however, it should be noted that Durkheim's and Merton's versions of anomie theory were constructed to explain *group-based rates* of deviant behavior, rather than the actions or thoughts of individuals. Returning our focus to group-based rates, and away from individuals, allows us to consider the historical roots of differential opportunity structures, and their ultimate consequences for individuals caught in the resulting social and economic circumstances. This point is conveyed best with an example: a social-historical case study of Africville, Nova Scotia, conducted by Donald Clairmont (1974).

An Example: The Case of Africville

Until its displacement for industrial and harbour development in the middle 1960s, Africville was a predominately black community located close to Halifax. The community was founded before 1850 by the descendants of refugee blacks who fled slavery in the United States during the War of 1812. Clairmont's research reveals that in the beginning Africville was a viable community with a few fine houses, some small-scale businesses, plenty of space, and a strong community spirit based on a stable kinship system. However, Africville developed in a period when the Nova Scotian economy was sluggish, if not stagnant; furthermore, whatever new economic opportunities that could have helped channel blacks into the economic mainstream were not made available. This context provides the basis for Clairmont's clear statement of the hypothesis of differential opportunity: "Minority group members, if oppressed and discriminated against, often find a mode of adjusting to their situation by performing less desirable and sometimes illegitimate services for the majority group." (36.)[11] Clairmont demonstrates that these conditions made Africville a "deviance service centre" for the rest of Halifax.

Two factors were essential in the development of Africville as a deviance service centre. First, Africville was located close to the dockyards and general port activity. Second, the community was given the "functional autonomy" by city fathers to develop the

FIGURE 3-1

1919 AFRICVILLE PETITION TO HALIFAX CITY COUNCIL

We, the undersigned ratepayers, do hereby make application for better police protection at Africville. We base our application on the following grounds: that a police officer seldom or never visits this district, except for a warrant or subpoena; that conditions that now prevail here are worse than at any time before; that these lamentable conditions tend to turn the majority away from the good teaching which they have received; that there is now an utter disregard of the Lord's day by many residents; that there are many persons, strangers in our midst, living openly in a state of debauchery, which must corrupt the minds of youth for we are more or less subject to our environment; that there is nightly confusion, carousel and dissipation which disturb the night; that these carousels have been the centres for spreading infection throughout the village; that we believe, if this disgraceful state of affairs continues there will be some grave crime or crimes committed.

Our earnest desire is that your Honourable Body, in this period of reconstruction, carefully consider our application so that the omission of the past may be rectified and by your assistance the evil influences now at work may be greatly reduced; then shall we be better able to train the young in the way of good citizenship and place the village on a better plane of Social Welfare.

Reprinted with permission of Donald Clairmont and the Canadian publishers, McClelland and Stewart, Ltd., Toronto.
Source: Clairmont (1974:37)

conditions of anomie described by Durkheim and Merton: " . . . that is, not sharing fairly in society's wealth, they . . . (were) allowed by the authorities a range of behavior, that would not be countenanced elsewhere." (36.)[12] These two factors came together during the First World War in the form of a growing bootlegging trade. Fearing a growing problem, residents of Africville petitioned the City Council of Halifax (see Figure 3-1) requesting police surveillance and protection. The response came in the form of a recommendation that Africville form its *own* police department.

In the period that followed the First World War, Africville continued to grow as a deviance service centre. Thus, as bootlegging gradually gave way to more hazardous forms of vice, the predictions of the petitioners of 1919 eventually were confirmed. Summarizing, it can *not* be said that community residents neglected opportunities for a better fate. Legitimate opportunities simply were not available. Clairmont summarizes the situation this way: "They played the 'mainstream game'; unfortunately the game was fixed, and they were compelled to play it in a way which profoundly and negatively affected their community life." (41.)[13]

NEUTRALIZATION THEORY

Neutralization theory brings with it a shift away from the objective conditions of lower class life, and a new emphasis on the *subjective* manner in which crime-producing situations are *interpreted*. At base, neutralization theory assumes that people's actions are guided by their thoughts. Thus, the question asked by this theory is "What is it about the thoughts of otherwise good people that sometimes turn them bad?" It can be noted that the question posed assumes that most people, most of the time, are guided by "good" thoughts. In other words, neutralization theory, like anomie theory, assumes that there is general agreement in our society about "the good things in life" and the appropriate ways of obtaining them. Thus, Sykes and Matza are able to observe that the juvenile delinquent " . . . recognizes *both* the legitimacy of the dominant social order and its moral 'rightness.' " (1957:665n.) With Morris Cohen, the neutralization theorists suggest that one of the most fascinating puzzles of human behavior is how individuals come to violate the laws in which they believe.

One of the most important contributions of this theoretical approach was to alter the emphasis of sociological theory on crime and deviance as lower class phenomena. Thus, applications of neutralization theory include the early work of Sutherland on *White Collar Crime*, the research of his student Cressey on embezzlement, and the connections drawn by Sykes and Matza between the acts of delinquents and the lifestyles of the "leisure class." The strand that ties these works together, across several generations of sociological research, is an interest in how the thinking of "good" people sometimes leads them to deviate. The answer is found in the willingness to neutralize, through the use of what we often call "rationalizations," the norms and values that inhibit deviant behavior.

Sutherland and Differential Association. Edwin Sutherland (1924) organized his work around the concept of "differential association." His focus was not only on associations among people, as the phrase suggests, but also on the connections of ideas to behavior. Sutherland's basic thesis was that people behave criminally only when they *define* such behavior as acceptable. Thus, "the hypothesis of differential association is that criminal behavior is learned in association with those who define such behavior favorably and in isolation from those who define it unfavorably, and that a person in an appropriate situation engages in such criminal behavior if, and only if, the weight of the favorable definitions exceeds the weight of the unfavorable definitions." (1949:234.)

Sutherland applied this hypothesis most provocatively in his study of *White Collar Crime.* This study was based on a sample of 70 large corporations, and their encounters with civil and criminal agencies of social control. From these data emerged several dramatic conclusions:

- that corporate criminality is both common and persistent;
- that convictions generally do not result in a loss of status for offenders among their business associates;
- that there is widespread corporate contempt for government regulatory agencies and the personnel involved in their administration; and
- that most white collar business crime is organized crime, in the sense that the violations are often either internally organized corporate affairs or are extended through several corporations.

Theoretically, Sutherland was concerned with how white collar criminals come to define their illegal business practices as acceptable. His conclusion was that a general ideology grows out of involvement in specific practices, and that this ideology in turn serves to justify the practices involved. The ideology itself is transmitted in a collection of common commercial cliches, including:

"We're not in business for our health."

"Business is business."

"It isn't how you get your money, but what you do with it that counts."

"It's the law of the jungle."

These cliches are, of course, multi-national in their currency. As Snider (1976) poignantly observes, " 'What's good for General Motors is good for the United States' is a philosophy that does not stop at the 49th parallel." Furthermore, Sutherland suggests that this justificatory ideology is diffused in an atmosphere that is isolated from competing points of view. Thus, "The persons who define business practices as undesirable and illegal are customarily called 'communists' or 'socialists' and their definitions carry little weight." (247.)

Sutherland, then, laid the broad outlines for neutralization theory with the suggestion that variable definitions determine whether social conduct will be considered lawful or unlawful. It remained, however, for Sutherland's student, Cressey, and later Sykes and Matza, to give more specific content to this perspective. Cressey's contribution was to make the causal structure of the theory emphatic.

Cressey and Other People's Money. Donald Cressey (1953; 1971) developed his theoretical perspective in a study of embezzlement, and later expanded his explanation to cover a variety of "respectable crimes." (1965.) The original research was guided by a demanding methodology, called "analytic induction" (Znaniecki, 1934: Lindesmith, 1947), in which the investigator is bound by the provision that the discovery of a *single* negative case requires rejection of the hypothesis under investigation. Using this approach, Cressey tested and rejected several hypotheses before settling on an explanation that reportedly survived interviews with 133 imprisoned embezzlers, and a rereading of some 200 cases in Sutherland's files. The result was a four part explanation of the violation of financial trust.

Cressey's explanation requires first that the subjects be in positions of financial trust; second, that they think of themselves as having non-shareable (usually financial) problems; third, that they be aware of techniques for violating the financial trust; and fourth, that they have access to a set of verbalizations that rationalizes their crimes. The two most important features of this explanation are the presence of the non-shareable problem, and the rationalization of guilt.

The presence of the non-shareable problem in Cressey's theory reflects the assumption that deviants and conformists alike share the basic values of the surrounding society, and that therefore some source of strain is necessary to stimulate the violation of these values. Thus, Cressey's embezzlers are assumed to be moral people who accept in good faith the positions of trust that they occupy. A non-shareable financial problem is required to initiate their decline. This problem is assumed to be so serious that it cannot be shared, discussed, or otherwise resolved with the help of others.

However, the non-shareable problem *alone* is not enough to bring embezzlement. Driven to *thoughts* of trust violation, the potential embezzler is subject to the *guilt* produced in the conflict between societal values and personal needs.

Verbalizations are the key to the neutralization of this guilt, and they are similar in form to those found by Sutherland:

> "Some of our most respectable citizens got their start in life by using other people's money temporarily."
>
> "All people steal when they get in a tight spot."
>
> "My intent is only to use this money temporarily so I am 'borrowing', not 'stealing.' "
>
> "I have been trying to live an honest life but I have had nothing but troubles so 'to hell with it.' " (1971:chapter 4.)*

We will argue in later sections that the non-shareable problem and verbalization components of Cressey's theory are subject to challenge, using the very methodology of "negative cases" that he suggests. However, for the moment, we will simply note that Cressey believes the verbalization component of his theory to have a more general application: "The generalization I have developed here was made to fit only one crime—embezzling. But I suspect that the verbalization section of the generalization will fit other types of respectable crime as well." (1965:15.) Sykes and Matza expand on this observation in suggesting that there may be a further link between the "respectable" acts of the leisure class, and the more commonplace acts of delinquents.

Sykes, Matza, and the Techniques of Neutralization. Although many theories of deviance assume that the deviant, particularly the lower class delinquent, is a markedly different type of person from "the rest of us," Sykes and Matza (1957; 1961) suggest that the similarities actually outnumber the differences. Their argument is based in part on the observations that delinquents usually exhibit guilt or shame when they violate the law, that they frequently accord approval to certain conforming figures, and that they often distinguish between appropriate and inappropriate targets for deviance. The delinquent, say Sykes and Matza, is an "apologetic failure" who drifts into a deviant lifestyle through a subtle process of justification: "We call these justifications of deviant behavior techniques of neutralization; and we believe these techniques make up a crucial component of Sutherland's 'definitions favorable to the violation of law.' " (1957: 667.)[14]

Sykes and Matza suggest that there are five techniques of neutralization:

Reprinted with permission of Donald R. Cressey.

The Denial of Responsibility. Here delinquents picture themselves as the helpless agents of social forces (e.g., unloving parents, bad companions, or a slum neighborhood). Thus the lament of the delinquent to Officer Krupke in *West Side Story*, "I'm not a delinquent, I'm misunderstood, I'm psychologically disturbed."

The Denial of Injury. Here delinquents argue that their behavior does not really cause any great harm. Thus vandalism is seen as "mischief," auto theft as "borrowing," and gang fighting as a "private quarrel."

The Denial of the Victim. Here delinquents conceive of themselves as avengers, while victims are transformed into wrongdoers. For example, the delinquents might here describe themselves as "Robin Hoods," stealing from the rich to give to the poor.

The Condemnation of the Condemners. Here delinquents allege that their captors are either hypocrites, deviants in disguise, or impelled by personal spite. The effect of this approach is to "change the subject" of concern, placing the focus instead on the alleged misdeeds of others.

The Appeal to Higher Loyalties. Here delinquents see themselves as caught between the demands of society, its laws, and the needs of smaller groups (siblings, the gang, or the friendship clique). The appeal is to "friends and family first."

It can be noted that none of these neutralizations are without some support in society at large. Beyond this, Sykes and Matza suggest that, "The delinquent has picked up and emphasized one part of the dominant value system, namely, the subterranean values that coexist with other, publicly proclaimed values possessing a more respectable air." (1961:717.) These subterranean, or latent, values include a search for adventure, excitement, and thrills, and are said to exist side by side with such conformity-producing values as security, routinization, and stability. Further, Sykes and Matza cite Arthur Davis (1944) and Thorsten Veblen (1967) in arguing that delinquents conform to society, rather than deviating from it, when they add the desire for "big money" to their value system. Summarizing, then, subterranean values make delinquency desirable, while the techniques of neutralization allow this desire to take direction.

Some Critical Comments on Neutralization Theory. Where Cressy postulates a non-shareable problem as the stimulating factor in embezzlement, Sykes and Matza suggest the simple attraction of the "good life" as the source of delinquency. It can be observed, however, that if the attraction is "big enough," then the need for neutralization might seem superfluous. Support for this view is available in the Schwendingers' (1967) finding that delinquents, when offered the opportunity to rationalize projected deviant behaviors, seldom do so (cf., Hirschi, 1969). Instead, delinquents observed in this study assessed their situations tactically, comparing the pains, versus gains, of contemplated acts. A major criticism of neutralization theory, then, is that it may underestimate the pleasures of a deviant lifestyle, while at the same time overestimating the guilt experienced by those who choose to pursue such pleasures. This point is clarified in a Canadian study of embezzlement considered next.

An Example: Embezzlement Without Problems

It will be recalled that Cressey developed his theory of embezzlement with the provision that, " . . . the discovery by the investigator or any other investigator of a single negative case disproves the explanation and requires a re-formulation." (1971:16.) Operating under this provision, Gwynn Nettler (1974b)[15] interviewed six Canadian embezzlers convicted during the past decade of stealing from a low of $60 000, to more than $300 000. Included among the six were two male attorneys, one female bookkeeper, one female bank cashier, one male social worker, and one male investment counsellor. Only *one* of these six cases conformed to Cressey's requirement that a non-shareable problem be the stimulant to theft.

In contrast, Nettler suggests that the remaining five cases " . . . are more clearly described as individuals who wanted things they could not afford and who were presented with (or who invented) ways of taking other people's money." (75.)[16] In all of these cases there was *desire*—things one could do with the money, and in each of the cases there was *opportunity*—ways to take the money with little apparent risk. In fact, Nettler suggests that in two of the cases the opportunities were so open, for so long, that it would have required strong defences or weak desires to resist the temptations offered.

For example, a social worker in charge of a welfare agency resisted for seven years stealing the inadequately guarded funds entrusted him. Only after these years of handling easy money did he succumb to the pleasures of acquiring some $25 000 annually in "welfare payments" made to non-existent clients. These benefits accrued for eight years before his arrest. The thefts were *not* engaged to meet a secret financial difficulty. They did, of course, *produce* an unshareable financial embarrassment. In this case, money was stolen because it was, like Everest, there." (75.)*

It is our suggestion that most individuals possess *neither* strong defences *nor* weak desires, and that in attractive circumstances neutralizations are more likely to occur after the fact, than before the act. In other words, neutralizations, verbalizations, or rationalizations may justify, rather than cause, embezzlements and other acts of deviance (cf., Hackler, 1971:72). We will consider this point in more detail in a later section, but first we will need to review the control theories of deviance.

CONTROL THEORY

Most sociological theories of deviance assume that people are "good," unless they are driven "bad"—either by social injustice or some other social problem beyond their legal control. In contrast, control theory takes a less optimistic view of the human condition, assuming that most people have an equal propensity for both "bad" and "good." In this view, people become "good" as society makes them so. "Good" and "bad" must be placed in quotes here because they have little or no intrinsic meaning outside of the society that defines them. That society does define these qualities through its norms and values; that these norms and values are widely (although not thoroughly or enthusiastically) shared; and that every society attempts to impose its norms and values on its members are the key assumptions of control theory.[17] The interest of the control theorist, then, is in that which restrains us. Instead of asking of the deviant "why do you do it?", the control theorist wonders "why don't we all do it?" Agreeing that "vice is nice," one control theorist, Travis Hirschi, answers that "we would if we dared." (1969:34.)

Traditionally, control theory sees constraints as operating inside and outside of the individual. Thus, Walter Reckless (1961) offers a broad outline of the concerns of control theory by focusing on "inner" and "outer containment." On the one hand, "Inner containment consists mainly of self components, such as self-control, (and) good self-concept . . . " while "outer containment represents the structural buffer in the person's immediate social world which is able to hold him within bounds." (44-45.) Inner containment is seen as resulting primarily from the success of the family at internalizing the "good values of society" in the minds of its offspring; when the family fails, control theorists are interested also in the role of the

From Gwynn Nettler "Embezzlement Without Problems," British Journal of Criminology *14(1):70-77. Reprinted with permission of the Institute for the Study and Treatment of Delinquency.*

community, the police, and other formal agencies as means of outer containment.

In large part, control theory tends to regard deviance as the result of "bad" (said politely, "inadequate") socialization into "good" (said sociologically, "conforming") values. Parsons (1951) says it this way: "The relevance of tendencies to deviance, and the corresponding relevance of mechanisms of social control, goes back to the . . . socialization process and continues throughout the life cycle." (320.) More simply stated, the problem is that of making people believe (whether through childhood socialization or adult resocialization) that they *want* what society defines as the "good life." This shared desire is the essence of what control theorists call the "social bond." According to control theory, when the social bond is weak or broken, deviant behavior is likely to follow.

Hirschi and the Elements of the Social Bond. If it is the social bond that keeps people from deviating, then we will need to know what it is that constitutes this bond, and how the absence of its binding character is associated with deviance. Travis Hirschi (1969) suggests that there are four elements of the social bond: (1) attachment, (2) commitment, (3) involvement, and (4) belief. In turn, we will consider briefly each of these elements.

The importance of *attachment* to others is that it arouses in us a sensitivity to their wishes and expectations. To be attached to siblings, parents, teachers, or anyone else is to be concerned about their feelings. Thus, although we "always hurt the ones we love," we usually do so unintentionally. More commonly, we seek to protect our loved ones from the type of hurt, loss, and embarrassment that deviant behavior can bring. It is this type of attachment that can make a person feel "tied down" or "locked in," that the "swinging single" seeks to avoid by refusing to "get involved," and that the transient anti-hero of the movie *Five Easy Pieces* calls the "auspicious beginning," and desperately leaves behind. But for most of us, most of the time, the wishes and expectations of others seem to add a meaning to our lives. An act of deviance is an act against these wishes and expectations. Conversely, to be unattached is to be unaffected by these constraints. In other words, *de*tachment provides the freedom to deviate.

Commitment refers to the investment of time and energy towards achieving a goal, like getting an education, building a business, paying off a mortgage, or building a reputation. Society is structured so that many, but not all of us, develop such commitments. As a part of our normal social life, most of us acquire goods, reputations, and prospects; in other words, a way of life that we do not want to risk losing. Hirschi refers to these accumulations as society's "insurance policy" against the violation of its rules. To deviate is to risk losing these accumulations, and control theory assumes that it is this commitment (or "stake in conformity," as we will call it later) that keeps most of us "honest." In other words, it is not so much that most of us wish to be honest, but that we fear the costs of being dishonest. Alternatively, the problems of deviance involve those people who feel they really have "nothing to lose."

To be *involved* is to be busy. Too busy, hopefully, to deviate. The thinking behind this proposition is as old as the homily that "idle hands are the devil's workshop," and as perennial as the desire to *do* something. The assumption is simply that if a person is busy doing *conventional* things, then there will be little time or opportunity to deviate. The catch, of course, is that the subject of involvement must be conventional, or, in other words, conforming.

Belief in society's values is the last of the elements of the social bond. Hirschi stresses that deviance is not caused by beliefs that *require* such behavior; rather deviance is made possible by the *absence* of beliefs that forbid deviance. Said differently, it is not that the deviant holds different values from the rest of us, but rather that he or she holds the dominant values in reduced amount. The assumption is that persons unconstrained by society's values feel no moral obligation to conform to its norms. The concluding hypothesis is that the less people believe they should obey the rules, the more likely they are to deviate from them.

According to control theory, the less committed, attached, involved, and believing individuals are, the less is their bond to society. The question, then, is how is this bond created? To this the control theorist has as many answers as there are people and processes that touch the individual. Two answers, however, receive particular attention: the first involves relationships within the family, and the second the personal stake an individual developes in conforming to the rules of society.

Nye and Family Relationships. To focus on the family as a causal factor in deviant behavior is to run the risk of seeming old-fashioned (cf., Hirschi, 1973). Wilkinson (1974) notes that family breakdown was first emphasized as a causal factor at the turn of the century, and was accepted as an important variable until about 1930. For the next 20 years, family breakdown was rejected as a causal factor, and although some signs of renewed interest emerged in the 1950s, to date, concern with the family remains limited. In explanation, Wilkinson suggests that in the early 1900s the family was seen as important because of its near exclusive control over the development of children, and because of a very negative attitude toward divorce. However, in the 1930s the family's protective, religious, recreational, and educational functions began to shift dramatically to other institutions. At the same time, attitudes toward divorce were softening. Of course none of this meant that the family was now of *no* importance, but Wilkinson suggests that we began to think and act more and more as if this was the case. Wilkinson summarizes our situation this way: " . . . the decline in concern for the . . . home . . . came about not because scientific evidence provided conclusive grounds for rejecting it, but because cultural and ideological factors favoring its acceptance early in this century became less important . . . ." (735.) The research of F. Ivan Nye (1958) and the control theorists serves to correct this trend.

Nye suggests that the family contributes to the creation of the social bond in four ways: through the provision of (1) internalized controls, (2) indirect controls, (3) direct controls, and (4) need satisfaction. *Internalized controls* are assumed to operate through the medium of the child's conscience. Such controls consist primarily of internalized norms and values, whose binding power is based in feelings of anxiety and guilt, conditioned through parental rewards and punishments (Eysenck, 1964; Trasler, 1962). *Indirect controls* consist primarily of the desire not to hurt or embarrass one's family by *getting caught* acting against their wishes or expectations. This sort of control, then, depends on affection for, or an attachment to, the family. *Direct controls*, on the other hand, depend more on restrictions and punishments. Examples here consist of rules about time spent away from home, choice of friends, and types of activities. Finally, the family's role in *need satisfaction* eventually involves its ability to prepare the child for "success": at school, with peers, and often in finding work. That some families are better able to do all these things is proposed as an influential factor in insuring conformity, and avoiding deviation.

It is interesting to note that Nye and others (Gibbons and Griswold, 1957; Toby, 1957b) find the family more influential in preventing delinquency with girls than boys. This is explained in terms of the larger role assigned to parents in our society in restricting the activities of girls. Also interesting is the finding of a "U" shaped relationship between the strictness of direct controls and delinquency. In other words, as Durkheim would have suggested, delinquent behavior is at a minimum where there is a *moderate* amount of direct control exercised. The explanation is that when direct controls become too pervasive, it becomes impossible for adolescents to function as normal members of their peer group. Finally, Nye reports that it is not so much whether a home is *legally* broken, but the happiness of the home, that influences the prospects of deviant behavior. Thus, "The *happiness* of the marriage was found to be much more closely related to delinquent behavior in children than whether the marriage was an original marriage or a remarriage or one in which the child was living with one parent only." (51.)

Toby and the Stake in Conformity. Although it is the family that is in large part responsible for the preparation of its offspring, it is society itself that must receive the final product. Thus, one measure of a "just" society is that it provides meaningful places for its members. For those persons who find a meaningful place in society, and for those who believe in the promise of such a place, there is a "stake in conformity." The problem, of course, is that individuals vary in the stake they feel in conformity. This problem begins in the family, gains significance in the school, and ends in the workplace.

In both the United States and Canada, education and occupation are closely associated, and in turn highly correlated with class position and ethnic background. Thus, Jackson Toby (1957a) notes that an upper class white Anglo-Saxon Protestant schoolchild is heavily favored to have a high stake in conformity.

> He comes from a "good" family. He lives in a "respectable" neighborhood. His teachers like him; he gets good marks and he moves easily from grade to grade. These social victories provide a reasonable basis for anticipating future achievements. He expects to complete college and take up a business or professional career. If he applied his energies to burglary instead of to homework, he would risk not only the ego-flattering rewards currently available but his future prospects as well. (516.)*

But the development of a stake in conformity is not *entirely* class-based. In both Canada and the United States, some immigrant groups, most notably the Jews and the Asians, have assumed an immediate stake in conformity that in spite of prejudice and discrimination moved them from poverty to affluence in a single generation (Porter, 1965). Toby (1957a) notes that in the case of the Jews, their social ascent was grounded in generations of respect for religious learning. In the New World, this faith was transferred to the educational system, yielding a commitment to conformity that paid off in occupational advancement. Alternatively, Porter suggests that, "Those who are reared in a milieu indifferent to education are not likely to acquire a high evaluation of it. . . ." (1965:172.) It is these instances that challenge a society to demonstrate that a faith in conformity is productive for all. Without this faith in conformity, there can be no perceived stake in conformity, and the probability of deviation increases.

Reprinted with permission of the Journal of Criminal Law, Criminology and Police Science. © *1957 Northwestern University School of Law, Vol. 48, No.1.*

Some Critical Comments on Control Theory. Most of the hypotheses of control theory are well supported by research (Hirschi, 1969; Nye, 1958; Hindelang, 1973; Jensen, 1969; Linden and Hackler, 1973; Linden, 1976; Dinitz, Scarpitti, and Reckless, 1962; Reiss, 1951; Hagan and Simpson, 1977).[18] Rather than question these findings, or minimize their significance, our central complaint will be that the implications of control theory have not been carried through to their logical conclusions. Theoretical discussion and research in the control tradition have focused on lower and middle class adolescents. Yet, it can be argued that the prevalence of social controls varies by social class. In particular, we are concerned with the widespread freedom to deviate that exists among established economic and political elites. Part of the problem at this level of society is that upperworld "indiscretions" are not consensually defined as disreputable, much less criminal, further freeing individuals to pursue their interests without moral or legal constraint. We will develop this point further by comparing neutralization and control explanations of the most dramatic set of upperworld crimes of our time: "Watergate." Our argument is that expanding the attention of control theory to upperworld deviance will serve to correct a limitation in its previous application.

An Example: "Watergate"

The American experience called "Watergate" is a chronology of events that spanned from June 12, 1972, to August 8, 1974. The outline of these events will be familiar to most readers, beginning with the unsuccessful break-in of the Democratic National Committee Headquarters in Washington's Watergate Complex, and ending with Richard Nixon's resignation as President of the United States. The most comprehensive view of executive activity during the course of these events is provided in the *Presidential Transcripts* (1974), the abridged 1200-page record of selected White House conversations. We will use these transcripts to evaluate competing neutralization and control explanations of the Watergate crimes. Of course, a problem in using these materials is that they are known to be incomplete. However, since the motives implied in the neutralization explanation of these crimes involve sympathetic representations of purpose, we will assume that material relevant to these theories is unlikely to be deleted from the transcripts. Further, we will argue that in spite of the self-serving potential of the transcripts, they actually provide support for an explanation of Watergate that is considerably less flattering than the neutralization approach (Hagan, 1975d).

At least five rationalizations, or neutralizations, of the Watergate cover-up are offered in the course of Nixon's conversations. They include: (1) the protection of national security: " . . . the whole thing was national security" (125); (2) protection of the presidency: " . . . it isn't the man, it's the office" (267); (3) support of the defendants: " . . . this was not an obstruction of justice, we were simply trying to help these defendants" (339); (4) loyalty: "Well, the point is, whatever we say about Harry Truman, etc., while it hurt him, a lot of people admired the old bastard for standing by people" (359); and (5) the country's future: "If there's one thing you have got to do, you have got to maintain the Presidency out of this. I have got things to do for this country . . . " (673.)

The most important of these rationalizations, judging from the attention it received from the participants, was the assertion that Administration agents were simply trying to "help" defendants by offering them cash payments. However, discussions relating to the support rationalization reveal that its importance was clearly as an excuse, or justification, rather than as a cause for the payments being made. For example, in the March 21, 1973 conversation in which the decision was made to pay Howard Hunt "hush money," the discussion is entirely tactical.

> PRESIDENT: That's why for your immediate things you have no choice but to come up with the $120 000, or whatever it is. Right?
> DEAN: That's right.
> PRESIDENT: Would you agree that that's the prime thing, that you damn well better get that done?
> DEAN: Obviously he ought to be given some signal anyway.
> PRESIDENT: (Expletive deleted), get it (133).*

Several weeks later, on April 14, the support rationalization appears for the first time, with little effort to deny its justificatory character. Here the former president reports that, "Support. Well, I heard something about that at a much later time." (242.) Later in this same conversation, the *ad hoc* character of the rationalization becomes even more obvious.

> HALDEMAN: What Dean did, he did with all conscience in terms . . . (of) the higher good.
> PRESIDENT: Dean, you've got to have a talk with Dean. I feel that I should not talk to him.
> EHRLICHMAN: I have talked to him.
> PRESIDENT: What's he say about motive. He says it was hush-up?

Excerpt from The Presidential Transcripts *in conjunction with the staff of the* Washington Post. © *1974 Dell Publishing Co., Inc. Reprinted with permission of Dell Publishing Co., Inc.*

EHRLICHMAN: . . . He says he knew, he had to know that people were trying to bring that result about (272).

Similar discussions surround the remaining neutralizations. In each case, the rationalization is introduced in a justificatory context. The concerns are tactical: the avoidance of legal prosecution, political embarrassment, and moral blame. These concerns relate to consequences, not causes, of upperworld crime.

Our argument is that a control theory of upperworld crime is more appropriate to the explanation of Watergate. Stated generally, the problem is to explain why all upperworld citizens are not criminals, or, viewed more candidly, why some of us are less criminal than others. Answers to the control theorist's question come from within and without. Unfortunately, the first line of defence, inner constraints, is problematic in a society whose conception of upperworld morality is badly defined. In lieu of a public morality that harshly condemns upperworld crime, the occurrence of such behaviors will depend largely on the risks and rewards (in other words, the perceived outer constraints) associated with violating public and financial trust. Watergate provides the example.

The actors involved in Watergate proved unconstrained by either moral ties or by a set of operating principles that were themselves unclear. A careful reading of the *Presidential Transcripts* reveals few references to, or considerations of, societal values. Occasional mention is made of the Nixon Administration's "commitment" to "law and order," however, the references are in passing (see page 362), and obviously not a matter of extended consideration. Repeatedly, the rights and obligations of the executive branch (e.g., the limits of "executive privilege," the meaning of "national security," and the scope of "high crimes and misdemeanors") were debated in terms of a vague Constitution and undecided public opinion. Similarly, the situational controls operative at the time of the initial Watergate offences were inadequate. White House aides were able to manipulate funds and personnel for criminal, political purposes with little expectation of detection. One reason why there was so little expectation of detection, of course, was that the criminals in this case were the people who controlled the institutions of social control (who could have been better positioned to deviate than those persons who controlled the FBI, the Justice Department, etc.?). Furthermore, once "caught," punishment became problematic in an atmosphere confused by promiscuous discussions of pardons. The uncertainties sur-

*Excerpt from The Presidential Transcripts *in conjunction with the staff of the* Washington Post. © *1974 Dell Publishing Co., Inc. Reprinted with permission of Dell Publishing Co., Inc.*

rounding these events emphasize, then, the porous nature of the controls operative in one upperworld setting.

The final irony of Watergate is that the people involved presumably had a high stake in conformity. The final costs of exposure outweighed any benefits the Watergate activities could ever have produced. Hirschi (1969:21) notes, however, that if a person can calculate the costs of a line of action, he or she is also capable of *mis*calculation. Clearly, Richard Nixon miscalculated these costs over and over again.

It should go without saying that Watergate is only one instance of a multi-national problem. We have selected Watergate as our example because it is both well-documented and dramatic. Our evidence on similar patterns in Canada is less complete, perhaps a comment on the aptitude of our thieves of the "white collar." Nonetheless, one partial glimpse of a similar pattern of upperworld crime in Canada is provided in Figure 3-2 in an unsettling news account of Canada's "Harbourgate."

If there is a message to the policy-minded in the experiences of Watergate and Harbourgate, and a control theory of upperworld crime, it is that checks and balances on power are crucial. Upperworld vocations, particularly politics and business, often carry with them a freedom to deviate unparalleled in the underworld. As control theory reminds us, unchecked freedom is a criminogenic condition.

SUMMARY AND DISCUSSION

The consensual theories of deviance begin with the assumption that we are generally agreed about what is "good" and "bad" in our society. In other words, we are agreed about our norms and values. The question asked, then, is why do some people violate the standards we share in common? Three types of answers are given to this question:

Anomie theory argues that the mechanisms of our society do not allow all people equal access to the things they are taught to value, and that therefore they develop deviant means of obtaining the things they want.

Neutralization theory argues that although we share norms and values in common, some of us develop ways of rationalizing, or neutralizing, the guilt that comes with their violation.

Control theory argues that some of us are bound less tightly than others to society's norms and values, and that those persons whose ties are weakest deviate most.

FIGURE 3-2

CANADA'S "HARBOURGATE"

POLITICIANS 'ON TAKE' DREDGE TRIAL TAPE SAYS

By JOHN BREHL
Star staff writer

HAMILTON—"A very high percentage" of politicians are on the take, but it's hard to prove, according to former Hamilton Harbor Commissioner Kenneth Elliott in a conversation tape-recorded by Royal Canadian Mounted Police and played in court today.

The recording, made on May 8, 1974, in Charleston, S.C., was the third one heard in the trial of Elliott, 42, and Reginald Fisher, a business consultant.

They face 10 charges of fraud, conspiracy and uttering in connection with three Hamilton harbor projects.

The RCMP took former dredging company executive Horace "Joe" Rindress to Charleston and wired him to record conversations with Elliott.

Got $1.2 Million

Rindress, 48, former president of J.P. Porter Co. Ltd., a Montreal-based firm, says his company got a $1.2 million Hamilton contract after two other firms co-operated by rigging tenders.

He says he paid off Elliott on behalf of his company.

Early in the four-hour tape, which began this morning, the pair commiserate with each other about the nervous tension put on them by the Mountie investigation.

Elliott remarked: "How come the . . . politicians are all the same, they've got everything of life and these assholes think they're going to nail me for any graft?"

Rindress: "A very high percentage of these guys are on the take but to prove it is something else again, eh?"

Elliott: "That's right."

Rindress: "It's funny when they die, they all end up with big estates and yet only make $20 000 a year."

Elliott laughed loudly and agreed. He remarked on the commissioner of Broward County in Florida who he said spent $1.25 million campaigning for a $22 000-a-year post.

After further discussion of this, Elliott remarked: "That's the democratic way."

Rindress: "Yeah, real democracy."

A few minutes later, Elliott remarked, when told that nine Quebec City women had won the $1 million first prize in the first Olympic lottery: "I think it's fixed, Joe."

Earlier in the conversation, Elliott spoke wearily of the "worry and aggravation" he had undergone through the RCMP investigation.

"I just made up my mind six months ago, f—— it. What can they really do. I've been all through it.

"The worst I can do is wind up with a fine and conflict of interest so they can criticize me in court and in the newspapers. F—— it. As far as the political payoff— they can kiss my ass. That's all he's after is political payoffs."

("He" was apparently a reference to RCMP Inspector Rod Stamler, to whom Elliott had referred a moment before.)

He added "if they want to put me in jail, then f—— them. They can put me in jail," he added with resignation.

Rindress, who is named as a co-conspirator but not charged, is testifying under the Canada and

Ontario Evidence Acts. This means his testimony can't be used against him except in case of perjury.

Premier William Davis' name came up yesterday in a brief reference in a tape recording made May 7, 1974.

A voice identified as that of Elliott told Rindress that "Bill Davis overruled the environment people" on what was apparently a Stelco harbor-land project.

Elliott: "The shit hit the fan again. Peter Gordon . . . told Davis you get off your . . . and tell those people we're taking . . . "

Rindress: "That meant a lot to those two companies."

'Big Kickback'

Elliott: "Oh, did it ever . . . "

Gordon is Stelco's president and chief executive officer.

The Davis reference was not amplified.

Elliott went on to laugh at a suggestion that he got a "big kickback" from Stelco, Hamilton's biggest firm.

"Can you imagine . . . All they got to do is pick up that phone to city council and say look it, tell that f——ing Elliott that we want that property . . . "

Reprinted with permission of the Toronto Star.
Source: The Toronto Star, *Wed., June 4, 1975*

We have noted weaknesses in each of these theories. We argued that Cloward and Ohlin's version of anomie theory demands a greater understanding by the deviant actor of the injustices of the class structure than may be necessary. Rather than being *pushed* toward deviance by a sense of injustice, the deviant may instead be *attracted* by the relative rewards and pleasures of the lifestyle involved. The *absence* of a stake in conformity leaves the deviant free to follow these inclinations. In addition, one consequence of a harsh class structure is to create social conditions that make the control of such inclinations by the family and other community groups less effective.

In response to neutralization theory, we suggested that verbalizations reducing feelings of guilt more frequently follow, than precede, deviant activities. In other words, neutralizations may be justifications, rather than causes, of deviance. This does not deny, however, that these rationalizations serve to facilitate the continuation of such behaviors.

Finally, we suggest that the implications of control theory need to be expanded into the upper regions of the class structure. The absence of decided public opinion about the seriousness of upperworld deviance, and the weakness of rules, regulations, and checks and balances on the powers and privileges of upperworld citizens, leave members of the upperworld seductively free to deviate. To ignore this is to deny a fundamental insight of control theory.

One final way of consolidating our understanding of the consensus approach is to indicate how this group of theories explains "the facts of deviance" reviewed in Chapter Two. The four issues raised by these findings are the basis of the discussion that follows.

• *Why is there so much more deviance than appears in the official records of our agencies of social control?* The consensus theories note that responding publicly to deviance fulfills a more important function than simply punishing all the individuals involved. Durkheim (1950) argued that the occurrence of deviance, and the selective response to it, is a part of the larger "social health." What he meant was that by publicly responding to *some* forms of deviance, we *selectively* demonstrate our symbolic disapproval of those acts that threaten important norms and values. More recently, Erikson put it this way: "Each time the community censures some act of deviance, . . . it sharpens the authority of the violated norm and reestablishes the boundaries of the group." (1962:310.) The important point here is that not *all* acts, even if they could be, need be punished. Each society selects those acts for punishment that seem best suited to insure the maintenance of the system in its desired form.

• *Why are rates of deviance increasing?* The consensus theories suggest that rates of deviance will increase (a) when the gap between perceived goals and means widens for many people, and (b) when the social bond is weakened further by a reduction in the influence of the family and community. In the context of rapid urbanization, attachments, involvement, and commitment to the family and neighborhood are all seen as declining. Nisbit (1953) describes our plaintive response to these conditions as "the quest for community." Combined with an increasing sense of economic deprivation, these conditions can provoke a feeling of "having little to lose." It is under these conditions that the consensus theorists expect rates of deviance to increase most rapidly.

• *Why is there a relationship between class background and rates of deviant behavior?* The consensual theories emphasize that the under-classes are systematically denied opportunities. Unequal opportunities, particularly when perpetuated over generations, reduce the commitment of disadvantaged groups to conformity. The point is that as class-linked differences in life chances are experienced, individuals' conceptions of their stakes in conformity diminish. One assumed result is a class-specific feeling of having little to lose, and much to gain, by exploring deviant success routes. In addition, economic hardships are assumed to produce a disorganization of family and community life that weakens the control mechanisms restricting involvement in deviance. Combined, these conditions encourage a relationship between underclass background and deviant lifestyles.

• *Why is there less deviance in Canada than in the United States?* Consensus theorists argue that Canadians and Americans vary in their values, and particularly in their relative respect for law and order. Two factors are emphasized in explanation of these differences. The first factor focuses on the ideological debate underwriting the political structure of each country, and the correlated link between

Britain and Canada. The second factor involves the economic development of the western and northern frontiers in Canada and the United States.

Seymour Martin Lipset (1968; see also 1963, 1964) argues that different patterns of deviance in Canada and the United States follow first from the carry-over of British values into Canada. Some have called this the "Imperial Connection." The resulting values are said to encourage an increased acceptance and respect for an orderly, elite-based society. Thus, where the United States began in revolution, Canada served as a sanctuary for counterrevolutionaries. Lipset argues that over time, " . . . the failure of Canada to have a revolution of its own, the immigration of conservative elements, and the emigration of radical ones—all contributed to making Canada a more conservative and more rigidly stratified society." (51.) These conservative values are said to discourage deviance on the one hand, and encourage its strict control on the other.

It is argued that strict policies for the control of deviance emerged early in the process of developing the western and northern frontiers. Harold Innis and later S.D. Clark (1976:Chapter III) argued that while the United States was able to develop a relatively "soft" frontier, Canada, in contrast, struggled with a relatively "hard" frontier. Canada's resources were very difficult to develop, while at the same time being extremely vulnerable to American efforts at expansion. To facilitate and secure the development of the Canadian frontier, the Northwest Mounted Police and the military moved into new settlements before, and along with, the original settlers (see Macleod, 1976). Clark describes these conditions of Canadian development as constituting a "closed" frontier.

On the other hand, in the United States, local authorities were free to develop their own law enforcement policies, or to ignore the problem altogether (see Figure 3-3). In Clark's terms, the American west amounted to an "open" frontier. In turn, Lipset concludes that, "This contributed to the establishment of a greater tradition of respect for institutions of law and order on the Canadian frontier as compared with the American." (1968:57; cf., Clark, 1962:192.) It is this Canadian tradition of relative value consensus, grounded in a greater respect for law and order, that is assumed to have kept Canadian rates of serious crime and deviance lower than those in the United States.

It must be emphasized that the consensual theories reviewed represent only one possible explanation of the "facts of deviance" we have considered. The conflict theories offer an alternative viewpoint. In particular, the conflict theories reject the assumption of value consensus, and argue that what is *considered* disreputable is itself a matter to be explained. It is to these sociological explanations of disrepute that we turn next.

FIGURE 3-3

"HOW THE WEST WAS WON"
IN THE UNITED STATES AND CANADA

The United States

The American frontier was Elizabethan in its quality—simple, childlike, and savage. It was a land of wilderness to be approached afoot, on horseback, in barges, or by wagon by only the most durable with a readiness for adventure. It was a land of riches where swift and easy fortunes were sought by the crude, the lawless, and the aggressive, and where written law lacked form and cohesion.

The professional outlaws emerged during the period following the surrender at Appomattox in 1865. Many were Union and Confederate veterans who wandered the country as penniless vagabonds searching for excitement. Many of them drifted to the Southwest when Congress opened millions of acres there for settlement and development. In these free lands were herds of cattle, left untended and free to roam during the war years. Much of this stock was also unbranded, proof of ownership was practically impossible, and "possession was nine points of the law." Branding these mavericks provided a natural opportunity for rapid economic security for the newly arrived homesteader, as it was considered legitimate cow hunting.

But there were those who claimed a prior right to this public domain in Texas, Oklahoma, and Wyoming, which had been staked by them decades before the war. Their relentless and violent persecution of the homesteader and small rancher made cattlemen in general the common enemy of many settlers, and the mavericking of random steers evolved into

Canada

It was in the established tradition of British North America that the power of the civil authority should operate well in advance of the spread of settlement. It was also desirable in view of frontier conditions in the United States and their tendency to spread across the border . . . . "An imaginary line," wrote a later Westerner, "separated Canada from the United States for a distance of 800 miles. South of that line strategic points were garrisoned by thousands of United States soldiers; an almost continuous condition of Indian warfare prevailed, and the white population in large measure ran free of the restraints of established authority. There had been an overflow of 'bad men' from Montana into what is now southern Alberta and southwestern Saskatchewan, who repeated in Canada the exploits by which they had made Montana infamous. In large measure the world took it for granted that lawlessness must accompany pioneer conditions. Canada's Mounted Police was the challenge to that idea."

This famous force was organized in 1874. To the 300 men who composed it was given the task of seeing that the law was obeyed from Manitoba to the Rockies and from the forty-ninth parallel to the Arctic Circle. Their fulfillment of that task is a record of patience and endurance, of courage and resourcefulness. Organized whisky traffic with the Indians was broken up within a year. Horse stealing was made so precarious that there was rustling as an organized business. To this new collective of frontier predators were added the miscreant soldiers of fortune—the thieves, prostitutes, and whiskey peddlers—who sought refuge in the territory west of Fort Smith, Arkansas. This seventy-four thousand square miles of Indian country from Texas and Kansas to Colorado had "rights of sanctuary," for there was no court or formal law under which a fugitive could be extradited.

Surpassing the efforts of the cattle thieves and adding to professional organized banditry were the robbers of stage, train, and bank.

Reprinted with permission of Rand McNally College Publishing Co.
Source: Inciardi (1975:88-89)

seldom need for the drastic community action which was the normal procedure in many parts of the American West. Perhaps most important of all, Canada was enabled to avoid the series of desperate conflicts with the Indians which was necessary to clear the way for the final advance of settlement in the United States.

From Edgar McInnis, The Unguarded Frontier. © 1942 Doubleday and Co., Inc. Reprinted with permission of Doubleday and Co., Inc.
Source: McInnis (1942:306-307)

Compare with Brown and Brown, 1973: Chapter 1.

---

1. From Emile Durkheim, *Suicide*. Free Press. Reprinted with permission of Macmillan Publishing Co., Inc., New York, and Routledge and Kegan Paul, London.

2. Ibid.

3. Ibid.

4. Durkheim's interest in the possible consequences of the absence of social restraints is a theme that is elaborated by the control theories considered later in this chapter.

5. From Robert Merton, *Social Theory and Social Structure.* © 1957 Free Press. Reprinted with permission of Macmillan Publishing Co., Inc.

6. Ibid.

7. Ibid.

8. Ibid.

9. Ibid.

10. From Cloward and Ohlin, *A Theory of Delinquent Gangs.* © 1960 Free Press. Reprinted with permission of Macmillan Publishing Co. Inc.

11. From Donald Clairmont, "The Development of a Deviance Service Centre," in Jack Haas and Bill Shaffir (Eds.), *Decency and Deviance.* 1974 McClelland and Stewart, Ltd. Reprinted with permission of Donald Clairmont and the Canadian publishers, McClelland and Stewart, Ltd., Toronto.

12. Ibid.

13. Ibid.

14. From Sykes and Matza, "Techniques of Neutralization," *American Sociological Review* 22:664-670. Reprinted with permission of the *American Sociological Review.*

15. From Gwynn Nettler "Embezzlement Without Problems," *British Journal of Criminology* 14(1):70-77. Reprinted with permission of the Institute for the Study and Treatment of Delinquency.

16. Ibid.

. Why societies do these things is not the immediate concern of the control theorists of deviance. However, it should be noted that consensus theories generally in sociology assume that the societal purpose involved is that of maintaining a smoothly functioning, stable system of the existing variety. The other side of this argument *is* raised by the conflict theorists of deviance, who we consider in the following chapter.

18. The most useful empirical criticism and elaboration of this theory has consisted of integrating it with a version of differential association theory (Linden, 1977).

IV

EXPLAINING DISREPUTE:
The Conflict Theories

"Why do the behaviors that seem acceptable to some, seem disreputable to others?" This is the question the conflict theories try to answer. The nature of this question indicates a basic difference between the consensus and conflict theories: where the former explanations assume a basic societal agreement about values, the latter do not. The importance of this difference lies in a change of focus. The new focus is on how behaviors become valued or disvalued within particular groups, and how these evaluations in turn influence future behaviors. In other words, the conflict theorists are not interested simply in deviant *behaviors*, but are concerned further with the disreputable *status* of these behaviors, and the consequences of disrepute.

Some of the theories we consider in this chapter are critical of the group processes that result in disrepute; others are accepting, non-committal, or indifferent. Moving from the non-critical to the critical conflict theories,

the subcultural theories argue that sub-groups promote values that oppose those of the surrounding society, thereby producing behaviors that society considers disreputable,

the labelling theories argue that it is the societal *response* to behaviors that defines them as disreputable in the first place, and

the group conflict theories link this labelling of disrepute with the activities of socially and economically dominant groups in society.

There is, of course, more to each of these theories than these summary statements suggest. These statements reflect, however, the emphasis placed in the conflict theories on the role of group processes in defining deviance. Our task in this chapter is to examine each of the conflict theories in more detail.

THE SUBCULTURAL THEORIES

Sociologists and anthropologists use the term "subculture" in various ways. Two common usages are outlined by Yinger (1960). The first points to basic differences in norms and values between subordinate and dominant groups in society. The second usage adds to the first a social psychological sense of frustration that stimulates the development and maintenance of the conflicting norms and values. Yinger distinguishes this second usage with the term "contraculture." For our purposes, we will consider the contracultural approach as a special form of subcultural theory.

Cohen's Contracultural Theory of Status-Deprivation. Albert Cohen (1955) characterizes North American society in terms of a dominant set of middle class values, including ambition, individual responsibility, the cultivation and possession of skills, a readiness and ability to postpone gratification, rationality, personableness, the control of physical aggression and violence, wholesome recreation, and respect for property (88-91). Contrasted to this are the characteristics Cohen attributes to the working class: a dependence on primary groups, spontaneity, emotional irrepressibility, a freer use of aggression, and a reduced likelihood of valuing the "good appearance" and "personality" necessary to make it in a middle class world (97).

Middle and working class values come into conflict as the working class child enters the "middle classified" school. Here, says Cohen, the working class child is assessed against a "middle class measuring rod." The problem of the child becoming an adolescent is simply stated:

> To win the favor of the people in charge he must change his habits, his values, his ambitions, his speech and his associates. Even were these things possible, the game might not be worth the candle. So, having sampled what they have to offer, he returns to the street or to his 'clubhouse' in a cellar where 'facilities' are meager but human relations more satisfying (117).*

The reader will note that unlike the consensus theorists, Cohen does *not* assume that our adolescent actively wants (i.e., values) what he or she cannot obtain. Rather, Cohen implies that middle class values exist as a *repressed* and *unrecognized* source of status anxiety for the working class adolescent (Short and Strodtbeck, 1965:53). What hurts is not so much the denial of valued goals, but rather the

From Albert Cohen Delinquent Boys. © 1955 Free Press of Glencoe. Reprinted with permission of Macmillan Publishing Co., Inc.

more immediate degradation of classroom comparisons: "The contempt or indifference of others, particularly of . . . schoolmates and teachers, . . . is difficult . . . to shrug off." (123.) Thus, the problem of the working class adolescent is that of adjusting to a status that they have little alternative but to accept. The delinquent contraculture facilitates this process by creating alternative criteria which working class adolescents can meet.

The delinquent contraculture performs its service by reapplying that old maxim, "do the best with what you've got." Said sociologically, it redefines the criteria of status so that present attributes become status-giving assets. Significantly, however, this redefinition is accomplished with a vengeance. Working class norms and values are reworked until they become an "explicit and wholesale repudiation of middle class standards . . ." (129.) They "express contempt for a way of life by making its opposite a criterion of status." (134.) In short, the deliquent contraculture defiantly insists that we're everything you say we are and worse."

The result, according to Cohen, is a delinquent contraculture that is *non-utilitarian, malicious,* and *negativistic* in its values. Translated, this seems to mean that members of the delinquent contraculture "raise hell for the hell of it." Cohen does not insist that all delinquency is produced by the observance of contracultural norms and values. However, he does argue " . . . that for most delinquents delinquency would not be available as a response were it not socially legitimized and given a kind of respectability, albeit by a restricted community of fellow-adventurers." (135.) Within this *confined community of peers,* juvenile deviance is seen as an acceptable response to an unacceptable environment. The problem, of course, is that the surrounding society does not agree.

Miller's Theory of Lower Class Culture. Where Cohen sees the delinquent contraculture as a response to, and repudiation of, middle class values, Walter Miller (1958) sees it as a simple "by-product of . . . the lower class system." (19.) The importance of this distinction is that it grants an historical independence to the conditions of lower class life. According to Miller, " . . . lower class culture is a distinctive tradition many centuries old with an integrity of its own."

Miller argues that the enduring lower class traditions are built around six "focal concerns." (See Table 4-1). The first of these concerns is with "trouble." According to Miller, getting into and out of trouble are the major preoccupations of life in the lower class. For men, "trouble" particularly means fighting, drinking, and sexual adventures (as R.P. Murphy cogently describes it to the psychiatrist in *One Flew Over the Cuckoo's Nest,* "fucking and fighting"); for women, it is sexual involvement and the risk of its consequences.

Table 4-1

FOCAL CONCERNS OF LOWER CLASS CULTURE

| | *Perceived Alternatives* | |
Area	*(state, quality,*	*condition)*
1. Trouble:	law-abiding behavior	law-violating behavior
2. Toughness:	physical prowess, skill; "masculinity"; fearlessness, bravery, daring	weakness, ineptitude; effeminacy; timidity, cowardice, caution
3. Smartness:	ability to outsmart, dupe, "con"; gaining money by "wits"; shrewdness, adroitness in repartee	gullibility, "con-ability"; gaining money by hard work; slowness, dull-wittedness, verbal maladroitness
4. Excitement:	thrill; risk, danger; change, activity	boredom; "deadness," safeness; sameness, passivity
5. Fate:	favored by fortune, being "lucky"	ill-omened, being "unlucky"
6. Autonomy:	freedom from external constraint; freedom from superordinate authority; independence	presence of external constraint; presence of strong authority; dependency, being "cared for"

Reprinted with permission of Walter B. Miller and the Journal of Social Issues.
Source: Miller (1958:7)

Added to the emphasis on sexuality is a concern with "toughness." The model here is the "tough guy" of movies and television—hard, fearless, undemonstrative, and skilled in physical combat. It is the Clint Eastwood figure of the spaghetti westerns and the Charles Bronson anti-hero of more contemporary tales of vengeance.

Combined with toughness is a further concern for "smartness." As conceptualized by Miller, "smartness" involves the capacity to out-smart, "take," "con," or "hustle" others. The media model here is the card shark, the professional gambler, the pool hustler, the con artist, and the promoter.

According to Miller, the preceding qualities are combined in the "search for excitement." Miller here notes that lower class lifestyles fluctuate between periods of exhaustive and repetitive work, followed by short, weekend bursts of excitement. This weekend search for "cheap thrills" leads commonly to "trouble" in the form of a "Saturday Night Special"—a cheap handgun that is frequently used to resolve deadly disputes among friends and relatives.

Acceptance of these fatal outcomes, Miller argues, is one reflection of a resignation to "fate" in lower class culture. Here a man is believed lucky or unlucky at cards, horses, sex, and by extension, in other areas of life, not by plan or intent, but by chance. Good luck is dealt, not developed.

Finally, Miller suggests that in lower class culture there is an ambivalent desire for "autonomy." Overtly, this desire for autonomy is verbalized in such assertions as "No one's gonna push *me* around," and the frequent and pointed reminder that "you know where you can stick it." Covertly, however, Miller suggests that restraint is actually *desired*: "Since 'being controlled' is equated with 'being cared for,' attempts are frequently made to 'test' the severity or strictness of superordinate authority to see if it remains firm." (13.) As illustration, Miller suggests that lower class patients in mental hospitals will exercise considerable ingenuity to insure continued commitment while voicing the desire to get out, and that delinquent boys will frequently "run" from a correctional institution to activate efforts to return them. Miller describes these patterns as reflecting "powerful dependency cravings" (13), and goes on to link these "cravings" to the structure of many lower class families.

The overt concern with autonomy, and a heightened emphasis on the remaining focal concerns, are presumed to have their basis in a type of "female-based household" disproportionately found in lower class communities. Miller estimates that about 15 per cent of all North Americans make up the "hard core" lower class group, ". . . defined primarily by its use of the 'female-based household' as the basic form of child-rearing . . . . " (6.) Miller's concern is that persons, particularly males, growing up in such families are deprived of appropriate role models.

The one-sex peer group of early adolescence offers these individuals in lower class communities an alternative opportunity to learn the male role, but in the company of others facing similar sex-role problems. Miller submits that it is not surprising, then, that these sub-cultural groupings are particularly anxious to emphasize those themes of lower class culture—toughness, smartness, and autonomy—that symbolize adulthood around them. The unfortunate outcome, Miller concludes, is that "following cultural practices . . . of . . . lower class culture automatically violates certain legal norms." (18.) In other words, simply acting on the basis of lower class culture can mean becoming the subject of legal disrepute. Where the group conflict theorists were later to link this conclusion into a rather radical set of inferences, Miller is content to offer his conclusions without critical comment.

Banfield and The Unheavenly City.[1] If Miller seems resigned in his view of lower class culture, Banfield (1968) will seem just plain reactionary to many students of sociology. So reactionary, in fact, that in his one attempt to speak at a Canadian university, Banfield was prevented from delivering his remarks by an angry group ironically self-proclaimed "Students for a Democratic Society." The source of their discontent is signalled in Banfield's choice of an introductory quote from Henry George to begin his discussion of crime in the city.

> . . . let the policeman's club be thrown down or wrested from him, and the foundations of the great deep are opened, and quicker than ever before chaos comes again. Strong as it may seem, our civilization is evolving destructive forces. Not desert and forest, but city slums . . . are nursing the barbarians who may be to the new what Hun and Vandal were to the old (158).

Banfield's view is that subcultural groups emerge in the city with varying likelihoods of crime. This *proneness* to crime is based on two factors: *propensity* and *incentive*. Propensity for crime is said by Banfield to be relatively constant, depending on the individuals' class culture, personality, sex, and age. The second factor, incentive, is said to vary, depending on situational factors, such as the number of police in an area and the value of things immediately available for the taking. Together, propensity and incentive are said to determine an individual's proneness to crime, so that "A city's *potential* for crime may be thought of as the average proneness of persons in various 'sex-age-culture-personality' groups times their number." (159.)

For our purposes, it is Banfield's discussion of propensity that is most important, for it is the assumption of a constant propensity to crime that makes Banfield's theory subcultural. Five elements determine propensity: type of morality, ego strength, time horizon, taste for risk, and the willingness to inflict injury. Each of these elements represents a value position potentially in conflict with the surrounding society.

There are three types of morality, each referring to the way in which an individual is presumed to conceptualize "right" and "wrong":

- *preconventional morality* understands a "right" action to be one that serves one's purpose and that can be gotten away with; a "wrong" action is one that brings failure or punishment;
- *conventional morality* defines "right" action as doing one's "duty" or doing what those in authority require;
- *postconventional morality* defines "right" action as that which is in accord with some universal (or very general) principle that is considered worthy of choice.

The remaining elements of propensity are largely self-explanatory. "Ego strength" refers to an individual's ability to control himself or herself; "time horizon" refers to an individual's concern for the future; "taste for risk" refers to a person's desire to take chances; and the "willingness to inflict injury" refers to just that, the willingness to impose pain on others.

Banfield's argument is that the five elements of propensity come together to reinforce one another in various social roles. In particular, it is argued that males, adolescents, and persons of lower class background are most likely to adopt a "preconventional morality," to be low in "ego strength," in addition to having a short "time horizon," an advanced "taste for risk," and a greater "willingness to inflict injury." Thus, ". . . when male adolescence and lower class culture meet in the same person, they will interact, reinforce each other and produce an extraordinarily high propensity toward crime." (168.) What is true for the individual is said to be even truer for the group. This theory, then, like those subcultural theories that precede it, makes crime and delinquency a normal response to the social context in which it emerges. The problem is that a high propensity for crime places the indigenous group in probable conflict with the prevailing societal values that surround it.

Wolfgang, Ferracuti and The Subculture of Violence. Although we have talked to this point about subcultural processes generally, this approach is also used by Wolfgang and Ferracuti (1967) to talk about violence specifically. These authors note that patterns of violence plague particular parts of the world as a part of their history. For example, in Columbia *La Violencia* has claimed thousands of lives in a wave of violence that spans several decades. In Sardinia, the *Vendetta Barbaricina* provides another bloody example of a long tradition characterized by deadly quarrels. Closer to home, we noted in Chapter Two strikingly higher homicide rates in the United States than in Canada. In one American city, Philadelphia, Wolfgang (1958) reports additional differences in homicide rates within and between ethnic groups. For example, non-white males aged 20-24 had a rate of 54.6 homicides per 100 000 population, compared with 3.8 for white males of the same ages. Further, non-white *females* were found to have higher homicide rates (10.2) than white males, as well as white females (0.6).

In explanation of these cross-culturally located pockets of violence, Wolfgang and Ferracuti suggest that " . . . there should be a direct relationship between rates of homicide and the extent to which the subculture of violence represents a cluster of values around the theme of violence." (1967.) These values include the significance attached to human life, and the manner in which individuals interpret the cues of others as calls to violent action. The concern is with a lifestyle in which violence becomes a quick and definitive response to difficult problems and frustrating circumstances.

The role of group processes in mediating the acceptability of violence is dramatized when subcultural norms gain cultural accept-ance. For example, during periods of war, whole nations become anxious participants in violence against the enemy. Wolfgang and Ferracuti's point is that subcultural environments can approximate the conditions of war. Thus, "Homicide . . . is often a situation not unlike that of confrontations in wartime combat, in which two individuals committed to the value of violence come together, and in which chance, prowess, or possession of a particular weapon dictates the identity of the slayer and the slain." (1967:156.) This process of identification of offender and victim becomes crucial, of course, as the subcultural environment gives way to the legal restrictions of the surrounding culture whose values have been violated. It is in this context that what is subculturally acceptable becomes legally dis-reputable.[2]

Some Critical Comments on Subcultural Theory. A basic problem of the subcultural approach is its tendency to *infer* (rather than identify independently) subcultural values from subcultural behaviors. Thus, subcultural theories frequently explain subcultural behaviors by reference to the prevalence of the behaviors themselves. Nettler (1974a) notes that, "It is as though one were to say that 'People are murderous because they live violently,' or 'People like to fight because they are hostile.' " (152.) Such statements are not, of couse, false, but rather descriptive of what we already know. Subcultural descrip-tions approach explanatory status as they widen their net of descrip-tion so that in accuracy and detail they begin to isolate new and independent components of the phenomenon under study.

Unfortunately, a second problem with the subcultural approach is an emphasis on juvenile gang life that often seems to exaggerate the prevalence of gang activity. For example, attempts to study gang be-havior, usually stimulated by the type of news account (see Figure 4-1)

FIGURE 4-1

10 000 IN NEW YORK STREET GANGS 'FEAR NOTHING, NOT EVEN PRISON'

By MANNY TOPOL
and ERNEST VOLKMAN
Special to The Star

NEW YORK—The elderly man walks slowly toward his apartment in the early afternoon, carrying a small bag of groceries. He is stopped by two youths, who throw him to the ground and demand money. The old man says he has none and begs for mercy. The youths then stomp on his legs, saying: "You'll never walk again, whitey."

—Two young boys are suspected of giving information to the police. They are seized one night, strung up in the basement of an abandoned building, tortured, and killed by five youths who slowly cut pieces of flesh from the boys' bodies.

—A man is the big winner in a dice game with a group of youths. They take him into an apartment building, where he is thrown from the top floor down an elevator shaft, but he lands atop an elevator. To ensure that the man is killed, the youths then push the elevator button, raising the elevator to the top floor, where the man is crushed.

Small, divided army

—A wino, wandering the streets after dark, is accosted by two youths, who steal whatever they can find from him. Disappointed by the meagre pickings, the youths douse the wino with lighter fluid and set him afire. He is burned to death.

These are items in a catalogue of crimes, ranging from murder to purse-snatching, that have been committed by gangs of youths who are mostly younger than 18. Many were committed in broad daylight.

During the past four years, New York city's youth gangs have become a criminal force that now amounts to a small though divided army. Police experts say there are at least 10 000 members in dozens of gangs. In some cases, a gang has taken over an entire neighborhood.

Two characteristics

Centred in the South Bronx, some areas of Manhattan and Brooklyn's Coney Island and East New York sections, the gangs live like maggots on the decaying areas of the city. They call themselves the Tomahawks, the Savage Skulls, the Nomads, the Crazy Homicides, the Ghetto Brothers, the Jolly Stompers.

Aside from criminal activity, the two characteristics of street gangs that cause police the most difficulty are (1) the sophisticated leadership and organization of some of the gangs, including Mafia-style ruling councils and assignment of crime specialties to individual members; and (2) the cold-bloodedness of gang members, many of whom haven't the slightest fear of arrest and imprisonment.

"They kill whoever they have a mind to kill," says one policeman. "And there isn't a damn thing you can do about it. They fear nothing, not even prison."

In one Brooklyn case, he noted, police prepared a case against a gang leader accused of ordering the murder of a rival. Police had located a key witness, and the case looked solid. But then the witness told the district attorney's office that his sworn statement was a lie.

Told he now faced perjury charges, the witness replied: "It's better than being dead."

Statistics show that the problem is steadily getting worse. In 1972 there were 2176 arrests of gang members for criminal acts including homicide, assault, robbery, rape, and burglary. In 1973 there were 3588 such arrests. Last year, 4141.

One Brooklyn police official estimates that at least 74 per cent of the robberies in his precinct are committed by gang members.

Even more serious is the fact that there is something of an arms race among the street gangs. Police have encountered large-calibre pistols, shotguns, and rifles and are beginning to turn up evidence of automatic rifles and hand grenades.

The popular image of street gangs was portrayed in the 1950's musical West Side Story.

Then, they were protective associations, formed to control individual streets or ghetto areas ("turf"). Members wore gaudy jackets ("colors") and occasionally had fights ("rumbles") with other street gangs over territory or girlfriends.

The fights, waged with such weapons as fists, clubs, car radio aerials, and occasionally zip guns, usually did not result in deaths.

During the 1960's, the street gangs virtually disappeared—mainly because more members turned to heroin and were arrested or struck out on their own.

But in early 1971 there was a sudden resurgence, not only in black and Puerto Rican neighborhoods but in middle class areas of Queens. No one is quite sure why, but two commonly cited factors are the emergence of the Black Liberation Army, Black Panthers, and Black Muslims and the return of Viet Nam veterans to ghetto areas.

Vying for control

The Black Liberation Army and, to a lesser extent, the Black Panthers, police say, are vying for control of entire gangs.

Whatever the cause, the street gangs of the 1970's have become something far different from the street gangs of the 1950's.

For one thing, the street gangs of the 1970's have been organized for virtually a single purpose: to make money from crime.

The crime is straight out of the days of the old Black Hand terrorists who preyed on Italian immigrants in the city during the early 1900's: extortion from local merchants, robberies, the shaking-down of students for money, intimidation of local residents, and the selling of stolen goods.

Acts suspiciously

"These gangs know exactly what they're doing," says the security manager of a large grocery store in Brooklyn.

"They'll send two guys in here. One guy deliberately acts very suspicious, to draw our attention; meanwhile, his confederate is boosting (stealing) stuff. We lose about $800 a week in meat they steal from us.

"You know what happens with it? They have a regular 'meat route' nearby, a list of people they sell the meat to. They'll even take orders before going out to grab the stuff."

'I DIDN'T LIKE HIM . . . HE HAD A BIG MOUTH'

NEW YORK—Antonio Colon (street name: TC) is 18 years old and heads a division of the Crazy Homicides, one of the city's predominantly Puerto Rican gangs. He commands about 100 youths, police say, throughout the East New York section of Brooklyn.

Q. What would you do if you were not in the gangs?

A. When you're not in the gangs, there's nothing happening. You stay in the house. No place to go. It's like nothing, man. Then you got nobody behind you. You're dead if they get you.

Q. How many times have you been arrested?

A. I've been arrested five, maybe six, times. They never put me away. Let's see, I've been picked up for unlawful assembly three times. And also for unlawful imprisonment.

Q. Unlawful imprisonment? Kidnapping?

A. Yeah, like the gang that was around here before I got here was the Unknown Savages. One of their guys, I kidnapped him. I didn't do nothing to him. Just held him for a couple of hours. I was going to kill him. I didn't like him. He had a big mouth. I put the gun to his head. I seen the tears come down. I just couldn't do it. I went soft on the guy . . . He was only a kid.

Q. How about rules and regulations?

A. Yeah, we have some of that. Like the girls can't go out with guys from another gang. Can't fly colors on certain days. Things like that.

Q. What happens when you violate the rules and regulations?

A. You either get lashes or the Apache Line (gauntlet). Two lines of guys, and he goes right through the middle, and those got belts or other things. The worst thing to do is to run out on a friend. If there's 2 of you and 10 of the other guys, and one of your guys stays and fights, you got to stay right there with him. Because if that guy gets away alive and tells the other guys you ran, forget it.

Q. Well, what happens then?

A. Consider yourself dead. I'll put the guy through the Apache Line 5 or 10 times until he can't walk. Until he can't talk no more. Until he's dead.

Q. How about yourself? What do you think you will be doing in 10 years? Still with the gangs?

A. No, man. I want to get married and have children. Yeah, don't laugh. That's what I really want. Why not? Why can't I want that?

represented above, cast doubt on the organizational reality of gangs. Yablonsky (1959), in a field observation study of "gang life" in New York City, found the gangs he observed to be loose affiliations of real (and sometimes imagined) individuals that were most accurately described as "near-groups." Yablonsky concluded that the reported size of the gangs was determined frequently by the shifting needs of a psychologically disturbed leadership. As illustration, he reports that,

In one interview, a gang leader distorted the size and affiliations of the gang as his emotional state shifted. In an hour interview, the size of his gang varied from 100 members to 4000, from 5 brother gangs or alliances to 60, from about 10 square blocks of territorial control to include jurisdiction over the 5 boroughs of New York City, New Jersey, and part of Philadelphia (217).*

Research in other American cities (Thraser, 1937; Short and Strodtbeck, 1965; Klein and Crawford, 1967) as well as in Paris (Vaz, 1962), London (Scott, 1956; Downes, 1966), and Cordoba, Argentina (deFleur, 1967) reveals similar conclusions.

However, perhaps most significant to the subcultural approach is research on the assumed value conflict between conforming and non-conforming groups. Short and Strodtbeck (1965) used detached workers as interviewers and informants in gathering data on the value positions of gang delinquents and non-delinquents in Chicago. A central finding of this study was that the acceptance of middle class values encouraging rewarded behaviors was quite *general*, but that middle class norms prohibiting deviant types of behavior declined in force, or were rejected more strongly in the lower class. A finding of similar interest is that lower class delinquents endorsed "middle class" conceptions of family life (e.g., stable monogamous relationships) in private interviews, but not in the presence of peers. These findings suggest that the subcultural values described by Cohen, Miller, and others may result in part from a shared misunderstanding of individual viewpoints within the context of the subcultural group (Matza, 1964:53-59). This type of finding suggests that it is the *group process itself* which is of primary importance in understanding the influence of subcultural values. One way of reinforcing this final point is to consider a particularly Canadian example of a (deviant?) subculture in action.

An Example: Violence in Hockey

Hockey Night in Canada means many things to many people, including, inevitably, the sociologist. Showing a distinctively absent-minded detachment from the things that really count, like the score, the sociologist wonders why it is that assault (with a sometimes deadly instrument) is acceptable on the ice, and disreputable in the alley. Said differently, why is the latter seen as criminally deviant, while the former is taken for granted as "part of the game"? In a recent study of secondary school hockey, Michael Smith (1975)[3] suggests an answer: "Perhaps in Canada, players and supporters of hockey form a subculture sharing values supportive of violence. . . ."

From Lewis Yablonsky The Violent Gang © *1959 Macmillan Publishing Co., Inc.*

Noting that the penalty average is over 20 minutes per game in the National Hockey League, Smith suggests that, "A great deal of the officially proscribed violence in the National Hockey League is, in fact, normal behavior." (73.) What makes violence normal on, but not off of, the ice is the support it receives from those surrounding the sport. To demonstrate this point, Smith asked 83 players from 7 school teams to estimate their fathers', mothers', teammates', coaches', and non-playing peers' approval of violence in hockey.

Predictably, hockey players' mothers and non-playing peers defined the two ends of the continuum of approval. Thus, 67 per cent of the players perceived their mothers as approving of hard but legal body-checking, while only 3 per cent perceived their mothers as approving of the starting of fights (the significance of this small but assertive minority is suggested in Figure 4-2). The comparable figures for non-playing peers were 100 per cent and 65 per cent respectively. In short, when one looks for an explanation of violence in hockey, the answer seems to lie most dramatically in the group support of non-playing peers. Typically, players summarized their peers' interest in hockey with the observation that "most of them come to the games just to see someone get killed." Smith concludes from this that " . . . much of the legal and illegal violence in sports is in no way aberrant; rather it is socially acquired normative behavior." (79.) Our legal system generally acknowledges this bit of sociological wisdom by leaving sports to their own subcultural standards of "sportsmanship."[4] Only the sociologist is surprised.

LABELLING THEORY

Subcultural activities are normal within the groups where they emerge. Whether these behaviors become the subject of disrepute, therefore, depends on their discovery by representatives of the surrounding society. One concern of labelling theory is that defining subcultural *or other* behaviors as deviant may intensify the problems underlying these behaviors, and thus maintain or even escalate the behavior patterns involved. Kitsuse and Dietrick (1959) put it this way: " . . . the delinquent subculture persists because, once established, it creates for those who participate in it, the very problems which were the bases for its emergence." (215.) The provocative suggestion of labelling theory is that many of these problems could be avoided by modifying the societal response to deviance; in other words, by avoiding the disreputable labels that define deviance.

Franklin Tannenbaum and "The Dramatization of Evil." Franklin Tannenbaum (1938) provides an early statement of the labelling

FIGURE 4-2

ATTACKS BY PARENTS ON REFEREES ARE INCREASING

By ARLIE KELLER
Star sports writer

When the Metropolitan Toronto Hockey League season opened last fall there were 125 referees on staff. Today, with the season all but concluded, only 91 remain.

Why?

"Of the 34 who left, half were either released by the MTHL, had job changes or left for some other reason," said Bob Stride, secretary of the MTHL. "The other half left because they no longer could take the aggravation from parents and coaches."

Stride admits the MTHL is worried and doesn't know what to do next.

"The way things are going we won't have any referees left," he said. "The abuse they have taken this year is unbelievable. There have been a dozen cases this season where referees were bodily assaulted by either parents or coaches."

When a coach assaults a referee, the MTHL can handle the situation.

"We have suspended a couple of coaches for a year," said Stride. "We also do the same with players if they attack a referee. But what can you do about the parents?"

The situation has become so bad the MTHL now lays charges against parents who attack referees.

"But we just had a case against a man dismissed by a judge," Stride said. "What can we do now? I tell you, it's a serious situation. These referees can't take the aggravation. And why should they?"

What about police protection?

"We have games in between 25 and 30 arenas a night," replied Stride. "There wouldn't be enough police available. And the cost would be extremely high even if they were."

The latest incident occurred Tuesday night when a scuffle took place between a referee and a woman fan after a bantam game.

According to Stride, the woman punched the referee who, near the end of the game, had broken up a fight between her son and another player. The son also is reported to have hit the referee . . . .

Source: Toronto Star, *April 26, 1973:19. Reprinted with permission of the* Toronto Star.

viewpoint in his textbook discussion, *Crime and the Community*. His view is that initial acts of juvenile delinquency are a normal part of adolescent street life—"Breaking windows, annoying people, running around porches, climbing over roofs, stealing from push carts, playing truant—all are items of play, adventure, (and) excitement." (17.) The larger community, however, sees such activities as a nuisance, evil, or delinquency. Tannenbaum explains that, "This conflict . . . is one that arises out of a divergence of values." (17.) He then focuses on the translation of this value conflict into an official response to the individual involved. The concern is that, "There is a gradual shift from the definition of the specific acts as evil to a definition of the individual as evil, so that all his acts come to be looked upon with suspicion." (17.) Within this process, Tannenbaum singles out one particular step as crucial: "The first dramatization of 'evil' which separates the child out of his group for specialized treatment plays a greater role in making the criminal than perhaps any other experience." (19.) In other words, it is the first application of a legal label that has the greatest impact.

Tannenbaum argues that this initial "dramatization of evil" is particularly detrimental in its effect on the individual's self-concept. The individual is overwhelmed by the response to his or her acts and begins to think of himself or herself as the "type of person"—a delinquent or criminal—who would do such things. Further, "The young delinquent becomes bad because he is defined as bad and because he is not believed if he is good." (17-18.) Thus, although officials involved in this process may intend to "reform" the individual, Tannenbaum suggests that these very efforts may serve to intensify the problem by calling more attention to it. "The way out," he suggests, "is through a refusal to dramatize the evil. The less said about it the better." (20.)

Lemert and Primary and Secondary Deviance. Edwin Lemert (1951; 1967) expanded Tannenbaum's discussion of the dramatization of evil by suggesting two terms to designate those acts occurring before and after the initial societal response. Thus, *primary deviation* refers to the initial acts of the individual which call out the societal reaction. Lemert emphasizes that these primary acts may occur at random, or they may be stimulated by a broad diversity of initiating factors. Significantly, however, these initial acts have little impact on the individual's self-concept: "Primary deviation ... has only marginal implications for the psychic structure of the individual. . ." (1967:17.)

Secondary deviance, on the other hand, refers to the problems that arise from the societal reaction to the initial deviance. For Lemert, the dramatization of evil is causally connected to a traumatization of self-concept, " . . . altering the psychic structure, producing specialized organization of social roles and self-regarding attitudes." (1967:40-41.) Most importantly, however, Lemert suggests that secondary deviance can bring with it a stabilization of the deviant behavior pattern involved.

Objective evidences of this change will be found in the symbolic appurtenances of the new role, in clothes, speech, posture, and mannerisms, which in some cases heighten social visibility, and which in some cases serve as symbolic cues to professionalization (1951:76).*

The implication, again, is that "leaving the deviant alone" might reduce or even eliminate some of these problems.

A classic example of secondary deviation is found in Lemert's (1962) discussion of paranoia. As commonly conceived, "paranoid persons" are those who engage in defensive or vengeful acts on the basis of an (inaccurate?) perception that surrounding individuals are conspiring against them. Lemert's point is that while these perceptions may or may not be accurate in the beginning, they usually *are* accurate in the end. Thus, " . . . while the paranoid person reacts differentially to his social environment, it is also true that 'others' react differentially to him and this reaction commonly if not typically involves covertly organized action and conspiratorial behavior in a very real sense." (3.)[5] Specifically, as fellow workers or even family members begin to perceive "problems" with the persons involved, their interaction with them changes in character: "In our words, it becomes *spurious*, distinguished by patronizing, evasion, 'humoring,' guiding conversation on to selected topics, under-reaction, and silence, all calculated either to prevent intense interaction or to protect individual and group values by restricting access to them." (8.)[6] All of this can be quite accurately perceived by the persons involved, producing a *new* set of communication problems for them. Following Lemert's logic, the eventual outcome is a spiraling pattern of secondary deviation in which the problems of paranoia escalate beyond the possibility of any other resolution but exclusion from the group. This outcome, of course, only serves to provide final confirmation for the "paranoid person's" original (but no longer inaccurate) expectations!

Becker and The Outsiders. Returning our focus to subcultural groupings, Howard Becker (1963; 1964) emphasizes that societal rules designating disrepute have the effect of creating groups of outsiders. At the same time, however, Becker notes that persons so designated may have an entirely different view of the matter: " . . . the rule-breaker may feel his judges are outsiders." (1963:2.) This two-sided conceptualization of the problem denotes the political character of the rule-making process. Said differently, Becker's perspective reminds us that " . . . social groups create deviance by making the rules whose infraction constitutes deviance, and by applying those rules to particular people and labelling them as outsiders." (9.)[7] One important aspect of this viewpoint is that it stimulates a distinction

*Reprinted with permission of Prentice-Hall, Inc.

between rule-breaking *behavior* on the one hand, and the disreputable *status* of being called a deviant on the other.

Thus, Becker suggests that, " . . . it might be worthwhile to refer to such behavior as *rule-breaking behavior* and reserve the term *deviant* for those labelled as deviant by some segment of society." (14.)[8] The question that follows from this distinction is "who makes the rules?" Becker's answer—"Those groups whose social position gives them weapons and power . . . " (18)—anticipates a view more fully developed by the group conflict theorists. However, Becker's more pressing concern is with the consequences for individuals of the imposition of disreputable labels.

Becker suggests that patterns of deviant behavior can be understood as unfolding in career-like progressions. The analogy is to more typical occupational careers involving a sequence of movements from one position to another. Crucial to the movement from one position to the next are "career contingencies"—including both objective facts of social structure and changes in the perspectives, motivations, and desires of the individual. The ultimate career contingency in Becker's description of the deviant career is the application of a disreputable label. Thus, "One of the most crucial steps in the process of building a stable pattern of deviant behavior is likely to be the experience of being caught and publicly labelled as deviant." (31.)[9] The assumption behind this assertion is that the imposition of a disreputable label sets in motion a process in which the individual's self-concept is stigmatized (cf., Goffman, 1961; 1963) or degraded (Garfinkel, 1956) to the point where he or she becomes what others expect. In other words, the labelling process is a self-fulfilling prophecy which " . . . sets in motion several mechanisms which conspire to shape the person in the image people have of him." (34.)

Scheff and Residual Rule-Breaking. Before the new interest in labelling theory that emerged with Becker's work, the field of mental illness was left largely to psychologists and psychiatrists. Thomas Scheff (1966) changed much of this by applying Becker's notion of rule-breaking to the occurrence of mental illness. Scheff suggests that our society uses the notion of mental illness in much the same way that other societies use conceptions of witchcraft and spirit possession—that is, as a residual category to contain all the forms of rule-breaking for which our society provides no explicit labels. An example of one such "rule without a name" is the expectation that a person appearing in public should be involved or engaged in *doing* something—a rule that explains why so many of us feel constrained to smoke, drink coffee, or otherwise appear occupied when we "take a break" from our daily routines (Goffman, 1964). Said differently, a person who lingers in public places aimlessly, without clear purpose, violates rules of public appearance and thereby runs the risk of being called "odd," if not "crazy," or "degenerate." It is the existence of these unnamed rules of life that provokes Scheff to redesignate the symptoms of mental illness as "residual rule-breaking."

Scheff goes on to suggest that we all learn the role behavior presumed to go with insanity as a part of growing up—in other words, we are all aware of stereotyped conceptions of mental illness. On the basis of this knowledge, Scheff argues that, "When societal agents and persons around the deviant react to him uniformly in terms of the traditional stereotypes of insanity, his amorphous and unstructured rule-breaking tends to crystallize in conformity to these expectations, thus becoming similar to the behavior of other deviants classified as mentally ill, and stable over time." (82.)[10] Once again, the corollary to this proposition is that if unpatterned incidents of residual rule-breaking are ignored, they will remain isolated and unproblematic (93).

One of the most significant aspects of Scheff's work is to call particular attention to the role of social stereotypes in stabilizing patterns of deviance. An "ethnomethodological" extension of the labelling viewpoint that we consider next suggests that stereotypes have a further role in determining the very process by which potential deviants are discovered in the first place.

Cicourel and the Ethnomethodology of Juvenile Justice. Aaron Cicourel (1968) introduces his work by noting that, " . . . following an ethnomethodological perspective . . . directs the researcher's attention . . . particularly to theories employed by police, probation, and court officials when deciding the existence of delinquency." (24.) The interest is in understanding how these official "theories" influence the process of labelling delinquents. Cicourel's argument is that official decision-makers develop stereotyped views, or theories, of what causes delinquency, and therefore what types of adolescents are likely to be delinquents. The result is said to be a process of "typification" in which "The language and physical behavior employed by different types of adolescents provide law enforcement officials with the 'evidence' or 'data' for employing a typology of typical delinquents and 'good kids' whereby juveniles are labelled, and categorized for further action." (40.)

Cicourel's concern is that this type of decision-making process bypasses traditional safeguards of due process and the associated assumption of innocence. In their place, Cicourel argues that a presumption of guilt is introduced for certain types of suspects:

"Thus the officer's preconstituted typifications and stock of know-ledge at hand leads him to prejudge much of what he encounters . . . . " (67.) In the end, Cicourel argues that this process of typifi-cation is class-linked, operating through common sense assumptions of the police about where delinquency is most likely to be found.

> My observations suggest police and probation perspectives follow community typifications in organizing the city into areas where they expect to receive the most difficulty from deviant or 'difficult' elements to areas where little trouble is expected and where more care should be taken in dealing with the populace because of socioeconomic and political influence (67).*

The issue that underlies much of this discussion, of course, is the accuracy of official stereotypes, and therefore the extent of the biases involved.

Some Critical Comments on Labelling Theory. Where labels are applied, mistakes will occur, and unintended consequences may follow. Admitting all this, the question is how large are the biases, and how great are the consequences? Approaching labelling theory from this angle encourages us to restate some obvious truths that an enthusiasm for the labelling viewpoint frequently ignores. First, deviance is not *entirely* a matter of societal response, with no deviant stimulus (Bordua, 1969). Labelling theory tends to portray the deviant as a passive victim of one-sided societal abuse. However, labels frequently may identify *pre-existing* and *enduring* behavioral differences correctly, and in some cases may even assist in changing these behaviors (Tittle, 1975). An awareness of when this may or may not be the case is the essence of Justice Holmes' advice that, "even a dog knows the difference between being stumbled over and being kicked." The urgency of Holmes' advice can be recognized when we consider seriously some labelling theorists' suggestions that we "refuse to dramatize evil"—in other words, that we stop imposing legal labels. The optimistic risks implied in such recommendations become formidable when we consider removing the labels from the Charles Mansons and Richard Specks of this world (Nettler, 1974a). Labelling theorists will probably respond with the protestation that this is not what they meant. Hopefully so, for this allows us to suggest the logical next step that no labelling theorist has yet taken in developing this perspective.

If labelling theory is to become useful in practice, we will need to determine some very basic regularities. We will need to find out

*Reprinted with permission of Professor A. V. Cicourel.

what types of subjects in what types of situations respond in which ways to varying types of labels (Hagan, 1973a and b, and 1975d). In other words, we will need to develop interrelated typologies of subjects, situations, and societal penalties so that we can predict with some degree of accuracy what types of responses produce what types of outcomes. Research of this variety will begin to tell us those instances where labels have positive effects, negative effects, and no effects at all. That the latter may often be the case is suggested in the following research conducted with Canadian and American junior high school students.

An Example: Delinquency and the Schools

A perennial concern of labelling theory is that the application of a deviant label brings with it a general stigmatizing effect that spills over into almost all aspects of the subject's life. The argument, again, is that labels imply a typification process that sets in motion a self-fulfilling prophecy. To test the accuracy of this assumed process, Sethard Fisher[11] (1972; and Fisher and Paranjape, 1969) designed a series of studies using grade seven, eight, and nine students in Edmonton, Alberta and Santa Barbara, California. The design of this research involved comparisons between groups of students placed on probation (an "experimental" group) and others without such experience (a "control" group). The criteria of comparison were academic (i.e., grades for academic courses) and non-academic (i.e., grades given for work habits, character, personality factors, etc.). Fisher (1972:79) summarized the theoretical basis of the test comparisons as follows: "If definition as a deviant leads to increased imputation of negative attributes, and thus to increased deviance, this should be reflected in a comparison of performance of 'deviants' and 'non-deviants' in the school system."

The distinctive features of Fisher's research that make his study an important test of labelling theory are the use of both "before" and "after" probation data (i.e., measures before and after the imposition of the label), and an attempt to control for pre-labelling measurements of academic ability. Fisher's initial findings seemed to support labelling theory in that his data revealed the theoretically expected relationship between being placed on probation and lower academic and non-academic performance. However, further analysis demonstrated differences between experimentals (i.e., the labelled) and controls (i.e., the non-labelled) *prior* to probation that were nearly as great as those found after the probation label was acquired. In Fisher's words, "This means that the essential difference between the two groups may not begin with the label but may have to do with school adaptation prior to the label." (82.) Additional evidence in favor of this conclusion is provided in several statistical controls for academic ability in the post-probationary data. In three out of four such controls, the initial relationship between probationary status and school performance is eliminated. As a consequence, Fisher (83) notes among his conclusions that " . . . deviance theorists do not sufficiently consider the extent to which those who acquire a public label are themselves a distinctive population group based on some common pre-existing characteristic."

None of what has been said, of course, denies that there is considerable importance to the labelling viewpoint. What is being emphasized is that we will want to be particularly careful in the future to determine *which* labels, in *what* situations, may actually *cause* the particular effects with which we are concerned. Thus, some of the more interesting research in this area currently is examining the possibility that labelling effects may occur earlier in the schooling process with initial "tracking" or "streaming" decisions (for example, see Frease, 1973, and Kelly, 1974). In any case, *the obvious importance of the labelling approach is that it emphasizes the need to study the societal response to deviance as a topic in its own right.* This interest in the societal response is developed further in the group conflict theories we consider next.

GROUP CONFLICT THEORY

Group conflict theory adds to the labelling theorist's interest in the application of labels a more detailed concern for the role of self-interested groups in the development of legal labels in the first place. The assumption that underwrites this approach is that various groups have specific interests in laws that require the imposition of labels, and that these groups therefore play an active role in guiding particular legal labels through the law-making process. In this way, dominant societal groups are seen as imposing disrepute on the activities of subordinate groups. The fact that subcultural groups typically are also subordinate groups ties group conflict theory to earlier parts of our discussion in this chapter.

Vold's Group Conflict Theory of Crime. George Vold (1958) was the first North American sociologist to write explicitly about a group conflict theory of crime.[12] He began with the assumption that crime involves both human behavior (acts) and the judgments or definitions (laws, customs, or mores) of others as to whether specific behaviors are appropriate and acceptable, or inappropriate and disreputable. Of the two components, Vold regarded the judgments and definitions as more significant. His salient interest was in the influence of groups in imposing their value judgments by defining the behaviors of others as criminal.

For Vold, crime and delinquency are "minority group" behaviors. For example, he argues that, "The juvenile gang . . . is nearly always a 'minority group,' out of sympathy with and in more or less direct opposition to the rules and regulations of the dominant majority, that is, the established world of adult values and power." (211.)[13] In this struggle, the police are seen as representing and defending the values of the adult world, while the gang seeks the symbolic and material advantages not permitted it under the adult code. At root, Vold argues, the problem is one of inter-generation value conflict, with adults prevailing through their control of the legal process.

Vold did not argue that his theory of group conflict was applicable to all types of crime, suggesting instead that, " . . . the group conflict hypothesis should not be stretched too far." (219.)[14] He did, however, indicate that his theory was relevant to a "considerable amount of crime," and suggested four types in particular.

The first type of crime considered involves political protest movements. Vold notes that, "A successful revolution makes criminals out of the government officials previously in power, and an unsuccessful revolution makes its leaders into traitors . . . . " (214.)[15] The fates of more than 400 suspected members of the *Front de Libération du Québec* during the October Crisis of 1970 provide examples in point.

The second type of crime considered includes clashes between company and labor interests during strikes and lockouts. Here Vold notes that, " . . . the participants on either side of a labor dispute condone whatever criminal behavior is deemed 'necessary' for the maintenance of their side of the struggle." (216.)[16] So justified was the government's violent response in Canada to the Winnipeg General Strike of 1917. This, and the incarceration of workers following the confrontation, demonstrate that governments, like corporations, have vulnerable interests that are subject to protection through violence (Jamieson, 1971; Masters, 1950).

The third type of crime included under Vold's theory involves disputes within and between competing unions. Vold notes that, "such disputes often involve intimidation and personal violence, and sometimes they become entangled with the 'rackets' and gang warfare of the criminal underworld." (217.)[17] Well-publicized examples here include incidents involving the Seafarer's International Union in Canada and the construction industry in Quebec and Ontario.

The final type of crime included in Vold's discussion involves racial and ethnic clashes. Vold observes that, "Numerous kinds of crimes result from the clashes incidental to attempts to change, or to upset the caste system of racial segregation in various parts of the world . . . . " (217.)[18] Among the most significant of such clashes in Canada was the Riel Rebellion of 1885 (Stanley, 1961).

While Vold directed his theory specifically to the types of crimes outlined, other sociologists have been interested in expanding the focus of attention. One of the most systematic of these efforts is found in the work of Austin Turk.

Turk and Criminality and the Legal Order. Austin Turk (1969) begins his discussion by arguing that criminality is a defined status conferred by others: " . . . criminality is not a biological, psychological, or even behavioral phenomenon, but a social status defined by the way in which an individual is perceived, evaluated, and treated by legal authorities." (25.)[19] The question, then, is who defines this status called criminality. Turk's answer is that in principle there are two types of people in society, "There are those . . . who constitute the dominant, decision-making category—the authorities—and those who make up the subordinate category, who are affected by but scarcely affect law—the subjects." (33.)[20] In other words, the authorities make the laws that make criminals out of subjects. Next question: how does this occur?

Turk's preliminary answer to this question involves a learning process, based on power, in which " . . . both eventual authorities and eventual subjects, learn and continually relearn to interact with one another as, respectively, occupants of superior and inferior statuses and performers of dominating and submitting roles." (41-42.)[21] Said more succinctly, the authorities learn "social norms of domination," while subjects learn "social norms of deference." The problem is that there can never be complete agreement on the normative lessons to be learned, and the resulting conflict becomes a challenge to authority. Thus, " . . . *lawbreaking* is taken to be an indicator of the failure or lack of authority; it is a measure of the extent to which rulers and ruled . . . are not bound together in a perfectly stable authority relationship." (48.)[22] Turk goes on to specify particular conditions under which this conflict is most intense, and therefore the situations in which crime rates will be highest. Among the conditions considered is the relative power of the persons involved. For example, it is suggested that it is the poor and the non-white who have least power, and are therefore subject to the highest rates of criminalization. The process by which this differential criminalization occurs is the subject for much of the work on conflict theory that follows.

Chambliss and Seidman and Law, Order and Power. William Chambliss and Robert Seidman (1971) begin with the assumption shared by all the theories considered in this chapter, that is, that our society is made up of groups with widely varying norms and values. These authors do not insist that this conflict is, or was always, present across all societies. Rather, they suggest that the less complex and stratified societies may resolve internal differences through compromise and reconciliation, allowing a condition of relative consensus. However, as societies become more complex and more stratified, reconciliation becomes progressively more difficult, and rule enforcement increasingly more common. The issue becomes that of which rules will be enforced, and how. Chambliss and Seidman observe that it is the character of our modern, complex, and stratified societies that such issues are assigned to bureaucratically structured agencies. The result, according to Chambliss and Seidman, is the influence of what we shall call the "primary principle of legal bureaucracy"; that is, that "rule creation and rule enforcement will take place when such creation or enforcement increases the rewards for the agencies and their officials, and they will not take place when they are conducive to organizational strain." (474.) Said more simply, the guiding principle of legal bureaucracy is to maximize organizational gains, while minimizing organizational strains.

Chambliss and Seidman go on to argue that the result of the above principle is to mobilize a "rule of law": "The rule is that discretion at every level . . . will be so exercised as to bring mainly those who are politically powerless (i.e., the poor) into the purview of the law." (268.) In other words, because the poor are least likely to have the resources necessary to create organizational strains, they become the most attractive targets for organizational activities. Probably the most important consequence is that, " . . . those laws which prohibit certain types of behavior popular among lower-class persons are more likely to be enforced." (475.) Chambliss and Seidman conclude that it is hardly surprising, therefore, that the poor form such a large component of our official crime statistics. In sum, the explanation lies more in the class bias of our society, and the dynamics of our bureaucratic legal system, than in the behavior of the poor themselves.

Quinney and The Social Reality of Crime. The work of Richard Quinney (1970) parallels that of the previous authors we have considered, but in addition attempts to link the formulation and application of criminal definitions with the occurrence of actual behaviors. Quinney suggests various sources of criminal behavior, including (1) structured opportunities, (2) learning experiences, (3) interpersonal associations and identifications, and (4) self-conceptions (21). The first two factors, structured opportunities and learning experiences, suggest that *prior* to legal response there are class-based differences in *behaviors* that later are called criminal.

This is because "Persons in the segments of society whose behavior patterns are not represented in formulating and applying criminal definitions are more likely to act in ways that will be defined as criminal than those in the segments that formulate and apply criminal definitions." (21.) In other words, the rich typically criminalize the behavior patterns that are learned, often in response to differential opportunities, by the poor.

The second set of factors discussed by Quinney, interpersonal associations, identifications, and self-conceptions, suggest that class-based behavior patterns called criminal exist as a *response* to encounters with the law. In Quinney's words, "Because of others' reactions, therefore, persons may develop personal action patterns that increase the likelihood of their being defined as criminal in the future." (22.) Said again, more clearly, " . . . those who have been defined as criminal begin to conceive of themselves as criminal; as they adjust to the definitions imposed upon them, they learn to play the role of the criminal." (21-22.)

In the end, Quinney argues that the various factors we have discussed are brought together by the *conceptions* of crime held by powerful segments of society. Here Quinney is concerned with the conceptions of crime portrayed in personal and mass communications, particularly as these conceptions represent the interests of the socially and economically powerful. The assumption behind this concern is that the conceptions of crime held by the powerful (i.e., their definitions of the "crime problem") become *real* in their consequences; in Quinney's terms, these conceptions ultimately determine "the social reality of crime." Quinney summarizes his formulation this way:

> In general . . . the more the power segments are concerned about crime, the greater the probability that criminal definitions will be created and that behavior patterns will develop in opposition to criminal definitions. The formulation and application of criminal definitions and the development of behavior patterns related to criminal definitions are thus joined in full circle by the construction of criminal conceptions (23).*

An overview of Quinney's theoretical formulation is presented in Figure 4-3.

The New Criminology. If there is a logical progression to the sociology of deviance, its most recent and critical juncture is found in the work of the "New Criminologists": Ian Taylor, Paul Walton, and Jock Young (1973). These authors critically review the development of

Reprinted with permission of Little, Brown and Co.

FIGURE 4-3

MODEL OF THE SOCIAL REALITY OF CRIME

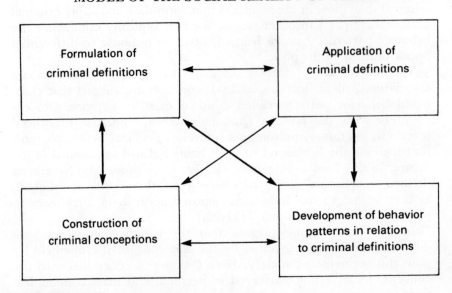

Reprinted with permission of Little, Brown and Co.
Source: Quinney (1970:24)

criminological theory, including group conflict theory, promising that the product of this critique will form the basis for a "New Criminology."[23] For our purposes, two key features of this new view of crime are a reconstituted perspective on the evolution of criminal laws, and a revised image of criminal offenders.

Taylor *et al.* argue first that the group conflict theorists have erred in seeing the criminal law as the outcome of a plurality of interest groups. For the new criminologists, there is only one prevailing interest: that formed in the alliance of the capitalists and the state. The institutions of capitalism are said first to have insured their interests by masterminding the victory of "an ethic of individualism." This ethic, as described originally by Kennedy (1970), has the effect of holding individuals responsible for their acts, while in turn, presumably diverting attention from the environmental structures in which these acts emerge. More to the point, however, this ethic has its primary effect on the *disadvantaged*, for it is "the labour forces of the industrial society" that are bound by criminal law and penal sanction. In contrast, "The state and the owners of labour will be bound only by a civil law which regulates their competition between each other." (264.)[24] The consequence of this societal arrangement, the new criminologists argue, is to create two kinds of citizenship and responsibility, the more advantaged of which is "beyond incrimination" and therefore beyond criminal sanction.

The new criminologists argue second that the modern group conflict theorists have continued to maintain " . . . a conception of the criminal man as pathological." (267.)[25] Taylor *et al.* acknowledge that the character of the new pathologies is more likely to be economic or political than psychological or biological. Still, the picture is one of determination and " . . . the overwhelming impression is one of determination at the expense of *purpose* and *integrity*." (267, emphasis in the original.)[26] For Taylor, Walton, and Young, the "new criminal" is a "purposive creator and innovator of action" whose crimes are the product of " . . . individual or collective action taken to resolve . . . inequalities of power and interest." (267.)[27] In other words, the "new criminal" is a product of an informed "class consciousness."

In the end, the new criminology is a call to arms, urging that, "The retreat from theory is over, and the politicization of crime and criminology is imminent." (281.)[28] This programme for action finds its expression through "direct action revolutionaries," whose activities include, for example, the work of recent Scandinavian criminologists.

The normative prescription of the new Scandinavian criminology led to the formation of the K.R.U.M., a trade union for inmates of Scandinavian prisons, and a union which was able, two years ago, to coordinate a prison strike across three national boundaries and across several prison walls (281).*

We will argue in the following section that this "call to the barricades," whether valid or invalid in its own right, has infected the new criminology with a set of ideological constraints that distort, as well as illuminate, the conflict theories of disrepute.

Some Critical Comments on Group Conflict Theory. All theories contain some truth; the more difficult question is "how much?" Our argument will be that some of the recent statements of group conflict theory, particularly those found in the new criminology, outdistance the credibility of the earlier formulations.

For example, Vold was careful to warn that the conflict hypothesis "not be taken too far"—indicating that this viewpoint applied to some forms of legal disrepute better than others. We made a related point in Chapter One by separating the consensus crimes (e.g., premeditated murder, kidnaping, etc.) from the conflict crimes and

Reprinted with permission of Routledge and Kegan Paul.

other forms of deviance. Our point was that most people, most of the time, across several centuries, and in most nations, have called some acts criminal. In other words, there is consensus about the evaluation of such acts. Group conflict theory works best as an explanation for other forms of deviance about which less consensus exists.

A second set of warnings delivered by Austin Turk (1976) notes that, "Conflict-coercion theory does not imply that most accused persons are innocent, nor that more powerful and less powerful people engage in conventional deviations to the same extent. It does not even imply that legal officials . . . discriminate against less power-ful and on behalf of more powerful people." (292.) The importance of these warnings is to acknowledge a set of findings often ignored by the new criminologists, that there are class-linked differences in behavior (see Chapter Two), and that patterns of differential treat-ment by legal officials are smaller than frequently assumed (see Chapter Five). These issues aside, it becomes possible to reaffirm a more fundamental assumption of group conflict theory, that activities common among the disadvantaged are more likely to be designated criminally disreputable than are other activities more common among the socially and economically powerful. We will argue in following chapters that public drunkenness laws provide one impor-tant example of this tendency.

Most damaging to the new criminology, however, is its effort to remake our theories of deviance to conform to a preferred image of crime (cf., Ericson, 1974:114-115), an image that makes the crim-inal a conscious catalyst for a classless society. To question this assumption is not to say it is entirely false. Rather, it is to note with Turk that, "Challenges to authority range from inadvertent and momentary deviations from relatively insignificant legal norms . . . to deliberate and determined efforts to alter or destroy the authority-subject relation." (1969:45.) The fact that the most frequent violation of legal norms in Canada is public drunkenness (see Chapter Six) suggests that many, if not most, deviant acts are of the former, rather than the latter, variety.

Having said all this, it is important to review some of the evidence that exists in support of the group conflict approach. The single most important effort to test the group conflict perspective is Lynn McDonald's (1976) cross-national study, *The Sociology of Law and Order*. This study is significant first because in a sophisticated manner it brings data to bear on a perspective that has often resisted empirical test. Second, the hypotheses of the study are organized such that they compare consensus and conflict viewpoints. Third, the findings of the study carry significant policy implications. Given the importance we attach to the study, we will attempt not only to cite its major findings, but also to suggest some important issues it raises.

The most dramatic finding of McDonald's research is that across nations, and specifically in Britain and Canada, the variables that predict crime rates best include measures of police force growth and economic prosperity. In other words, it is the growth of the power structure and economic interests of a society, and the corresponding growth in policing activities, that predict the rate at which crime rates will increase. Of course, the crucial question in response to the later finding is that of what comes first: an increase in the crime rate or an increase in police force size and expenditure. McDonald is able to address this issue only briefly (194), but concludes that, "Recommendations for increases in police force size and expenditure to reduce crime would seem to be badly based in view of these facts." (285.) The pessimistic response to such recommendations can be seconded, while at the same time noting that police growth and crime rates probably are related *reciprocally*, each having a causal impact on the other. Further research inevitably will address this issue. Meanwhile, we can agree that police increases apparently are an ineffective means of *reducing* crime (see Chapter Six).

An interesting exception to the trend of McDonald's findings is that police increases do *not* predict murder rates. Rather, variables emphasized in consensus theory are salient here, most notably the levels of economic deprivation. Although this finding cannot make up for the weakness of these variables in other phases of the analysis, it does again suggest the importance of the distinction drawn between consensus and conflict crimes in Chapter One. It should also be noted that one variable that has variously been linked with both the consensus and conflict traditions, unemployment, proves a potent predictor in much of McDonald's analysis, leading her to the conclusion that, "A revised conflict explanation would include the level of unemployment in a society as one of the factors affecting the *need* for formal control measures." (51.)[29]

A final important finding of McDonald's study is that the severity of court sentences in Canada does not appear to correspond well with the public's evaluation of the relative seriousness of the crimes involved (see also Grindstaff and Boydell, 1974). Thus, McDonald presents the data reproduced in Table 4-2 (with offences grouped by type and sentences recorded alongside) to indicate the disparity between public evaluation and court response. McDonald concludes that ". . . apart from the seriousness accorded murder and the most heinous crimes of violence . . . . the priorities exhibited in actual practice reflect the interests of the owners of private property and the owners and managers of industrial and commercial enterprises."

Table 4-2

SENTENCES AND SERIOUSNESS OF OFFENCE

Offences against the person	*No. of Prison Sentences*	*No. of Convictions*	*% Convicted sentenced to prison or jail*
murder	27	27	100.0
manslaughter	67	70	95.7
rape	64	65	98.5
criminal negligence—death (motor manslaughter)	14	14	100.0
criminal negligence in operation of a motor vehicle	14	28	50.0
criminal negligence in operation of a motor vehicle (summary)	36	412	8.7
dangerous driving	26	94	26.6
dangerous driving (summary)	150	1 991	7.5
impaired driving (summary)	1 216	24 762	4.9
driving ⟩ 80 mg alcohol (summary)	284	24 734	1.1
assault causing bodily harm	664	1 879	35.3
offensive weapons (summary)	156	1 119	13.9
duty to provide necessaries (summary)	4	136	2.9
duty to safeguard dangerous places (summary)	4	14	28.6
Protection of Children	8	4 241	0.2
Deserted Wives & Children's Maintenance	66	9 626	0.7

Offences against property and others—lower- and working-class offences

armed robbery	42	48	87.5
breaking and entering	3 587	6 785	52.9
theft	4 305	20 238	21.3
damage under $50 (summary)	325	3 291	9.8
vagrancy (summary)	1 179	3 281	35.9
disorderly conduct/disturbance (summary)	1 167	12 530	9.3
drunkenness (summary)	7 438	69 284	10.7

Offences against property and others—middle- and upper-class offences

fraud and corruption	535	1 049	51.0
Income Tax	3	7 366	0.04
Weights and Measures	0	0	—
Weights and Measures (summary)	0	95	0.0
bankruptcy	0	0	—
Combines Investigation	0	1	0.0
Excise	0	1	0.0

Source: *Statistics of Criminal and Other Offences, 1971, pp. 38, 40, 140, 141 in* McDonald, *The Sociology of Law and Order. Westview Press, Inc., Boulder, Colorado.*

Data excludes Quebec & Alberta, Number of prison sentences computed from total number sentenced less numbers fined and sentence suspended. Offences are indictable unless otherwise noted.

(67.) Unfortunately, a problem in confirming this conclusion is that the data provided do not take into account prior convictions the offenders may have experienced. Traditionally, we have regarded those persons convicted more than once as more deserving of incarceration. In addition, as McDonald notes, these data do not consider what probably *is* the most salient problem in current sentencing practices: the imposition of fines that indigent offenders are unable to pay. These problems are examined in more detail in following chapters. For the moment, we can simply acknowledge the significance of the issues raised by this set of findings.

The comments we have offered in response to McDonald's findings can be taken as one measure of the significance we attach to her work. This research demonstrates in sophisticated and provocative form that the propositions of conflict theory are not only capable of being tested, but apparently are also supported by an interesting body of research. The challenge of McDonald's research is to explain in additional detail the meaning of these findings. One further way of emphasizing the importance of this pursuit is to offer a final example of the insight group conflict theory can add even to the understanding of a consensual crime: rape. An interesting point implicit in this example is that group interests are sometimes pursued with the apparent support of the subordinate group involved.

An Example: The Case of Rape

Across many nations and many centuries rape has been considered a serious, consensually defined crime. Recently, however, Lorenne Clark (1976, see also Clark and Lewis, 1977) has argued that Canadian rape laws are shaped by male interests. These laws are said to have their origin in two sexist assumptions: (a) that a woman is the exclusive sexual property of a particular male, and that (b) the primary value of a woman lies in her sexual and reproductive function. The central hypothesis is that our rape laws are formulated to maintain female sexual property as the exclusive possession of those men who have established their rights of ownership.

Clark goes on to argue that the harm suffered in rape is most significantly economic: the unauthorized taking of a sexual commodity. In this context, the offence committed by the rapist is basically one of theft: the stealing of one man's property by another. Thus, Clark notes that in Canada rape carries the same statutory maximum and average sentence as robbery. Variations in the likelihood of conviction and the severity of sentence are, however, substantial. The problem, Clark suggests, is that sexually "valueless" women are inadequately protected, while sexually "marginal" men are overzealously punished. The classic example is found in the selective use of the death penalty for rape in the southern United States. In a 20 year period, based on 11 southern states, Wolfgang and Riedel (1973) report that black men raping white women were primary targets for the death penalty, while white men raping black women almost never received this sanction. From Clark's viewpoint, this disparity is one of the cruel prices of "coercive sexuality."

Clark's solution is to legally recategorize rape as a form of assault. This approach would hopefully do away with many of the special rules which make rape convictions so difficult (see Figure 4-4) and the occasional sentences so severe. In this new context, "rape" would be merely one form of unprovoked attack on one's physical person, whether perpetrated *on* a man or a woman, *by* a male or a female.

FIGURE 4-4

RAPE CRISIS CENTRES HELP WOMEN TO COPE WITH SHOCK, SHAME

By MARY JANIGAN
Star staff writer

OTTAWA—It was rape—so she didn't tell anyone.

Not then, six years ago, when she was 16 and a virgin and was attacked in a suburban parking lot.

Not the police, not her parents, not her friends, not even a doctor. But several months ago, she finally confided in her husband after four months of counselling to save a year-old marriage chilled by that single incident.

She says to let her name be Cindy now because at last she's talking in a small bare room upstairs after one of the first official meetings of Ottawa's three-month-old Rape Crisis Centre.

Two police force members and a social worker have just told the group downstairs that many cases of rape go unreported because of the woman's shame and fear and because of laws that place her private life under attack at the rapist's trial.

The social worker adds that only an estimated 1 in 10 rapes is reported.

The women here know this. So in crisis centres here and in Toronto, Montreal and Vancouver, they're honing their demands as voters, lobbying for law changes, more support for the victim, and more concern from a public that has often regarded rape as "she done him wrong—and then called the police."

About 30 women now are taking turns on a 24-hour crisis telephone line, comforting women, urging them to report to the police and persuading them to talk out a trauma that all too often turns to self-abasement.

"I get very emotional speaking about this—I mean, it's not the nicest thing to talk about," says Cindy. "It was hard enough to admit to myself that this had happened to me.

"So how could I tell anyone else that this had been done to me in such a degrading, humiliating way? I just blamed myself for so many years."

It happened after classes one November evening, 1968, when she and a friend were crossing a university parking lot on their way to a bus stop. A friend of Cindy's boyfriend stopped and offered them drives home.

"He dropped her off . . . and then all of a sudden he turned off my route . . . and he wouldn't talk to me or look at me anymore and I started to get panicky," she says. "I kept thinking that I was imagining this so I kept asking where we were going.

"Then we were in the suburbs and I was really terrified . . . and he pulled off into a parking lot . . . I got really scared, fighting him and hitting him and the car door wouldn't open. He laughed and said 'Don't move or you'll wish you hadn't.'

"And then he pinned me down and raped me."

She's small, slight, shaking and her face is pale without any make-up.

"I became really introverted after that, didn't go anywhere, didn't want to go out with anyone any more," she says. "I started thinking 'I'm terrible, really terrible' and I blamed myself.

"My activities, all of them, completely changed."

Never punished

The man, now 24, was never punished—because Cindy was too ashamed and afraid to go to the police.

Next month, Justice Minister Otto Lang is moving to ease the ordeal faced by women like her. An omnibus bill with amendments to the Criminal Code will include changes in the rape laws.

"I examined the laws and didn't see any reason for holding back on changes," Lang says. "The changes and these crisis centres and more police support will create a better attitude of sympathy to the woman."

The proposed changes will prevent defence counsel from inquiring into the moral integrity of the witness except in limited circumstances where the lawyer can persuade the trial judge in the absence of the jury that it is essential her character be scrutinized.

At present, to spare his client a sentence of life imprisonment, the lawyer probes the victim's sex life, inquiring into the number and type of her love affairs in an attempt to show that she consented to the rape.

The tacit assumption is that if the woman has had a lover other than her husband, then she is prone to consent to the act.

"Relentless attacks on a woman's habits, her private life, her associations, and her past are commonplace at this type of trial," Lang said recently.

Taboo subject

"So we lobby for more sympathy and changed laws and we're seen as a group of women talking about a subject that is taboo," Vanhusen says.

"We're making our stand in support of the victims. A man is a big hero if he has a different woman every week. A woman gets on the stand as victim and is crucified for her past. How long do you think these laws would have been around if the man had to get on the stand?

"I think if lawyers were permitted to go into the rapist's private sex history and criminal life—instead of the victim's—you'd have no trouble getting convictions."

She says the centre offers support against the inevitable skepticism rape victims encounter from both men and women: "They think to themselves 'Now what did she do to encourage him?'

"It's the old phony image of the beautiful woman walking down the street, seductive and mean and she doesn't want a man," she says. "The man jumps her and she doesn't like it at first and then she starts to love it. We've got a lot to change."

Reprinted with permission of the Toronto Star.

Under this arrangement, the offence would no longer be linked to the special interests of a specific group. In all of this it is acknowledged, however, that we will need a period of transition in which the sentences for this form of assault will remain more severe. The point is that rape having been consensually defined as a serious crime for so long, many women will continue to believe that the social harms they have experienced are substantial, and that some suitably severe form of retribution is due them. This is one way of acknowledging that we are working in a transitional period in which the consensual acceptance of existing rape laws is only beginning to change. However, the end goal is to generate an atmosphere in which the primary concern is the physical, rather than the socioeconomic, injury sustained. In this manner, the influence of male group interests would hopefully be eliminated and consistent sanctions would be made more certain.

SUMMARY AND DISCUSSION

The conflict theories assume what the consensus theories neglect: disagreement among groups about what is acceptable and disreputable in society. The focus of the conflict theories of disrepute, then, is on the evaluation of behaviors within particular groups, and the influence of these group evaluations on future behaviors. Said differently, the conflict theories are less interested in deviant behaviors *per se*, and more concerned about the status of these behaviors as deviant, and the consequences of disrepute. These interests are focused in three ways:

subcultural theory attends to the role of sub-groups in transmitting values opposed to the dominant culture, and the role of these values in then producing behaviors that society considers disreputable;

labelling theory specifies the societal response as the key variable in designating and perpetuating the disreputable status of these behaviors, and *group conflict theory* examines the influence of socially and economically dominant groups in determining those behaviors regarded as disreputable.

Weaknesses of each of these theories were suggested. We noted first that the subcultural theories often are more a description than an explanation of the behaviors they examine. Second, we noted that the emphasis on juvenile gang activities in the subcultural theories frequently overestimates the organized size and constancy of the groups under study. Third, we argued that more important than the distinctive values presumably held individually by members of these groups is the effect of the group process in enforcing a public commitment to these values.

In response to labelling theory, we noted that the differences labelled frequently precede the societal response, and sometimes even are deterred by it. The point is that we will need to determine what type of labelling responses to which types of situations produce desired and undesired effects. As we will see in later chapters, a common finding is that most forms of labelling have little or no effect. Interestingly, this in itself is frequently a good argument against the application of a label.[30]

The most important comment to be made in response to the group conflict theories is that they serve best in explanation of what we have called the conflict crimes. For most consensus crimes, like homicide, the implications of the group conflict theories are limited. For other consensus crimes, like rape, the importance of the group conflict approach is in informing us of the basis on which consensus may have emerged.

Most significantly, however, the group conflict perspective provides an alternative view of many of the "facts of deviance" we reviewed in Chapter Two. We noted in that chapter that the official statistics of deviance can be thought of as consisting of two components: a behavioral component and an error term. While the subcultural theories uncritically described the behavioral background of these statistics, the labelling and later the group conflict theories adopted a more critical attitude. These theories regard the "facts of deviance" as largely influenced by error-producing factors. One final way of consolidating our understanding of the conflict approach, then, is to review these new explanations of the findings reported in Chapter Two.

Why is there so much more deviance than appears in the official records of our agencies of social control? For the conflict theorist, deviance is more a matter of public evaluation and official response than actual behavior. Thus, Becker (1963:12) is able to observe that, "The degree to which other people will respond to a given act as deviant varies greatly." An extremely important source of this variation is the knowledge and information the public has about how much deviant behavior may actually be occurring. Lynn Mc-Donald's research (1976: Chapter 7) in southern Ontario reveals that the public may be badly informed on these matters. A study by Davis (1952) of crime news in Colorado newspapers reveals a reason why. What Davis found was that public estimates of increases in crime in Colorado were associated with increases in the amount of crime news reported, but not with increases in the actual amount of official crime recorded. In other words, the newspapers were mis-informing the public. Quinney and McDonald would not be surprised at this finding. As conflict theorists, they argue that our impressions of how much deviant behavior occurs are manipulated by the interest groups in society that control the media portrayal of deviance. Through the mass communications industry, drives against new kinds of deviance are initiated and sustained. Quinney and McDonald would argue that two results follow: (a) deviant behavior common to powerful interest group members is ignored, while (b) the levels of deviant behavior among less powerful groups are exaggerated. From this viewpoint, the issue of "how much deviance" is one of *whose* definition is being applied to *what* sector of society.

Why are rates of deviance increasing? The conflict theorists argue that official rates of deviance will increase as the interest groups powerful in defining deviance increase the resources they have available to control deviance. From this view, the official response to deviance is seen as a means of tightening the hold of dominant groups over the less powerful. As economic resources grow, then, police forces expand in size and expenditures, and official rates of deviance will follow. Lynn McDonald (1976:51) adds to this the possibility that as unemployment rates grow, financial interests perceive a greater *need* for protection from the disadvantaged, and thus further intensify efforts at control. Together, these factors are said to encourage increasing rates of reported deviant behavior.

Why is there a relationship between class background and rates of deviant behavior? The conflict theorists offer two different answers to this question. On the one hand, they argue that agencies of social control discriminate in the handling of economic and ethnic minor-ities; that is, that the police and courts prejudicially prosecute and sentence minority group offenders, so that these offenders are more common in the official statistics of deviance. In other words, the argument here is that the law is *enforced* unequally.

A second argument is that the laws themselves apply unequally to economic and ethnic minority groups in society. Here it is sug-gested that many of our laws define acts that are more common among minorities as criminal, while defining more leniently those acts more common among majorities. Thus, we have noted that while many unethical business practices can be thought of as deviant, they are "regulated" by civil law, and are therefore immune from criminal prosecution. Instead, offences like public drunkenness make up a large part of the application of criminal sanctions. Some recent conflict theorists have argued that with laws like these, pre-judicial enforcement is unnecessary, and perhaps even counter-productive. Thus, Austin Turk suggests that, "Indeed, discrimination is not only in principle unnecessary but is likely to be counter-productive in contributing to the demystification of the structure of legal control." (1976:292.)

Why is there less deviance in Canada than in the United States? The consensus theorists, specifically Seymour Martin Lipset, argue that differences in rates of deviance in Canada and the United States are attributable to differences in values. In contrast, the conflict theorists, specifically Irving Louis Horowitz (1973), argue that the difference is one of "cultural lag." Furthermore, Horowitz observes (341-342) that the data on criminality reveal "marked tendencies toward closing the 'cultural gap,' " and that the remaining disparities are greatest among the crimes of violence—in other words, among what we have called the consensual crimes. It is, of course, the conflict crimes that hold greatest interest for the conflict theorists, and Horowitz goes on to construct an argument for a growing similarity in their respective national rates.

Where Lipset placed an emphasis on the "Imperial Connection" with Britain, Horowitz argues that Canada's rising reported crime rate has its origin in " ... the loosening of the ties of the Imperial Connection and the strengthening of the ties with the American Connection." (346.) Horowitz then adopts an argument drawn from the metropolis-hinterland model developed in Canada by Davis (1971). Said briefly, this argument is that, "Canada is in the same relationship to the United States as the agrarian sector of the United States is in connection to its industrial sector; or for that matter, the Canadian 'hinterland' is with respect to the Canadian 'metropolitan centre.' " (Horowitz, 1973:349.) In other words, the argument is that the economic centre (whether it be the United States in relation to Canada, or Toronto in relation to other parts of Ontario) dominates and exploits the periphery. Our interest is in what this argument says about rates of deviance.

McDonald argues that as economic growth occurs, the machinery for crime production grows apace. In fact, McDonald implies that crime production through increased policing is a means of insuring economic domination, by maintaining the privileged position of

Reprinted with permission of the Toronto Star.

some interest groups relative to others. The inference that one can draw is that as the Canadian economy grows and increases in its dependency on the United States, that its crime rate will become more and more like that of the United States. Horowitz suggests that this is in fact what is happening. Further, in support of the argument drawn from McDonald, Lipset's own data (1968:38) can be cited to note that at the same time Canada's crime rate has been lower than that of the United States, the ratio of police to population has also been lower in Canada. What remains at issue, as we indicated earlier, is whether this relationship is causal in the single direction that McDonald suggests.

We will not attempt to impose what would be a premature closure on the debate between the consensus and conflict theories. We have argued that the consensus theories work best in explaining consensual crimes, but that the conflict theories may also in some cases help to explain the emergence of consensus. Beyond this, we have argued that the conflict theories serve best in explaining the societal response to those forms of deviance about which little consensus exists. We also noted that the consensual theories are more interested in explaining behaviors, while the conflict theories are particularly interested in the disreputable status of these behaviors. From this point on, however, we must leave the readers to draw their own conclusions, or even better, to the accumulation of additional evidence. In the meantime, we turn our attention in the following chapters to a discussion of the response to deviance in Canada and other nations. Significantly, we will argue that both the consensus and conflict theories can be used to recommend important changes in the Canadian response to deviance.

1. *The Unheavenly City Revisited* by Edward C. Banfield. © 1968, 1970, 1974 by Edward C. Banfield. (Boston: Little, Brown and Company.)

2. It is interesting to note that attempts to reduce levels of violence, by law reform, can produce additional problems. Thus, advocates of gun control laws are placed in the uncomfortable position of adding to the value conflict surrounding the use of interpersonal violence and the right of indigenous persons to protect themselves against this violence.

3. From Michael Smith, "The Legitimation of Violence," *Canadian Review of Sociology and Anthropology* 12 (1):72-80. Reprinted from the *Canadian Review of Sociology and Anthropology*, Volume 12, Number 1, by permission of the author and publisher.

4. The courts have taken occasional interest in the violent world of hockey, most recently in Ontario, and previously in Minnesota. In the latter case, a Boston Bruin butt-ended a member of the Minnesota North Stars in the eye as the two players emerged from the penalty box during a stoppage of play. However, a split jury decision followed indictment, and a re-trial was not sought. More recently, the Attorney-General of Ontario has taken several hockey cases to court, arguing that, "criminal charges are a last resort when the owners and executives of leagues are reluctant to admit that they have problems and do something about them." However, a more common and probably prevailing view is expressed by the coach of some of the players involved: "sport has policed itself since the days of ancient Rome. That's the way it should be and the attorney-general of Ontario is overstepping his bounds when he gets involved." (Toronto *Star*, April 17, 1976:1-2.)

5. From Edwin Lemert, *Human Deviance, Social Problems, and Social Control*. 1967 Prentice-Hall, Inc. Reprinted with permission of Prentice-Hall, Inc.

6. Ibid.

7. From Howard Becker, *Outsiders: Studies in the Sociology of Deviance*. © 1963 Free Press. Reprinted with permission of Macmillan Publishing Co., Inc.

8. Ibid.

9. Ibid.

10. From Thomas Scheff, *Being Mentally Ill*. © 1966 Aldine Publishing Company. Reprinted with permission of Aldine Publishing Company.

11. From Sethard Fisher, "Stigma and Deviant Careers in Schools," *Social Problems* 20 (1):78-83. Reprinted with permission of the Society for the Study of Social Problems.

12. For an excellent historical discussion of the development of conflict theory outside North America, see McDonald (1976).

13. From George Vold, *Theoretical Criminology*. 1958 Oxford Book Company. Reprinted with permission of the Oxford Book Company.

14. Ibid.

15. Ibid.

16. Ibid.

17. Ibid.

18. Ibid.

19. From Austin Turk, *Criminality and the Legal Order*. 1969 Rand McNally. Reprinted with permission of Austin Turk.

20. Ibid.

21. Ibid.

22. Ibid.

23. For an insightful discussion of the political roots of the "New Criminology," see Ericson (1974).

24. From Ian Taylor *et al.*, *The New Criminology*. 1973 Routledge and Kegan Paul. Reprinted with permission of Routledge and Kegan Paul.

25. Ibid.

26. Ibid.

27. Ibid.

28. Ibid.

29. The alternative argument from a consensus viewpoint is that it is unemployment in the face of prosperity (i.e., relative deprivation) that causes criminal behavior, the *response* to which is increased policing. Again, the issue is what comes first: crime and then the police, vice versa, or both.

30. This argument is developed more fully in Chapter Six.

V

RESPONDING TO DEVIANCE:
The Reaction to Disrepute

One outgrowth of the developing conflict theories of disrepute is a new interest in the societal response to acts and persons called deviant. Sociologists study the response to deviance in various ways. However, much of this research is unified by a concern with the decision-making acitivities of agencies of social control. Such research is concerned particularly with inequality of treatment[1]—resulting either from the assumed prejudice of decision makers, or from the limited access of socially disadvantaged persons to resources for their protection. Interestingly, we will see that this research provides a more complicated picture of the societal response to deviance than is commonly portrayed.

We will organize our discussion in this chapter in terms of a typical sequence of agency responses to deviance, beginning with initial detection, and following through to final disposition. Thus, we will focus initially on the work of the police, and later on the various activities related to the courts. It is important to note that although the police and courts are usually thought of as responding exclusively to criminal matters, their scope of operations actually covers a wide range of deviant and non-deviant behaviors. This point will become clear as we turn first to an examination of the day-to-day character of police work.

THE POLICE

Nearly all studies of police work agree that policing is a diversified task. Thus, it is variously suggested that we consider the police as an "omnibus service agency" (Clark and Sykes, 1974:462), that we examine the police officer in his or her correlated roles as "philosopher, guide, and friend" (Cumming, Cumming, and Edell, 1965), and that we understand the activities of the police officer as a "peace keeper" (Bittner, 1967a). The message of these suggestions is that the police do many things other than catch criminals. One sociologist who *temporarily* traded his armchair for a badge reports that, "As a police officer myself, I found that society demands too much of its police: not only are they expected to enforce the law but to be curbside psychiatrists, marriage counselors, social workers and even ministers and doctors. . . ." (Kirkham, 1974.)

The problem, it seems, is that when in doubt or desperation, we call the police. As a result, the police become our front line gate-keepers of deviance, responding to all kinds of day-to-day variations from the norm, and deciding at this point of entry which of these many acts require further agency attention. Two factors encourage the police to persist in this role. First, it allows the police to avoid an exclusive image as oppressive keepers of the law (instead, they are able to perform a social service role as well). Second, the police frequently are the only 24-hour service agency available to respond to those in need. The result is that the police handle everything from unexpected childbirths, skid row alcoholics, drug addicts, emergency psychiatric cases, family fights, landlord-tenant disputes, and traffic violations, to *occasional* incidents of crime. The latter wording is deliberate, for Canadian and American studies agree that relatively little police time is spent on actual criminal cases.

A Montreal study reported by Evans (1973:64) indicates that the police of that city spend as little as 13 per cent of their total working hours on "anti-criminal" activity. Similarly, across Canada, Evans (61) estimates that the average police officer brings criminal charges against only 1.25 individuals every month. Even in a major city like Toronto the volume is not much higher—with district detectives and patrol officers averaging 15.5 criminal charges per *year*. The explanation of this pattern seems to lie in the character of the requests the police receive. Thus, in an American study, Wilson (1968a) reports the following distribution of calls: 21.1 per cent asking for information; 37.1 per cent requesting service; 30.1 per cent seeking maintenance of order; and only 10.3 per cent dealing with the enforcement of laws. The importance of these varied demands on police time will become apparent as we see, in following sections, that the public gets, to a surprising extent, much of what it asks for.

Police-Citizen Encounters. The most extensive research carried out to date in the area of police-community relations is that of Donald Black and Albert Reiss (1970; Reiss, 1971b). Having designed their research as a field observation study, Black and Reiss trained 36 persons with law and social science backgrounds to record observations in 3 of North America's largest cities. The observers rode in patrol cars and walked with police officers on their beats, on all shifts, each day of the week, for 7 consecutive weeks, in each of the 3 cities. In the end, 5713 incidents were observed and recorded in "incident booklets" filled out by the observers. These results provide information on several important issues.

An important insight of the Black and Reiss study consists of the simple observation that *most* police work is "reactive" rather than "proactive." In other words, the police usually do not *seek out* deviant behavior, but rather they more often *respond* to complaints about such behavior. Black and Reiss make this point by distinguishing two basic types of mobilization of the police: "citizen-initiated" or "reactive mobilization," and "police-initiated" or "proactive mobilization," depending upon who makes the original decision that police action is appropriate. The importance of this point is to counteract a common image of police work that is portrayed in television and movies.

The media image of police work is often that of constant and penetrating efforts at surveillance that continuously result in the discovery of deviance—even when it does not exist. The common impression is that where there is no deviance to be found in a particular jurisdiction, the police will simply go out and cultivate their own "new business"—persecuting and prosecuting as they go. However, the Black and Reiss study suggests that there may be an oversight in this pattern of thought, for there seldom seems to be an end to the citizenry's capacity to find new supplies of deviance to complain about. In this context, there are limited opportunities for proactive police work; and the implication of this finding is that the people are the primary source of police intervention into the lives of others.

Thus it is the citizens of the community, and not the police, who most often initiate the societal response to deviance. However, once past this stage of initiation, the police officer rapidly becomes the central figure in an unfolding social drama. It is his or her role to make sense and introduce order into a frequently disorganized situation. For example, Hayduk (1976), in a study of police behavior in Edmonton (Alberta) describes police work as involving both "moment-to-moment sense-making" and "a concern for the managing of practical situations." The police must do this with the aid of specialized techniques they have developed for restructuring what are often potentially chaotic encounters. Reiss and Bordua (1967) argue that the basic tactic for accomplishing this goal is to "take charge." If successfully carried out, this tactic "freezes" the situation and avoids escalation of the incident involved.

The basic instrument utilized in the "take charge" strategy is the verbal and physical expression of authority. The importance of the successful implementation of the "take charge" strategy is revealed in the fact that when it fails, force may be imposed to compensate for the unsuccessful expression of authority. Following research on the mobilization of the police in Toronto, Shearing and Leon (1974; see also Shearing, 1973) observe that it is the residual access to the legitimized use of force that makes the police such a frequently summoned resource for the solution of public and private troubles. They conclude that, "The police officer in Canada is not only armed with both a baton and with a firearm but he has a much wider authority to use these and other weapons in maintaining order than do other citizens." (9.)[2] Of course, it is in the process of using the "take charge" strategy to gain control of socially disorganized situations that brutality and arrest are most likely to occur.

The Use and Abuse of Force. Stebbins and Flynn (1974), in a study of a police-community relations programme in St. John's, Newfoundland, propose a model for studying police encounters with citizens. This model outlines a sequence in which (a) the police enter the situation or happen on the event with one or more goals in mind (e.g., to keep order, to make an arrest), (b) they perceive what is happening (i.e., they see, hear, and feel what is occurring), (c) they interpret, give meaning, or define these perceptions, and (d) they ultimately perform their duties on the basis of this definition, at least until reinterpretation occurs.

It is within this context that the expression of authority becomes an extremely important factor in the police control of disorganized situations. Any slippage in the amount of respect officers are receiving may be perceived and defined as a warning signal that they are losing their authoritative edge. As our previous discussion indicated, the likely outcome of such a situation is that officers will turn to the use of force.

William Westley (1953), alarmed at the apparent willingness of the police to resort to the use of violence, designed a study to discover just how great the tendency to rationalize the use of brutality is. In pursuing his study, Westley found that the police regard the public as their enemy, feeling that their occupation puts them in conflict with the community. The police apparently see themselves as "social pariahs" who are assigned an essential, yet intensely disliked, role in our society (cf., Skolnick, 1966). Taylor Buckner (1974) makes a similar point in describing the relationship of the police to society as one of "antagonistic symbiosis." He observes that almost all societal institutions need the police to carry out their "dirty work," but these same institutions seldom value police services. At the same time, the police need the support of many social institutions, but they can only rarely satisfy all the conflicting demands placed upon them by these institutions.

However, Westley indicates that this is not the full extent of the patrol officer's problems. There are additional pressures with which to contend. Among these are the competition between patrol officers and detectives for important arrests, the publicity value associated with *solved* cases, and public pressures for the strict control of certain offences (e.g., sexual assaults and drug abuse). All of these factors combine in pressuring officers to enlarge the area where violence is legally prescribed. The results, Westley contends, are police secrecy, an attempt to coerce respect from the public, and a belief that almost any means are legitimate in completing an important arrest.

Evidence for Westley's conclusions come in the form of questionnaire responses secured from members of a large urban police force in the United States. After analyzing his data, Westley reports that, "37% of the men believed that it was legitimate to *coerce* respect." (1953:39, emphasis added.) The implication, of course, is that violence may all too readily be utilized in an effort to coerce an attitude of respect from the public. Some reassurance, however, that this may be less of a problem in Canada than in the United States is provided in a study of the RCMP in British Columbia by Dan Koenig (1975; see also Thornton, 1975). Koenig reports that, " . . . although public disrespect *does* bother the police, they appear neither to exaggerate its incidence nor to habitually respond to it with extra-legal force." (319.) Interestingly, this study also provides evidence that the police may be more restrained than many of the rest of us would be in similar circumstances: "The public *and* the police both consider police roughness . . . justified in response to disrespect, but the public (54 per cent) is about twice as likely as are the police (26.6 per cent) to consider such extra-legal force justified in this situation." (319.)

Still, Albert Reiss (1971b) suggests that as the factors we have discussed accumulate, and as they are combined with a perception that the courts are not proceeding in agreement with police views, the likelihood of police brutality will increase. In these circumstances, Reiss suggests that a "police subculture" with its own standards of justice may emerge. One dramatic example of the possible activities of such a subculture is found in the "Death Squads of Rio" described in Figure 5-1; this set of events, transposed into a fictional American context, formed the basis for the film *Magnum Force.* Clearly, the probability of a similar police subculture developing in Canada is debatable; however, the *seeds* of similar discontent are recorded with the Brazilian experience in Figure 5-1 in the form of an anonymous newspaper interview with what is probably a typical Toronto police officer (see also Morand, 1976).

FIGURE 5-1

THE DEATH SQUADS OF RIO

The Death Squads of Rio

Like policemen in almost every U.S. city, the police of Rio de Janeiro are convinced that their country's legal system makes it difficult and sometimes impossible to convict criminals. Furthermore, there is no capital punishment, and no matter how serious the offence, a convict never serves more than 30 years. Some of Rio's cops think that the coddling of criminals has gone so far as to become unendurable. Taking the law into their own hands, they have formed small, clandestine death squads, and now execute any criminal who they think has cheated the law.

Last year nearly 200 criminals were found dead in and around Rio, and the death rate shows no sign of slackening so far this year. In the last two weeks, nine new murders of hoodlums were in the local news. The details of their deaths were grimly familiar. Found on lonely roads outside the city, some of the victims had their arms tied behind their backs. The bodies of at least two were marked with cigar burns. Two more had nylon ropes looped around their necks. One man had been shot five times in the mouth, another three times in the neck; a third had been riddled with 38 bullets of various calibers. In all, 102 bullet holes were found in the nine bodies. It was a foregone conclusion that the torture murders would never be solved.

RED ROSE. In official statements, Rio police have frequently and vociferously denied that they have anything to do with the killings; they claim that warring gangs are to blame. Last week, however, a TIME correspondent reported that several lower- and middle-echelon police officers have admitted to him that death squads are indeed manned by off-duty cops. They claim that the majority of hoodlum killings are disguised gangland slayings, but they concede that many are summary police executions. According to one informant, who was a charter member, the first squad was organized in 1958. It was a tightly knit group of 16 policemen who rubbed out an average of a hood a week for six years. When their most famous member was finally killed by a gangster, the squad stayed together long enough to avenge his death (the gangster's body was ravaged by some 100 slugs), then gradually went out of business.

It has now been replaced by less tightly organized groups that have sprung up spontaneously in different police districts. According to one police captain, victims are usually murderers, armed robbers, dope peddlers, or auto thieves. A man is generally marked for death on the basis of his record and the likelihood that he will escape just punishment in the courts. Once condemned, he is picked up, sometimes as he leaves a police station after being released for lack of evidence. Usually he is taken to a remote jail, where he is held under a false name for a week in case his disappearance upsets any important friends.

If the kidnaping goes unnoticed, the victim is taken to an isolated spot, beaten or tortured, and then killed by a salvo of bullets fired by all the assembled cops. A *coup de grâce* is finally administered above the ear, and often a piece of paper is left by the body bearing a skull and cross-bones and the initials E.M.—the sign of *Esquadrão da Morte*. Sometimes there is also a note saying "I pushed marijuana" or "I was a car thief."

Shortly afterward a man known as "Red Rose" will call police reporters and tell them where the body can be found. (Rose was nicknamed after telling one reporter that he got "an almost sexual pleasure from seeing a .45 bullet in a riddled body, blood bursting from the wound like a red rose from the earth.") As a result of all the violence, the Rio gangsters have not surprisingly begun to fight back. They have already executed several cops in direct imitation of the death-squad style.

Reprinted with permission of Time, *the weekly news magazine;* © Time, Inc.

Source: TIME, *April 25, 1969*

AN INTERVIEW WITH A TORONTO POLICE OFFICER

Q—In the time you have been on the force, how many beatings of citizens by policemen have you seen?

A—Four or five.

Q—How did you happen to see them?

A—A couple I was involved in. Not in the beatings, in the arrests. So maybe I was involved. They weren't really beatings in the sense that 25 guys jumped one individual and put the boots to him. They were more a case where an individual maybe got slapped around. You can only be provoked so much. You know—someone spits at you or calls you names. I've even seen policemen urinated on. I don't care who you are; you're going to lose your temper when that happens.

Q—Describe one such incident.

A—Once a policeman was assaulted and the men who did it were stopped behind a storage building of some kind. One of the men, the guys who did it, actually swung first, if you can imagine it. There were four policemen—three or four—and they thumped those two guys pretty good. Back at the station, same thing. What you have to understand is that when you work with a guy, you've been in tight situations with him, and he gets hurt, you want revenge. That's what happened in this case.

Q—How badly were the men, the suspects, beaten?

A—Enough to require medical attention. But the courts didn't do their job because those two characters were back on the street in a few months. There is that nagging doubt that the courts will administer a suitable penalty and so street justice is administered.

Q—Is street justice common?

A—No matter what you see on television, it's common in big cities all over the world. There are people who would stab you in the back as soon as look at you and given the opportunity, they will do just that. The only thing that stops them is the fear of what will happen to them. Not when the courts get them. When the police get them. If you ever lose that fear of consequences, you might as well pack up the police force.

Q—In other words, you feel you have a responsibility to maintain a deterrent which is the knowledge of what will be done to you by the police, not the courts?

A—Yes.

Q—And that has come about because the courts aren't doing their jobs?

A—Largely, yes, as a generalization.

Q—What, then, is the police attitude toward the courts?

A—A lot of policemen generally are disgusted with the court system. A lot of this so-called police brutality would never happen if you could rely on the courts to do their jobs. When you hear about some of the sentences that are handed out, well, hell. Some of those guys are back on the street before the copper has finished the paper work. I know of a policeman who was badly beaten and it was just about even: around the time the policeman got out of hospital, the guy got out of jail.

Reprinted with permission of the Toronto Star.
Source: Saturday, November 30, 1974 Toronto Star, *Page B1*

Suspect Demeanor and Police Response. A hypothesis that easily suggests itself from research we have reviewed is that it would be suspects who do *not* show respect for the police who are most likely to be caught and labelled as criminals or delinquents. Just this sort of hypothesis formed the basis for a study by Piliavin and Briar (1964). Stressed throughout this research is the belief that it is the "demeanor" of juveniles that forms the basic set of cues used by the police to make their decisions for the disposition of juvenile cases. Thus the authors report that both the decision on the street (i.e., whether to take the juvenile in) and the decision made in the station (i.e., whether to release or detain) are contingent upon the more salient personality and background characteristics of the juvenile in question. In particular, it is found that other than previous record, it is the juvenile's general demeanor that is the most crucial determinant of his or her fate. In other words, Piliavin and Briar indicate that it is specifically the degree of "contriteness" projected by juveniles that determines whether they are to be labelled delinquent or non-delinquent. They conclude that the official delinquent is the product of a social judgment made by the police.

The provocative implication of the Piliavin and Briar study is an implicit explanation for higher arrest rates among juveniles from minority groups. In short, Piliavin and Briar suggest that racial imbalance in the severity of police decisions is attributable to the fact that blacks in large American cities demonstrate a demeanor that provokes punitiveness on the part of the police (see also Ferdinand and Luchterhand, 1970). If this were true of American blacks, then it may also be true of Canadian Native Peoples. An indication that this may be the case is provided in a survey prepared by the Canadian Corrections Association:

> It is ... obvious that the Indian people, particularly in the cities, tend to draw police attention to themselves, since their dress, personal hygiene, physical characteristics, and location in run-down areas make them conspicuous. This undoubtedly results in more frequent arrests.
>
> The feeling is widespread among the Indian and Metis people that the police push them around and arrest them on the slightest provocation (1967:37).*

Clearly, the question that emerges is whether cultural or class factors are an explanation for the differential handling of offenders. Although this issue remains under-researched in Canada, some interesting implications can be drawn from a review of American research on this question. In other words, we can use the American research to form a background for a discussion of the Canadian situation.

Police Bias and Minority Group Relations. In evaluating the findings of the various studies of class bias in police work, it will be useful to call upon two sources. First, we can utilize Bordua's (1969) able review of several studies directed to this question. Second, we will report more recent findings in this area as described in a study, referred to earlier, by Black and Reiss (1970).

Bordua includes four studies in his review. Each of these research efforts involved an attempt to determine the factors most often associated with police decision-making in juvenile cases. In other words, the researchers sought an answer to the question, "What determinants operate in police decisions regarding the handling of juveniles taken into custody?"

The studies cited by Bordua are those conducted by Goldman (1963), McEachern and Bauzer (1967), Bodine (1964), and Terry (1965). Bordua reaches the following conclusion regarding those factors that *did* influence disposition of juvenile cases in three of the four studies: "If we put together the findings of McEachern and Bauzer and Bodine we find that offence type, arrest record, probation status, age, department, and officer all seem to affect disposition; of the factors common to these studies, and also in Goldman's, offence and previous record seem the most securely established." (1969:158.) The fact that stands out in Bordua's summary is that social class factors achieve *no consensual recognition* as influences on the police handling of juvenile cases.

Reprinted with permission of the Canadian Corrections Association.

The final study included in Bordua's summarization is an analysis by Robert Terry of police work in a midwestern city. The results of this research are perhaps the most convincing yet considered. " . . . Terry found that offence, previous record, and age held up as correlates of disposition decision of twelve factors studied. Terry points out that his results imply a rather 'legalistic' handling of juveniles and also that the much claimed socio-economic bias of the police simply does not appear." (1969:158.) It must be noted that not *all* studies confirm Terry's legalistic viewpoint (e.g., Ferdinand and Luchterhand, 1970). However, among those studies that take legal factors into account, the relationship between social class and disposition usually is either weak or removed (Green, 1970; Hirschi, 1975). In other words, a class bias in police work may exist, but it apparently is not as large as is frequently asserted.

Bordua offers a compelling explanation for the failure of a substantial class bias to show up in police statistics. The police are severely constrained in the number of juveniles that they can refer to court and, beyond the court appearance, there is very little in the way of institutional space for juveniles. Thus the police know that they are going to have to return the great majority of juveniles to the community. As an example, in Terry's study nearly 90 per cent of the juveniles were returned to the community without a court appearance. It appears that the police must reserve the use of court referrals for only the most severe cases. Thus Bordua concludes that we should not be surprised at the failure of class bias to show up in police figures: " . . . in order for socio-economic bias to appear, it would have to be monumental since after all the police must pay *some* attention to the law." (1969:158.)

The findings reported by Black and Reiss in their most recent study allow us to look beyond the more general problem of class bias to the possible details of racial differences in treatment. Again, the findings contain some surprises. Initial results of the study revealed a disparity between the proportion of black and white juveniles taken into custody and those later arrested: 21 per cent of the blacks were eventually arrested, as compared to 8 per cent of the whites. Part of this disparity was explained by the fact that black juveniles were disproportionately involved in more serious offences. However, a second major factor that influenced higher arrest rates for black juveniles was whether or not a *black complainant* participated in the encounter.

Black and Reiss observe that a complainant in search of justice can make direct demands with which the police officer has little choice but to comply. Of particular interest, in the case of complaints about black juveniles, is the fact that the complainants seeking more severe dispositions are themselves black. The white officer acting without a black complainant is considerably more lenient. Further, when no complainant is involved in the police-juvenile encounter, the racial difference in arrest rates nearly disappears (14 per cent for blacks, 10 per cent for whites). Black and Reiss conclude that, "Given the prominent role of the Negro complainant in the race differential then, it may be inappropriate to consider this pattern as an instance of discrimination on the part of policemen." (72.)[3]

A paradox of the finding that the police themselves seem to express relatively little racial prejudice in their decision making, is the fact that the police do *verbalize* racial prejudice in their attitudinal expressions. For example, in an earlier report, Black and Reiss (1967) indicate that during the observation period included in the study a large majority of the police expressed anti-black attitudes in the presence of observers. Thus, it would appear that there is a large slippage between police expressions of verbal attitudes and their actual overt behaviors.

The most convincing evidence for the preceding conclusion is found in another portion of the above study. Using data gathered in the previously described research, Reiss (1968) tabulated the infliction of brutality by both white and black police. The finding that emerges is that 33 per cent of the citizens victimized by white police were black, while fully 71 per cent of the citizens victimized by black police were black. In other words, black police inflict more than twice as much of their brutality on blacks as do white police. Reiss concludes that, "Though no precise estimates are possible, the facts just given suggest that white policemen, even though they are prejudiced toward Negroes, do not discriminate against Negroes in the excessive use of force." (1968:17.)

The American research that we have reviewed cannot be translated directly into the Canadian context (Hagan, 1974b). For one thing, whereas in the United States blacks are more frequently arrested for serious charges than whites, in Canada Native Peoples are more frequently charged with minor offences (cf., Bienvenue and Latif, 1974). As in the American situation, however, the problem may not so much be a matter of the prejudicial or discriminatory *application* of the law. Instead, the problem would seem to lie more prominently in *the character of the law itself*, specifically as it requires the enforcement of standards of public conduct (Stinchcombe, 1963) on Native Persons.

Until a 1969 Supreme Court decision in *Regina v. Drybones*, Canadian Indians were prohibited from becoming intoxicated away from a reserve (see Tarnopolsky, 1971). In this important decision, the Supreme Court of Canada determined that Section 95 of the Indian Act violated provisions of the Canadian Bill of Rights insuring equality before the law. Legal commentary on this and later decisions focused on whether the law itself was inherently unequal in that it applied *exclusively* and *disadvantageously* to Indians. Later in this chapter we will see that this question is crucial in determining the scope of the Canadian Bill of Rights. For the moment, however, we will accept the verdict of Hogg (1974:275) that, " . . . the Supreme Court distinctly held that the law itself, and not merely enforcement practice, was inoperative."

In sociological terms, the problems of Native Peoples and the law clearly did not end with the Supreme Court's legal housecleaning. In the absence of the Indian Act, provincial liquor statutes remain as an unequal imposition on Native Peoples. Again, however, the problem does not lie simply in the administration of these statutes, but in the character of the statutes themselves. Native Persons frequently come to towns and cities from surrounding reserves, usually for temporary periods. During these periods, involvement in alcohol-related activities is common, while availability of places for private drinking is limited. As a consequence, Native Persons must drink in public and the police are left with the responsibility of enforcing laws regulating public conduct. Our point, in short, is that limited access to privacy and laws controlling public drinking behavior are major explanatory factors in the disproportionate processing of Native Persons for alcohol-related offences. It makes little difference whether these laws are *applied* equally or not, for the laws themselves fall disproportionately on Native Persons without access to shelter. In later sections of this chapter, we will present evidence that illustrates the consequences of this situation.

Policing the "Apparently Mentally Ill." We noted earlier in our discussion that much police work is concerned with non-criminal events. Among the most significant of these incidents are those leading to involuntary psychiatric attention. Bittner (1967b) notes that the police are obliged to deal with the "mentally ill" in two ways: (a) as transporters of persons adjudicated by others to be in need of treatment, and (b) as front line decision makers who determine on their own whether a person is to be apprehended and conveyed to hospital for examination. Sociological interest focuses on the police in the second of these roles; in other words, in their role as psychiatric decision makers. Best estimates indicate that from 5 to 20 per cent of all hospitalizations involve the police. There is much evidence that the police do not seek, and in fact avoid, this role. As in other areas of police work, most of the involvement in psychiatric activities is reactive (i.e., in response to complaints) rather than proactive (i.e., police initiated). In addition, the police demonstrate some reluctance to take action in such cases, preferring, if possible, to deny the urgency of treatment (Bittner, 1967b). The result is that the police seem to adopt a working definition of mental illness as consisting either of violence or some other sustained and highly abnormal behavior (Mathews, 1970). Many of these points are effectively portrayed by Fox and Erickson (1972) in a study of the use of police psychiatric powers in Toronto.

All provinces in Canada include in their mental health legislation provisions allowing the police to apprehend persons for psychiatric examination. To determine how these powers are used in Toronto, Fox and Erickson examined police and hospital records, and conducted observations in a psychiatric admitting area. On this basis, it is estimated that up to 19 per cent of all hospital admissions involved the police. What this statistic does not reveal, however, is a finding that the police overlook much of what they see:

> Thus, while the researchers were accompanying officers on a routine patrol on a summer evening in a popular part of a busy downtown street, several known "weirdos" were pointed out by the police. One, a short spry middle-aged man, whose clothing included an over-sized sports jacket, was engaged in what appeared to be a tap dance on the sidewalk corner. Another was an old bearded man, wearing layers of tattered clothes, bobbing up and down and apparently talking to a fire hydrant. A third, a woman in her thirties, was said to have been taken by police to a mental hospital about five times and that she had been last reported on the street "putting candles up her nose and lighting them. Some citizens complained and we talked to her. She was quite capable of talking to us, she wasn't wanted and she wasn't hurting anyone and she lived nearby so we didn't pick her up." The police commented that these people, whom they knew by name, were "nutty as a fruit cake, but we don't bother them if they are getting by." On another patrol, an officer remarked that, "we leave them alone unless they are causing trouble or are a danger." During the pilot observation at Queen Street, one officer who had brought a person for examination stated, "I could go out and round up a dozen." (165.)*

One source of police reluctance to respond to these "diverse" forms of behavior is the ambiguity of their legal mandate. As an example of this ambiguity, Fox and Erickson note that no consistent

Reprinted with permission of Richard Fox.

label exists for the person who is apprehended and taken to hospital by the police; the authors find such persons variously referred to, sometimes in the same report, as the "accused," the "victim," or the "suspect." (167.) This ambiguity reflects the blurred criminal/civil nature of the procedures in which the police are involved, and the potential legal liabilities that can follow.

How, then, do the police decide who among these qualified candidates are "apparently mentally ill"? When compared with other hospital admissions, police admissions are disproportionately male, young, single, and of low educational background. A possible explanation of these findings is that such individuals are also disproportionately without persons other than the police willing to initiate their commitment (see Gove, 1975). Thus, when the police occurrence sheets are surveyed, Fox and Erickson find that the most common factors in the backgrounds of those processed are the existence of a history of mental illness and the occurrence of overt aggressive behavior. The picture is one of desperation; "when asked what would have happened if they had taken no action, the majority of the police respondents referred to a risk that the person might be a danger to himself or to others." (170.) The presence of such danger creates for the police a set of circumstances that corresponds well to their more typical role as "keepers of the peace." It is in this role that the police feel safest in acting.

The Organization of Police Work. The fact that the police must deal with such diverse kinds of behavior explains in part the highly organized, bureaucratic character of police operations. Concern for the "quality and efficiency" of these operations, in all areas of community service, has recently stimulated attempts to "professionalize" or "modernize" police departments. The hope is that the "new police officer," a well-educated and extensively trained public servant, working in an highly organized department, would be less prone to brutality and other patterns of decision-making which produce disparity in enforcement. James Wilson (1968a), among others, has attempted to evaluate this "new look" in the organization of police work.

Wilson begins his study by observing that juvenile codes allow considerable discretion on the part of authorities in their handling of delinquency. The result is that the organization of a department can make a large difference in the disposition of juvenile cases. Wilson's study characterizes two departments, one in a western city and another in an eastern city, and compares their respective styles in the handling of juvenile cases. Western City operates a "professional" police department. This department is described as highly organized with an emphasis on centralization. Officers are recruited on the basis of their achieved characteristics, with particular importance attached to the level of education attained by applicants.

Eastern City, on the other hand, operates a "fraternal" department. Decentralization is the organizational priority with this police force. Officers are chosen primarily for their ascribed characteristics, particularly according to their residence and recognition in the community. Training in this department is informal and characteristically of the "how to get along" variety. In short, one might summarize the situation in Eastern City and juxtapose it to the setup in Western City with the following bit of folk wisdom: "it's not what you know, but who you know that counts."

A comparison of official statistics for the handling of juveniles in Western and Eastern Cities presents some surprises. It seems that "professional" officers in Western City, invoking their impersonal standards, arrest a relatively large share of the juveniles encountered; the result is a release rate of only 53 per cent. The "fraternal" officers in Eastern City, on the other hand, arrest far fewer of the juveniles they encounter, and in the end release 70 per cent of the cases they handle. The conclusion that one must reach on comparing these figures is that Western City, with its professional department, follows a more punitive policy.

There is another dimension to this situation, however, and it involves black neighborhoods. The professional department shows no bias in terms of class or racial factors, while the fraternal department shows a significant disparity in its referral rate for blacks (blacks, apparently, are referred to court in Eastern City at a higher rate than whites). Given our earlier discussion of differentials in black-white referral rates, it is difficult to know whether this disparity represents discrimination. What we do know, however, is that this disparity in referrals is eliminated in the professional department by increasing the arrest rate for whites, rather than by reducing the arrest rate for blacks. This is presumably an unintended consequence of professionalization.

Wilson suggests an explanation for the generally higher arrest rate in the professional department. While professional departments employ officers who usually have no contact with the community they work in, other than patrol assignment, fraternal departments more often utilize officers who have an in-depth and personalized knowledge of the community they patrol. Often the officers in Eastern City have grown up in the community to which they are assigned. The implication is that officers in Eastern City are aware of means other than arrest for solving problems in encounters with juveniles. Knowing the details of a family's situation, or having lived through similar situations themselves, the officers from a fraternal department may often be able to find personalized solutions that avoid arrest.

Another investigation of the organization of police work is provided by John Gandy (1970) in his study of the Metropolitan Toronto Police Department. Gandy notes that in an organization as large as the Toronto Department bureaucratic subdivision is inevitable. Thus it was expected that in a department of this type there would be several, rather than only one, patterns of disposition in the handling of juveniles. To investigate this proposition, Gandy selected three administrative sub-units within the larger department, all dealing with the disposition of juveniles taken into custody by Metropolitan Police. After analyzing responses to open-ended interviews conducted with officers in each of the organizational branches investigated, Gandy concludes that, "There were significant differences between the administrative sub-units (a) in the emphasis and weight given to the same criteria in making choices among possible dispositions; (b) in their perception of the relative seriousness of certain types of behavior; and (c) in the frequency with which certain courses of action were selected." (342.)

The important insight emerging from the type of studies carried out by Wilson and Gandy is an awareness that it can make a great deal of difference where and by whom an offender is caught. In other words, the social transformation from conventional to disreputable status is at least partially contingent upon the particular organizational orientation that the officer of first encounter is following. Certainly these findings should alert us to the possible naivety of the universalistic and democratic values that underlie our systems of criminal and juvenile justice. This theme grows in in its importance as we turn next to the work of the courts.

THE COURTS

Police apprehension is, of course, only a first and tentative step toward a disposition that formally symbolizes disrepute. In this section, we will be concerned with the intermediary steps between apprehension and institutionalization. We will concern ourselves first with the role of the prosecutor in securing conviction and the role of defence counsel in representing the accused; second with the role of the probation officer in the preparation of pre-sentence reports; third with the role of the judge in the formation of sentencing decisions; fourth with the role of the psychiatrist as an arbitrator in involuntary commitment proceedings; and finally with the general role of the courts as they are involved in the societal response to alcoholism. We will begin with the interrelated roles of the prosecutor and defence counsel.

The Prosecution and the Defence. The media image of the court process is that of a trial by jury, with prosecution and defence attorneys assuming adversarial roles in a battle for justice. In fact, however, few criminal cases follow this adversarial pattern. The typical sequence, followed in more than 90 per cent of the cases in most jurisdictions, is for the defendant to plead guilty and forfeit trial. Thus, jury trials are not common in Canada, with less than 2000 trials by jury occurring annually. Jury trials are proportionally more frequent in the United States (Kalven and Zeisel, 1966:12-13); however, the far more common outcome is still a plea of guilty, and most sociologists who study the criminal justice system are skeptical about how these pleas are determined.

Abraham Blumberg (1967a, b) suggests that the process of criminal prosecution amounts to "the practice of law as a confidence game." His argument is that over time, court officials, prosecutors, and defence lawyers develop working relationships that place the defendant in the role of a potentially disruptive outsider. This situation is said to result from several factors. Court officials and prosecutors are under the strain of limited court resources, and are therefore anxious to move cases through the court system as efficiently as possible. Defence lawyers as well stand to gain financially by handling as many cases as possible in the shortest period of time. With this common resolve to complete cases quickly, Blumberg suggests that prosecutors, judges, and defence attorneys covertly conspire to encourage a guilty plea from the defendant.

To stimulate this plea, as well as to assure the payment of legal fees, Blumberg indicates that the defence attorney will commonly mobilize the defendant's family. Then, frequently with the help of adjournments offered by an understanding judge, the defence attorney seeks to convince the family of the financial and practical wisdom of the defendant's "pleading guilty for considerations." Donald Newman (1956; 1966) suggests that in about 33 per cent of these plea negotiations the result is an alteration in charges, while in about 66 per cent of the cases the expectation is a reduced sentence. We will note later that this expectation of a shorter sentence may be illusionary, a possibility that fits well with the analogy to a confidence game. For the moment, however, the interesting finding that Blumberg reports is that it is most frequently the lawyer for the defence who suggests first to the defendant that it would be better to plead guilty than to protest his or her innocence. Following such a plea, all that remains is to resign the defendant to fate—or, in the vernacular of the confidence game, "to cool the mark out." (Goffman, 1952.)[4]

There are various reasons why plea bargaining is a common part of the court process. Grosman (1969) observes, on the basis of interviews with prosecutors in York County (Ontario), that guilty pleas are an important way of avoiding the time, expense, and uncertainty of trials. Similarly, Blumberg (1967b) notes that metropolitan courts are bureaucratic organizations, and as such they demand a continuing rationalization of procedures whose primary measure is efficiency. Given these demands for efficiency, the question is not whether negotiations will take place, but rather how they will occur.

David Sudnow (1965) has attempted to spell out in sociological terms the procedures involved in bargaining for reduced charges. Sudnow notes first that the reduction of charges focuses on two types of offences: "necessarily included offences" and "situationally included offences." Necessarily included offences are those that by legal definition occur in association with one another; for example, "homicide" cannot occur without "intent to commit a murder." In contrast, situationally included offences are those that occur together by *convention*; "public drunkenness" *usually*, but not necessarily, occurs in association with "creating a public disturbance." Bargaining for charge reductions works on the general *premise* of reducing the initial charge to a lesser necessarily or situationally included offence.

Sudnow's point, however, is that the procedural rules followed in deciding what sort of a reduction is appropriate are not entirely defined by law. Rather, lawyers and prosecutors develop working conceptions of what they regard as "normal crimes": " . . . the typical manner in which offences of given classes are committed, the social characteristics of the persons who regularly commit them, the features of the settings in which they occur, the types of victims often involved, and the like." (259.)[5] According to Sudnow, it is on the basis of these conceptions of "normal crimes" that an initial legal categorization is established; attention is then directed to determining which (*possibly* necessarily or situationally included) lesser offence may constitute the appropriate reduction. As an example, Sudnow notes that in the jurisdiction he studied a burglary charge is routinely reduced to petty theft. However, "The propriety of proposing petty theft as a reduction does not derive from its . . . existence in the present case, but is warranted . . . (instead) by the relation of the present burglary to 'burglaries,' normally conceived." (263.)[6] Finally, Sudnow notes that there must be a balance established between the sentence the defendant might have received for the original charge, and that which will probably be received for the lesser charge. In Canada, this balance is assisted by the fact that our Criminal Code allows the judge so much discretion in sentencing that the likelihood of receiving the same sentence for *either* the greater or lesser charge is substantial.

The issue that follows from this description of criminal prosecution is what type of defendants will benefit most and least. Several views are expressed on this issue. Chambliss and Seidman argue that, "How favorable a 'bargain' one can strike with the prosecutor in the pretrial confrontations is a direct function of how politically and economically powerful the defendant is." (1971:412.) However, data collected by Donald Newman in interviews with convicted felons cast doubt on the class based hypotheses of Chambliss and Seidman. For example, when defendants are compared in terms of their initial pleas, no significant differences are found by education, occupation, and residence. Similarly, "(an) analysis of the sample of offenders showed no clear-cut categories separating bargained from non-bargained convictions. . ." (1956:789.)[7] Nevertheless, Newman concludes with the hypothesis that, "The way bargaining now works, the more experienced criminals can manipulate legal processes to obtain light sentences and better official records. . . ." (790.)[8] Fortunately, there is Canadian data to address these issues.

Wynne and Hartnagel (1975a, see also 1975b) provide a study of plea negotiation in a western Canadian province, focusing particularly on the pre-trial interaction between prosecutor and defence attorney that often leads to guilty pleas and charge reductions. Their study is based on a stratified sample designed to over-represent those cases where negotiation is thought to be most common; plea negotiation is in fact found to occur in more than 25 per cent of the cases examined. This study does *not* find more experienced offenders to be advantaged in the negotiation process, but white and upper socio-economic status offenders *are*. For example, 16 per cent of the native offenders charged with indictable offences experienced negotiation, compared to 29 per cent of the non-native offenders. Further, the presence of defence counsel is crucial to negotiations occurring, and the presence of multiple counts or charges also apparently gives something to negotiate about. Wynne and Hartnagel are cautious in their conclusions, noting that, " . . . there may be differences in the nature of offences engaged in by natives compared to non-natives which in turn could affect the chances of negotiation and the presence of such counts/charges." (51.) Furthermore, they conclude that, "the sentencing consequences may remain substantially unchanged even though the charge has been reduced." (52.)

A second study of criminal prosecution in a western Canadian province, by Hagan (1975a), focuses more specifically on charge alterations and their impact on the final disposition imposed. Based on a random sample of cases prosecuted in the city of Edmonton, this study again emphasizes the crucial role of defence counsel and the presence of multiple charges in generating a charge alteration. The latter finding is interpreted as an indication that some offenders may systematically be "overcharged" to set the bargaining process in motion. Again, like Wynne and Hartnagel's study, no clear evidence is found that experienced offenders receive more or better "bargains." *Unlike* Wynne and Hartnagel's study, however, the proportion of white and native offenders retaining counsel, pleading guilty, and receiving charge alterations is approximately equal. It is unclear whether this disparity between the studies is a result of differences in sampling techniques or the latter study's focus on charge alterations rather than plea negotiations. In either case, however, probably the most intriguing finding of Hagan's study is that charge alterations have no substantial impact on final disposition, unless the charges are dropped completely. In other words, where judges have the opportunity to pass sentence, they seem able to use the substantial discretion allowed by Canadian statutes to sentence as they would have in the first place. "This finding suggests that 'considerations' won in early stages of the legal process may ultimately prove illusionary, a finding that fits well with Blumberg's characterization of the bargaining process as a 'confidence game.' " (544.)

The Role of the Probation Officer. The influence of the probation officer in criminal and juvenile justice proceedings is frequently underestimated, particularly when compared to the prosecutor and judge. However, Wheeler *et al.* (1968) demonstrate in a juvenile court study that the probation officer sustains strategic contact with, and communicates crucial information between, all participants in the court process. The background to this aspect of the probation officer's role is described in part by Everett Hughes' (1951; 1962) concept of "dirty work"—those occupational activities that are socially necessary, but in some significant sense "unclean." In a graphic description of court work, Hughes (1958:71) notes that, "What the learned lawyers argue before an Appellate Court ... is but a purified distillate of some human mess." The question that follows from this observation is who must undertake, and by what means, the process of "purification." It has been argued that an important part of this task falls to the probation officer (Hagan, 1975b; see also Ericson, 1975b).

Although probation is now known as the "growth industry of corrections" (Wallace, 1974), the role of the probation officer originated with religious sponsorship. The Church of England Temperance Society appointed the first probation officers as "court missionaries" in 1876 (Chute and Bell, 1956; Timasheff, 1949; Madley, 1965). Their initial responsibilities were to provide lay supervision. However, as the role of the probation officer became professionalized, much of its identity was drawn from the field of social work. The result was to add a methodology to a vocation.

The method of the probation officer follows from the principles of casework (Diana, 1960; Towle, 1973). These principles outline techniques for objectifying (i.e., "purifying") the circumstances of "persons in trouble." (cf., Cicourel, 1968.) The primary step involves "observing, gathering, and recording" the social, legal, and historical facts of the case. These "social facts" are then assembled in the form of a "probation report." Gradually, jurists recognized the potential of such reports as guides for sentencing (Chute and Bell, 1956:136-151).[9] From here it was a small step to the elevation of the probation officer to an advisory role in the sentencing process: probation reports became pre-sentence reports, and diagnostic evaluations became prognostic recommendations. Thus, research by Wahl and Glaser (1963) indicates that as early as ten years ago probation officers were spending nearly as much time on pre-sentence work as on supervision. This arrangement is viewed by many observers as an efficient and rational division of court labor.

The work of Everett Hughes suggests another view of this process. Hughes notes that occupations within institutions often maintain symbiotic (i.e., mutually rewarding) status relationships. Thus, the judiciary reinforces its status by delegating to probation officers the "dirty work" of collecting information for sentencing. Senior probation officers, in turn, can enhance their own status by turning over to less experienced probation officers increasing responsibilities for case supervision. A consequence is that senior probation officers spend more time in office and court activities. Most importantly, however, the court activities of probation officers now involve prestige-conferring opportunities to offer pre-sentence recommendations. The results of these organizational rearrangements, then, may be socially rewarding for both groups.

Hughes (1958:77) warns, however, that such organizational innovations may often have unintended consequences. More specifically, Carter and Wilkins (1967) cite the close and apparently causal relationship between recommendations and dispositions, and suggest the hypothesis that probation officers are a source of disparities in judicial sentencing. Recent research by Hagan (1975b) examines this hypothesis by comparing cases where probation officers' recommendations are requested to cases where they are not. This research was carried out through adult probation departments in the Province of Alberta.

Looking first at cases where recommendations are received, this research finds that the offence and prior record of the offender play an important role in determining the type of sentence recommended.

Similarly important, however, are a succession of variables beginning with the offender's ethnic background, following with the probation officer's perception of the offender's demeanor, and culminating in the probation officer's perception of the offender's prospects for success on probation. More specifically, native offenders, whose demeanor was perceived unfavorably by probation officers, were evaluated as having poorer prospects for success on probation, and were less likely to receive a lenient recommendation for sentence. In contrast, when recommendations were not received, the influence of these variables was reduced. Finally, Hagan (1976b) reports in a follow-up study that the ethnic background of the offender had its primary impact on recommendations in rural jurisdictions, where Native Persons most frequently experience their first contact with the courts.

The Role of the Judiciary. Although the recommendation of the probation officer is an influential factor in determining the type of sentence imposed, this finding must be placed in a broader context. First, pre-sentence reports and probation officers' recommendations are not received in all, or even most, cases. For example, judges typically sentence minor offences without consultation. Furthermore, even when a judge accepts a probation officer's recommendation for the type of sentence (e.g., probation, fine, or imprisonment), the judge must still decide on the conditions of such a sentence (e.g., the length of probation or imprisonment, or the amount of fine). The discretion of the judge in these matters is substantial—particularly in Canada.

Legislation outlining the sentencing responsibilities of the criminal courts in Canada entrusts to presiding judges nearly complete freedom in the determination of minimum sentences. Similarly, a wide range of discretion is allowed in the establishment of maximum penalties. The nature of the problem, however, extends beyond the absence of statutory guides to minimum and maximum sentences. Also involved is confusion regarding a basic set of principles to be used in the determination of sentences. Thus Decore (1964) notes that even the utilization of precedents in sentencing is a matter of contradiction and doubt. A consequence is a heavy reliance on the discretion of the sentencing judge, with the implication that variation and disparity will follow.

Several studies have attempted to chart the effects of the use of this judicial discretion within Canada. The first of these studies, by Jaffary (1963), examined differences in sentencing patterns between provinces. Jaffary found that these disparities were substantial. For example, an offender convicted of theft was nearly five times as likely to be given a penitentiary sentence in Quebec as in Manitoba,

Saskatchewan, or British Columbia. One of Jaffary's conclusions, then, is that important discrepancies exist across provinces in the severity of the treatment of offenders in Canada. Perhaps even more significantly, however, Jaffary also presents data to support claims that Canadian courts generally make heavy use of imprisonment, combined with long sentences, when compared with other countries. Jaffary concludes that, "In both the quantity of imprisonment and the duration of imprisonment . . . Canadian courts . . . give evidence of the application of a strongly punitive philosophy." (54.) One historical illustration of this punitive philosophy is found in a letter written in 1871 to the warden of Kingston Penitentiary by then Prime Minister John A. MacDonald. This letter is reproduced in Figure 5-2.

FIGURE 5-2

COPY OF A LETTER FROM SIR JOHN A. MACDONALD TO JOHN CREIGHTON, WARDEN OF KINGSTON PENITENTIARY

Ottawa, October 31st, 1871.

Private

My dear Creighton—

I have yours of the 25th which I have read with all the attention you bespeak. I can quite appreciate your anxieties in your office, it is a most responsible one, not without care but as you remark, it has also its bright side. I never had any doubt of and do not now doubt your ultimate success in making the Penitentiary a school of reform, as well as a place of punishment, of course you feel that inexperience at first, that everyone does in a new situation. My only fear is that your natural kindness of disposition may lead you to forget that the primary [purpose] of the penitentiary is punishment and the incidental one reformation . . . .

Yours sincerely,

John Creighton, Esq.   (signed) John A. Macdonald.
    Kingston.

Reprinted with permission of the Macmillan Company of Canada Limited.
Source: Edminson (1965:Appendix)

More recently, John Hogarth (1971) has extended attention from differences between nations and provinces, to variation between judges. Hogarth begins by noting that judges in the lower provincial courts in Canada have broader jurisdiction (i.e., 94 per cent of all indictable cases are tried in these courts) and wider sentencing powers (e.g., to life imprisonment) than any comparable set of courts in the western world. Extending Jaffary's theme, Hogarth provides additional data suggesting that Canada in the mid-1960s had one of the highest rates of imprisonment in the western world (see also Cousineau and Veevers, 1972a; Matthews, 1972). However, Hogarth also presents evidence of a recent shift in this pattern (see Figure 5-3), with the heavy reliance on prison sentences giving way to an increasing use of fines.

The most recent evidence on Canada's use of imprisonment is provided in an exceptionally careful analysis by Waller and Chan (1975). This analysis indicates that Canada's overall imprisonment rate is now lower than that of the United States and several other countries (see Table 5-1a), with only the Yukon and the Northwest Territories remaining high relative to most American states (see Table 5-1b). Waller and Chan are careful to emphasize the difficulties of drawing any final inferences from the data they present, and to their cautions we will add several additional comments. First, it is not surprising to find Canada's imprisonment rate per 100 000 population low relative to some other countries, particularly the United States, for we have noted in Chapter Two that Canada's serious crime rate is also relatively low. The more crucial comparisons would involve ratios of incarcerations to occurrences and convictions. Waller and Chan appropriately note the complications in accurately computing these ratios with current official data. Second, it should be noted that where imprisonment rates are highest in Canada (i.e., in the north), Native Peoples are most likely to be experiencing the consequences. Finally, we can note that while efforts to avoid incarceration through the increasing use of fines may be successful on an aggregate basis in Canada, economic and ethnic minorities unable to pay these fines remain at a continuing disadvantage. These comments should discourage any sense of complacency with our condition, a complacency that Waller and Chan clearly disavow (see also Waller, 1974). We will be returning to these points as our discussion continues. However, for our immediate purposes, we will need to complete our discussion of Hogarth's research.

The primary goal of Hogarth's study was to explain variations in sentencing between judges through attention to their (1) attitudes and beliefs, (2) perceptions of social and legal constraints, (3) cognitive styles, and (4) perceptions of relevant case facts. As a group, Hogarth finds that judges vary widely in their penal philosophies. As *individuals*, however, they are quite consistent in their approaches to sentencing. Thus, the attitudes of individual judges influence the way they perceive and act upon the facts of cases, constraints of the law and social system, and other features of the external world.

FIGURE 5-3

TRENDS IN CANADIAN SENTENCING PRACTICE, 1960-7
(INDICTABLE CASES ONLY)

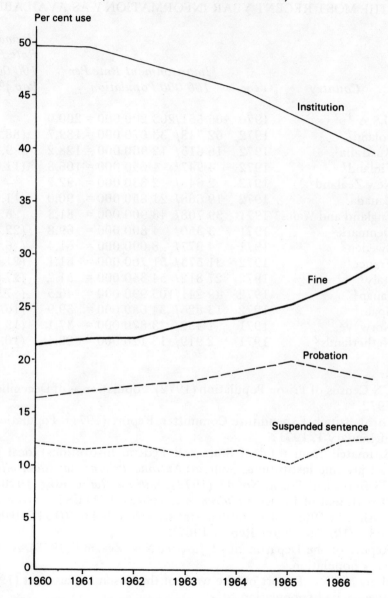

Reprinted with permission of University of Toronto Press and John Hogarth.
© *1971 University of Toronto Press.*
Source: Dominion Bureau of Statistics in Hogarth (1971:42)

Table 5-1a

SELECTED COUNTRIES RANKED IN ORDER OF THE NUMBER OF PERSONS IN PRISON PER 100 000 PERSONS IN THE POPULATION FOR THE MOST RECENT YEAR INFORMATION WAS AVAILABLE

Rank	Country	Year	Imprisonment Rate Per 100 000 Population	(Remand Rate Per 100 000 Pop.)[6]
1	U.S.A.[3]	1970	406 531/203 200 000 = 200.0	
2	Poland[1]	1972	62 748/ 33 070 000 = 189.7	(88.8)
3	Australia[1]	1972	16 615/ 12 960 000 = 128.2	(9.2)
4	Finland[1]	1972	4 947/ 4 630 000 = 106.8	(11.0)
5	New Zealand[4]	1972	2 643/ 2 850 000 = 92.7	—
6	Canada[1]	1972	19 668/ 21 850 000 = 90.0	(11.0)
7	England and Wales[5]	1971	39 708/ 48 900 000 = 81.3	(6.1)
8	Denmark[2]	1971	3 350/ 4 800 000 = 69.8	(22.0)
9	Sweden[2]	1971	4 977/ 8 090 000 = 61.4	(6.9)
10	France[1]	1972	31 573/ 51 700 000 = 61.1	(21.8)
11	Italy[1]	1972	27 812/ 54 350 000 = 51.2	(27.8)
12	Japan[1]	1972	49 241/105 990 000 = 46.5	(7.9)
13	Spain[1]	1972	13 826/ 34 680 000 = 39.9	(16.6)
14	Norway[2]	1971	1 432/ 3 870 000 = 37.1	(13.7)
15	Netherlands[2]	1971	2 919/ 13 120 000 = 22.4	(10.4)

Sources:
1. UN Census of Prison Population (1972). Population as of December 1, 1972.
2. Great Britain Expenditure Committee Report (1971). Population as of January 1, 1971.
3. Estimated from total of State and Federal Institutions, local jails, and juvenile institutions. Sources: *National Prisons Statistics Bulletin,* US Bureau of Prison No. 47 (1972); *National Jail Census* (1970) US Department of Justice; *Children in Custody* (1971) US Department of Justice. In 1965, the equivalent statistics were 404 049/194 240 000 = 208.0 (US Task Force Report 1967).
4. Report of the Department of Justice, New Zealand (1973). Average daily population.
5. Home Office. Report on the work of the Prison Department (1971). Average daily population.
6. Remand rate is not restricted to those awaiting arraignment or their first trial. In some European jurisdictions such as Italy, this includes those awaiting a hearing in a court of second instance.

Table 5-1b

COUNTRIES AND JURISDICTIONS GROUPED AS TO HIGH,
MEDIUM, OR LOW RATES OF PERSONS IN PRISON
PER HEAD OF POPULATION

Ranges	Countries	Canadian Provinces	Australian States	U.S.A.
Extra High Over 250/ 100 000	–	Yukon and North West Territories	–	California, Florida, Georgia, Nevada
High 150-249/ 100 000	Poland, U.S.A.	–	–	19 States mainly in South and West, but including Texas, New York, and Michigan
Medium 75-149/ 100 000	Australia, Canada, England and Wales, Finland, New Zealand	Nova Scotia, New Brunswick, P.E.I., Ontario, Saskatchewan, Alberta, B.C., Manitoba	N.S.W., Tasmania, South Australia, West Australia	20 States mainly North and East, including Illinois, New Jersey, Ohio, Pennsylvania
Low 0-74/ 100 000	Denmark, France, Italy, Japan, Netherlands, Norway, Spain, Sweden	Quebec, Newfoundland	Queensland, Victoria	Connecticut, Hawaii, Massachusetts, North Dakota, Vermont

Reprinted with permission of Irvin Waller, Janet Chan and the Criminal Law Quarterly.
Source: Waller and Chan (1975:58-59)

The results of this process are sometimes unexpected. For example, the judicial selection of prison sentences is associated with interpretations of facts which emphasize both punishment *and* treatment. In other words, judges come to believe that they can punish and treat offenders at the same time. Hogarth emphasizes that this "punishment as treatment" approach is a way in which judges mentally adapt themselves to the unpleasant task of having to send people to prison. The point is that sentencing is a very human, and therefore subjectively influenced, process.

Probably because Hogarth's research was based primarily in the large urban areas of Ontario, little attention was given to the social consequences of sentencing for ethnic and economic minorities— particularly Native Persons. We have already noted that Native Persons are present in Canadian court and prison populations far beyond their representation in the general population. To further understand the influence of race and other offender characteristics on judicial sentencing, we will need to consider briefly a large body of American research.

A variety of American studies focus on the role of race, sex, age, and socio-economic status of the offender in the formation of sentencing decisions (e.g., Bullock, 1961; Green, 1961, 1964; Nagel, 1969; Wolfgang and Riedel, 1973). A recent review of 20 such studies concludes that there is a generally small relationship between the extra-legal attributes of offenders and sentencing decisions (Hagan, 1974a). However, because the authors of many of these studies fail to take the seriousness of offence and prior records of offenders into account, it is difficult to know whether the relationships found can be taken as evidence of discrimination (i.e., do blacks in the United States receive longer sentences because they are discriminated against, or because they commit more serious offences and more frequently have prior convictions?). When these factors *are* controlled, the relationships reported between extra-legal offender characteristics and sentence usually are reduced or eliminated (Chiricos and Waldo, 1975). The importance of these considerations becomes apparent when we turn to the Canadian data.

Judges in Canada are as frequently charged with being differentially *lenient* with native offenders, as they are with being unjustly *punitive*. The charge of leniency reflects an attempt on the part of some Canadian judges to take cultural differences into account when sentencing native offenders (see Figure 5-4). However, recent evidence on this issue suggests that most judges sentence *primarily* on the basis of offence seriousness and prior conviction records. Thus, Hagan (1975c) divided a sample of Albertan judges into two groups scoring "high" and "low" on a "law and order scale." He then predicted that those judges scoring high would sentence native offenders punitively, while judges scoring low would sentence Native Persons leniently. Perhaps surprisingly, the results showed that "law and order" judges sentence almost exclusively on offence seriousness, while judges less concerned about such issues provided Native Persons only minimal leniency. More generally, this study suggests that most judges sentence most offenders mechanically—not taking the *time* to consider their social backgrounds. This is particularly the case, and becomes particularly problematic, with minor offenders.

FIGURE 5-4

DISPENSING JUSTICE IS A VERY SERIOUS MATTER TO "JUDGE OF THE NORTH"

CANADA'S JUSTICE MORROW TRIES TO UNDERSTAND NATIVE PEOPLE, FIT PUNISHMENTS TO CULTURES

By JOHN E. COONEY
Staff Reporter of
THE WALL STREET JOURNAL

"Oyez, Oyez, Oyez. All persons having anything to do before my Lady the Queen's Justice of the Supreme Court of the Northwest Territories at its sitting for trial of criminal cases draw near and give your attendance and you shall be heard. God save the Queen."

FORT FRANKLIN, Northwest Territories—It's a bitter 30 degrees below zero outside the large log cabin where Justice William G. Morrow's supreme court is in session.

Occasional growls of dogsled huskies curled in the icy snow filter through the walls and mingle with the muffled typing of the court reporter. A window to the judge's left silhouettes the distant bent form of an Indian fishing through a hole in the frozen Great Bear Lake.

Unmindful of distractions, Judge Morrow weighs the business at hand. Donald Yukon, a 24-year-old Indian, has just pleaded guilty to assaulting a woman during a drinking spree last May in this settlement of some 200 people.

Because the defendant is the son of a chief and because he had a similar charge against him previously, Orval Troy, the prosecuting attorney, whose blue snowsuit pants are visible beneath his black barrister's robes, solemnly demands that the book be thrown at young Yukon. But Malcolm McConnell, the defence attorney, who shuffles nervously in his knee-high furry mukluks, seeks leniency because Mr. Yukon is the major support of his family.

The judge listens attentively but occasionally stops the lawyers' arguments in order to beckon into seats some curious and timid people from this village in the upper western half of the Territories who have gathered in the back of the room. Finally, the judge firmly warns Mr. Yukon that things won't go well for him if he doesn't mend his ways. The lecture plus a $150 fine to be paid over two months ends the proceedings. The court party makes ready to move on to another settlement several hundred miles away.

Getting the Message Across

"I hate to give fines because these people depend so much on that paycheck," the judge confides a few minutes later. "But I have to get it across to that young man that he had better watch himself and change his ways."

Such is the way Justice Morrow, "the judge of the North," goes about his job in the vast, culturally complex Northwest Territories. He is the only judge in the Territories, an area nearly two-thirds the size of the United States and containing only 35 000 people. But because his supreme court often deals in remote outposts such as this with sensitive issues concerning the rights of Indians and Eskimos, his decisions frequently have ramifications throughout the rest of Canada as well.

"Judge Morrow is the best person who could be sitting where he sits now," says Jim Wahshee, president of the Indian Brotherhood, a national organization based in Yellowknife, the capital of the Territories. "More than most other white men up here, the judge understands Native People, our customs and cultures."

The judge's office over the Yellowknife post office is crammed with books on history, anthropology, and sociology. Many deal with the problems of the area's Native Peoples—who make up two-thirds of the population to the white man's third—as their cultures painfully confront the onslaught of the 20th Century with its oil rigs and gas pipelines and welfare and whisky. And many of the judge's decisions,

such as legally recognizing native adoption, which merely consists of informally giving a child to someone else, as well as his giving Native People lesser sentences than whites convicted of similar crimes, have been used as precedents by courts elsewhere.

Too Lenient?

"Why should an Indian or Eskimo go to jail for as long as a white when they don't live as long as whites?" asks Judge Morrow, 57, a friendly, hefty six-footer who has been sitting on the bench for seven years. "One of the reasons I took this job was to see if I couldn't help these people."

Such an attitude doesn't go uncriticized. There are those who say he is too lenient. And his recent decision contending that Indians have aboriginal rights to 400 000 square miles of the resource-rich Mackenzie Valley has raised the hackles of federal officials, who disagree as to what Indian treaty rights are in the area. "They went out of their minds in Ottawa when Morrow handed down that decision," a Justice Department lawyer says.

The judge brushes aside such reactions. "Probably every lawyer wants to be a judge and see if he can do better than the bastards who have been sitting in front of him," Justice Morrow says. "Now I'm the bastard."

Reprinted with permission of the Wall Street Journal, © *Dow Jones and Company, Inc. 1974. All rights reserved.*
Source: The Wall Street Journal, *January 14, 1974, page 1*

We noted earlier in this chapter that the police typically apprehend native offenders for minor alcohol related charges. In turn, judges typically sentence such offenders to "so many dollars or so many days." The outcome of this approach is predictable: Hagan (1974b) reports that nearly 66 per cent of all Native Persons who go to jail are incarcerated in default of fine payments. This is nearly twice the rate for whites. One result is that in this Albertan sample, Native Persons are represented in the prison population four times more frequently than in the general population. A follow-up study by Hagan (1976b) indicates that these differential consequences are concentrated primarily in rural jurisdictions. In the following chapter, we will consider ways in which fines can be used more "judiciously," for example, by linking the amount of the fine to the offender's ability to pay.

The Psychiatrist and the Court. As we turn our attention from criminality to mental illness, and later alcoholism, we begin to encounter some striking changes in the character of our findings. In the areas of crime and delinquency, there is limited evidence (with legal variables accounted for) that economic and ethnic minorities somewhat more frequently are labelled criminal and delinquent. This is no longer the case in the area of mental illness. To understand this change, we will need to consider first the process of being diagnosed and adjudicated mentally ill.

Many sociologists have indicated concern that psychiatrists in and out of the courts are too ready to assume the illness of a proposed patient. It is argued that as doctors, psychiatrists are more prone to making what in statistics is called a type two error. In other words, doctors are trained to take the risk of assuming something present (i.e., an assumption of illness), when in fact it may be absent, rather than run the risk of assuming something absent (i.e., an assumption of health), when in fact it may be present.[10] Thus, the medical patient who may or may not be ill is kept for hospital observation, rather than being allowed to run the risk of an unattended relapse. While we can all applaud such caution in medicine, sociologists are concerned that assuming the worst in the case of mental illness can sometimes *make* it happen. Recent research, however, suggests that as in medicine, it is the socially more "resourceful" person who is somewhat better able to obtain the psychiatrist's attention, and thereby *encourage* the assumption of illness.

Much of the research relevant to the issues we are considering is reviewed by Walter Gove (1975). Gove begins with a point made earlier: that most persons who receive psychiatric treatment do so *voluntarily*. The point is that this is one potentially disreputable status that is not necessarily avoided. One explanation of this finding is that mental illness, relative to other forms of deviance, is no longer as disreputable a status as it apparently once was. Thus among 13 types of deviants, Simmons (1969) recently found that ex-mental patients were less likely to be rejected than 11 other types of deviants, including "atheists, gamblers, beatniks, alcoholics, and adulterers." In any event, Gove and Howell (1975) present evidence that persons from the upper classes seek treatment more quickly, and for a wider range of behaviors, than persons from the lower classes.

There is related evidence that concerned friends and relatives do not frivously seek hospitalization for others. Smith *et al.* (1963) report that the typical psychiatric patient performs three or more "critical acts," each of which may justify hospitalization, before commitment procedures are initiated. Similarly, there is evidence that hospitalization is sought earlier for economically more important family members, than for those less consequential to family life (Hammer, 1963-64). Beyond this, Gove (1975) reviews a variety of studies leading to the observation that, " . . . officials do not assume illness but, in fact, proceed rather cautiously, screening out a substantial number of persons." (45.) Significantly, this results in a situation where (with the severity of personal disorder held constant) hospitalization is more readily obtained by members of the upper classes (Gove, 1975:57). One explanation for this situation, as it relates to the courts, is offered by Rock: "The more important problem today is not the filing of petitions (for institutionalization) that are without cause, but rather finding a person willing to petition." (1968.) Apparently there are class differences in the willingness to assume the role of petitioner for another person. A second explanation is that some forms of treatment for mental illness, or alcoholism, may be a fate preferable to others—particularly when the other forms of response carry the stigma of criminal disrepute. This point will become clear as we turn next to the problems of alcoholism.

The Courts and Alcoholism. The treatment of alcoholism is perhaps the area where the connection between class background and societal response is most apparent. The descending social rank of the persons typically receiving treatment in private sanitaria, from Alcoholics Anonymous, and from the Salvation Army will be obvious to anyone who has passed through the doors of each. The issue that underwrites this situation is how members of various classes find their way into these widely varying treatment arrangements.

One way of approaching this problem is to study the admission and treatment practices of a single institution that deliberately attempts to attend to persons of varying class backgrounds. The purpose of this type of study is to determine if there are intra-organizational patterns suggestive of more general principles in the treatment of alcoholism. Such a study was carried out by Schmidt *et al.* (1968) in the Toronto clinic of the Alcoholism and Drug Addiction Research Foundation. This study deals entirely with *voluntary* admissions, nonetheless, it carries larger implications for our concern with the courts. One of the major findings of this study is that lower class alcoholics in this clinic were more likely to receive drug related treatment from physicians, while upper class alcoholics were more likely to receive "talking" therapies from psychiatrists (87). These class related treatment differences could not be explained by differences in diagnosis or age, although differences in verbal skills are suggested as an explanatory variable. Even more interesting than these treatment differences, however, are variations by social class in the sources of referrals to the clinic. Upper class patients are more likely to find their way to the clinic through the intermediary services of private physicians, middle class persons by way of Alcoholics Anonymous, and lower class persons through general hospital and welfare agency referrals (80). Schmidt *et al.* offer the conclusion that, "These class patterns are probably attributable to the extent to which behaviors resulting from alcohol excess are tolerated in a given social milieu and to differences in the modal drinking patterns of the class." (81.) We are particularly interested, at this point, in the role the courts play in responding to these class differences.

An understanding of the role of the courts in the societal response to alcoholism requires that we use the findings of voluntary clinic studies as a source of leads to what may be happening across agencies, and particularly in the *involuntary* sector. Lowe and Hodges (1972) began a progression along this route in studying the treatment of black alcoholics in the southern United States. They began their research with the operations of a single voluntary clinic, but soon left this course with the finding that, " . . . any variation in amount of services given to patients within the clinic was insignificant beside the overwhelming fact that so few black alcoholics entered into service at all." (244.) This finding is eventually explained with the observation that black alcoholics are less likely to view admission as offering treatment, and are therefore unlikely to admit themselves *voluntarily* into any programme. Unfortunately, the result is that black alcoholics find themselves the involuntary subjects of law enforcement operations that start with the police, take fatal form in the courts, and end up in prison. Lowe and Hodges note that the courts very rarely attempt to reverse this situation with referrals to alternative treatment institutions (248). This pattern is apparent for Native Peoples in Canada as well.

Hagan (1974b) followed up the treatment received by native and white offenders in Alberta following incarceration. On the basis of either judicial recommendation or inmate request, offenders in Alberta are considered for transfer to an open institutional setting offering a programme particularly designed for alcoholic offenders. However, Hagan finds that although the "target population" of problem drinkers is nearly twice as large among native offenders as among whites, more whites than native offenders receive treatment in the open institutional setting. Thus, although only a minority of alcoholic offenders from either ethnic group experiences the open institution, white offenders are more than twice as likely as native offenders to find their way to this treatment setting. There are three plausible explanations for this situation. First, judges may less often recommend referrals of native offenders to the open institution. Second, native offenders may less often seek and accept such referrals. Third, correctional personnel may less often consent to the transfer of native offenders. It is important to note, however, that the three possibilities described are certainly not mutually exclusive, and in fact probably are mutually supportive. In other words, there may be general agreement that the open institutional setting, as organized, is less beneficial for native than for white offenders.[11] This possibility leads us to a set of significant class and ethnic-related conclusions.

CONCLUSIONS

The materials discussed in this chapter are relevant to two different issues: (1) how decision-making occurs within and between various agencies of social control, and (2) how this decision-making process in Canada may differ from that in other countries—particularly the United States. Our concluding argument will be that the various agencies of social control fit together in similar ways in Canada and the United States, but that particularly in the area of *crime*, Canadian policies and procedures have been more repressive. In other words, there are similarities *and* differences in the processing of deviance in Canada and the United States. We will summarize the similarities first, and the differences second.

Similarities in the Organization of Social Control. Materials reviewed in this chapter provide clear evidence that the perceived seriousness of a deviant act and the frequency of its prior occurrence are powerful predictors of the type and severity of societal response. For example, offence seriousness and prior convictions are important predictors of sentencing decisions. However, considerable evidence is also provided that these behavioral variables do not tell the *full* story.

Thus, probably the most fascinating finding of this chapter is that in both Canada and the United States there is evidence that an individual's *social resources* also have an influence on the application of disreputable labels. When this influence operates, less punitive labels are applied differentially to more "resourceful" persons, while more punitive labels are applied differentially to less "resourceful" persons (cf., Hagan, 1977). For example, when the relevant behavioral variables are taken into account, some research on police and court operations indicates that criminal and delinquent labels are applied somewhat more frequently to the socially disadvantaged, while alcoholic and psychiatric labels are reserved somewhat more frequently for those who *take* social advantage.[12]

It bears repeating here that social advantage implies not only access to resources, but also the ability and motivation to use these resources. It is the essence of social class that there is a differential learning of the ways and reasons to act to one's advantage. The point is that some labels, under some circumstances, become advantageous, and the ability to take advantage of these conditions varies by social class. Thus, it is perhaps unsurprising that when in a position that leads to being labelled deviant, middle and upper class persons are more likely to be labelled alcoholic or psychiatric cases. The other side of this coin is that socially disadvantaged persons more frequently become, and more frequently are labelled, criminals or delinquents. It is in this context that class related differences in the application of labels become more meaningful, and that the existence of different types of deviance and different agencies of social control becomes understandable. These observations seem as applicable in Canada as they are in the United States.

Policies and Procedures in Canada. A second issue discussed in this chapter is the possibility that the Canadian legal system is more repressive in its policies and procedures than other western nations, with specific attention to comparisons with the United States. Evidence reviewed indicated that in the past Canada incarcerated a larger proportion of its population, for longer periods of time, than did many other western nations. Evidence was then presented that (a) our use of imprisonment is decreasing, that (b) in proportion to population it now may be lower than the United States, but that (c) because of deficiencies in the data no final comparisons can be made. In short, we are hopeful that Canada's use of imprisonment has improved relative to other countries, but we cannot be certain that this is so. Given this uncertainty, let us turn to a second area of concern: the rights of individuals and minorities before the law.

Canadian and American traditions have differed in their efforts to prevent the arbitrary or unequal exercise of police or court related powers. American civil liberties, including the rights to due process and to equality before the law, are constitutionally entrenched in the American Bill of Rights. Through the American doctrine of judicial review, individuals and minorities look to judges and the courts as the guardians of their constitutionally protected liberties. In contrast, the Canadian approach places its ultimate constitutional faith in the supremacy of Parliament. Bruton (1962) reminds us that this faith must ultimately rest on a belief in the self-restraint of a parliamentary majority: "Consequently, faith in parliamentary supremacy as a protection against arbitrary government becomes faith that the majority can be depended upon not to work its will in arbitrary ways . . . . " (108.)

In Canada, on August 10, 1960, Parliament saw fit to supplement its role with the passage of "An Act for the Recognition and Protection of Human Rights and Fundamental Freedoms"—in other words, the "Canadian Bill of Rights." It can be argued, however, that the late appearance of the Canadian Bill of Rights signals a fundamental historical difference in concern for equality before the law and due process in Canada.[13]

Evidence for this view is found in recent judicial interpretations of the Canadian Bill of Rights. Instrumental in these interpretations are the views of Justice Ritchie, as expressed in the landmark *Drybones* decision discussed earlier in this chapter, and in the more recent case of *Attorney-General of Canada v. Lavell*. We have noted that it was the unequal character of the Indian Act's provision controlling native intoxication off a reserve that led to this law's being declared inoperative. This decision seemed to set a precedent for the judicial review of legislation violating the Canadian Bill of Rights. However, in the more recent *Lavell* case, Ritchie denies this meaning to the *Drybones* decision, arguing instead that " . . . the phrase 'equality before the law' as employed in . . . the *Bill of Rights* is to be treated as meaning equality in the administration or application of the law by the law enforcement authorities and the ordinary courts of the land." (cited in Tarnopolsky, 1975:15.) In effect, this decision indicates that the Canadian Bill of Rights is merely a statute of Parliament and, as such, cannot supersede another act of Parliament, such as the Criminal Code of Canada. This decision makes uncertain the direction in which the protection of individual rights is proceeding in Canada. The suggestion of our discussion is that historically Canada has adopted a more modest role than the United States in protecting these "rights." One quick way of dramatizing this point is to remind ourselves of some of the powers of the police in relation to the public in Canada, as indicated in Figure 5-5.

One final indication that Canada has historically adopted a more restrictive approach than the United States in its response to deviance is the pattern of penal reform in Canada.[14] Jaffary (1963) has

FIGURE 5-5

THE POLICE AND THE PUBLIC IN CANADA

Just to set the record straight, let's understand certain basic principles of Canadian law and jurisprudence:

• The police are under no obligation to inform you that you have the right to remain silent and that you have the right to counsel.

• If you insist on seeing a lawyer and the police refuse to allow you to see one, any voluntary statement you make to them without a lawyer present, is still admissible in court.

• Evidence, even if gathered illegally, can still be admissible in a Canadian court of law.

• Leads gathered by police as a result of unlawful wiretapping or tape recording can be admissible in a court of law even if the illegal recording isn't. This is directly opposite to the American practice where, under what is called "the fruit of the poisonous tree doctrine," no evidence gathered in this way can be produced at a trial.

• Under the narcotics laws, certain police officers have the unqualified right to enter *any* premises apart from your own home without a specific search warrant if they have "reasonable cause to believe" that drugs are present. And certain policemen—generally Mounties—armed only with a Queen's Writ of Assistance, can break into your home without a warrant. Ours is one of the few countries in the English-speaking world that allows such latitude.

Source: Berton (1976:9-10). Reprinted with permission.

---

compared the progress of penal reform in Canada, the United States, and Britain, and concludes that Canada again lags behind. One illustration of this fact is that penal reform really did not get under way in Canada until 1946, and only then after many years of activist support from the first woman Member of Parliament in Canada, Agnes Macphail. Jaffary notes that the United States and England were far ahead of this pace. However, more interesting than the comparative details of these reforms is the question that Jaffary asks and then attempts to answer, "Why had Canada come to the mid-century with its nineteenth century philosophy and services virtually unchanged?" (81.)

The answers Jaffary provides are in the tradition of the consensual theories we reviewed in Chapter Three. He suggests that the social and economic development of Canada posed great problems, with many of the difficulties traced to environmental factors of the type discussed by Innis, Clark, and Lipset. The size of the country, the problems of communication, and the difficulties of extracting resources are all mentioned as discouraging interest in such secondary issues as penal reform. Only after settlement, industrialization, and urbanization could such changes really begin.

The conflict theorists discussed in Chapter Four clearly would view this situation differently. From the conflict perspective, the repressive character of the Canadian response to deviance probably reflects the early influence of colonial, and later class, interests. If Canada were to be a successful colony, it would need to maintain the conditions of "law and order" essential to the development of uninterrupted trade and commerce. The use of imprisonment and restrictive legal procedures were one means of insuring the orderliness that allowed class interests to develop and prevail. According to the conflict view, we continue to live with this legacy.

Regardless of whether one accepts the conflict or consensus view, there is reason to believe that Canada can benefit from the reform of many of its laws and penal practices. Laws defining and controlling criminality are the cutting edge of a society's response to deviance, for the laws defining and punishing "crime" designate those acts most subject to disrepute. In the following chapter, we will indicate ways these laws could be changed and applied more judiciously. We will concentrate our attention on approaches taken to punishing, treating, and preventing crime and delinquency, for this is the area where our literature is best developed, and our problems most acute. However, what we will have to say will be relevant to other areas of deviance as well.

1. The phrase "inequality of treatment" is used here, in place of the more common term "discrimination," to avoid the definition problems that surround use of the latter concept in sociology (see Hagan, 1976a).

2. An interesting exception to this statement is St. John's, Newfoundland, one of the few remaining places in North America where the police do not carry guns.

3. For further discussion of the influence of the victim-complainant on charging decisions, see the discussion of Hogarth's (1974) research in Chapter Six.

4. For an indication of how legal aid programmes in Canada may help to overcome some of the types of problems we have discussed, see Wilkins (1976).

5. From David Sudnow, "Normal Crimes: Sociological Features of the Penal Code in a Public Defenders' Office," *Social Problems* 12 (3):255-276. Reprinted with permission of the Society for the Study of Social Problems.

6. Ibid.

7. From Donald Newman, "Pleading Guilty for Considerations: A Study of Bargain Justice." Reprinted with permission of the *Journal of Criminal Law, Criminology, and Police Science*, © 1956 Northwestern University School of Law, Vol. 46, No. 6.

8. Ibid.

9. Frankel (1972) points out that the conventional "rules of evidence" that minimize the influence of much of the type of information contained in probation reports at the conviction stage no longer apply at the sentencing stage.

10. In contrast, it is the expressed preference of our legal system to accept the risks of type one errors: "better that 100 guilty people go free than that 1 innocent person be punished."

11. Community-based programmes, operated by indigenous personnel, represent one mode of reorganization that may improve this situation.

12. This does not contradict the finding that the *under*classes may experience mental illness more frequently. Rather, when frequency is taken into account, it is found that members of the *upper*classes have better access to treatment.

13. For an empirical examination of some of the issues of due process in the Canadian courts, see the Canadian Civil Liberties Educational Trust (1971; cf., Wilkins, 1972).

14. It should go without saying that the United States cannot be taken as the "model" in any of the areas we have discussed. To be blunt: the Canadian experience is different, and the American example far from virtuous. Our purpose is to use the United States as a convenient and interesting point of reference. Clearly, Canada will have to solve its own problems in its own (and hopefully better) ways. We address ourselves to this task in the following chapter.

VI

LIVING WITH DEVIANCE:
The Lessons of Treatment and Prevention

Not all deviance is preventable, and we are learning to live with some of it. This is fortunate, for the absence of deviance is a symptom of a totalitarian society. Such societies lack the freedoms we value. What most of us desire, then, is not the elimination of deviance, but a reduction in its more *serious* forms. In other words, what most of us desire is a reduction in the level of what we have called the "consensual" crimes. Sociological thinking about the best means for accomplishing this goal is changing.

Past efforts focused on three approaches: individual treatment, social reform, and police deployment. We will argue that these efforts were well-intended, but largely ineffective. More recent efforts focus on community involvement—through law reform, environmental design, and the location of correctional programmes in the community. We will argue that these programmes outline a more efficacious means of dealing with conflict crimes, while at the same time freeing new resources for a more thorough response to the consensual crimes. In short, the latter programmes are more promising, although it must be acknowledged that the promise is as yet unfulfilled. We will begin by reviewing the less successful programmes of the past.

INDIVIDUAL TREATMENT

The time-honored approach to crime prevention is individual treatment. Emphasized in this approach is the social-psychological development of the criminal, with particular attention to the experiences of adolescence. The distinctive assumption of this approach is that if the delinquent or pre-delinquent can be identified, and corrective therapy applied, then juvenile and adult crime can be prevented. This assumption finds expression, and sometimes evaluation, in a variety of treatment programmes.

One of the earliest and most ambitious treatment programmes was the Cambridge-Sommerville Youth Study (Powers and Witmer, 1951; McCord, McCord, and Zola, 1959). In this project, teachers, police, social workers, and a psychiatrist were asked to predict future delinquents; the selected individuals were then assigned to either an intensive counselling programme or to a comparison (i.e., "control") group that received no treatment at all. A follow-up evaluation based on further contact with local police revealed no positive effects of the counselling programme.

A seemingly more successful, but less rigorously evaluated, programme was the Highfields experiment (Weeks, 1958). This experiment involved an intensive programme of guided group interaction with 16- to 17-year-old youths in a progressive institutional setting. The youths were later compared for recidivism with the inmates of a more typical reformatory. The results indicated that, " . . . for every hundred boys who complete residence, . . . the Highfields programme rehabilitates twenty-eight more than does the traditional programme of caring for such boys." (120.) However, youths sent to Highfields tended to be younger, better educated, first-time offenders. In other words, the Highfields boys may have been "better risks" in the first place, a possibility that jeopardizes the conclusions that safely can be drawn from this study. In addition, it is sometimes argued that simply *being* in a special programme may induce a "policy effect" on the part of the police and others, so that they respond more leniently to the boys involved. The difficulty is that this official reluctance to arrest may be confused with assumed "treatment effects" (Lerman, 1968).

Another programme similarly based on guided group interaction, the Provo Project, received a more stringent evaluation (Empey and Erickson, 1972). Here young "habitual offenders" were assigned randomly to either a community group therapy programme, probation, or institutionalization. A follow-up 6 months after "release" indicated success rates (i.e., absence of arrests) of 84, 77, and 42 per cent respectively. In other words, although the community-based project was superior to incarceration, it was approximately equal in success to a period on probation that involved almost no treatment at all. A second study by Empey and Lubeck (1971), the Silverlake Experiment, compared a residential community treatment programme with a private training school programme. Again there was little evidence that the experimental programme fared better than the control programme. It can be added that an interesting criticism of the group therapy programmes is that their use of group pressures can sometimes parallel the techniques of brainwashing.

Still another programme, the Opportunities for Youth Project, used employment and teaching machines in an experimentally designed effort to prevent delinquency (Hackler, 1966). The key variable in this design involved an effort to improve subjects' self-concepts by convincing them that (a) they were capable of working successfully, and (b) they were competent to assess the adequacy of teaching machines. Four years after the project began, data were gathered on police contacts. The results revealed that boys involved in the work programme were slightly *more* delinquent than those in the comparison group, while boys in the teaching machine programme were slightly *less* so. These perplexing findings leave the authors " . . . only faint optimism with regard to uncovering effective 'cures' for the ills of delinquency." (Hackler and Hagan, 1975:105.)

Probably the most controversial of the individual treatment approaches, however, are the behavior modification programmes. Using some of the same techniques dramatized in the movie *Clockwork Orange*, behavior modification programmes were used first in the treatment of alcohol, drug, and sex offenders. For example, an Alberta programme (see Figure 6-1) uses the drug succinylcholine to induce a simulated overdose experience among incarcerated drug addicts. The assumption is that repeated "aversive" experiences of this kind will condition subjects to avoid further drug use. In a similarly provocative programme, convicted sex offenders are wired to receive electrical shocks when they view sexually stimulating pictures on a screen before them, or while they listen to tape-recordings of their own sexual fantasies. An Ontario programme (Marshall, 1973) also reports the use of "orgasmic reconditioning"—the systematic replacement of "deviant" with "nondeviant" fantasies during masturbation, and the use of a "penometer"—a device used to predict post-treatment success by measuring penis circumference in response to various stimuli. The applications of these devices are left to the reader's imagination. Meanwhile, it should be noted that the limited success of such programmes is said to signal the development of a "new biotechnology" (Burton, 1974) and the new field of "electronic rehabilitation" (Schwitzgelel, 1971; Ingraham and Smith, 1972).

In their more positive form, behavior modification principles are also used in token reinforcement systems to control institutional behavior. These programmes systematically link increasing privileges to monitored changes in behavior. Short-term evaluations of the various versions of this type of programme give some promise of success (Costello, 1972; see also Hindelang, 1970). However, obscured in the evaluations of behavior modification programmes are some pressing problems.

FIGURE 6-1

A 'TASTE OF DEATH' . . .

By BARRY CRAIG
Of the *Journal*

The Alberta Hospital at Oliver is attempting to condition drug addicts into quitting their habit by giving them an actual "taste of death" without killing them.

The addicts, male and female criminals, volunteer to inject themselves with a drug that works the same as the poison used by some aboriginal head-hunters—it paralyzes their bodies and robs them of the ability to breathe for up to 30 seconds.

One heroin addict who has gone through the experience six times says it's like drowning. Another says it's like being strangled to death.

"It takes a lot of guts to go through with this," says Dr. B.W. Dorran, director of the forensic services unit at Oliver, where these behaviour-modification treatments are going on.

Dr. Dorran said there is now a waiting list of about 20 prisoners who have applied for these treatments. He mentioned that one patient actually came back wanting a second series of treatments. He had already had six of them and wanted and got four more.

The purpose is to give addicts an idea of what it would be like if they were dying from an overdose of drugs and were conscious to know it.

This "dying" experience, which Dr. Dorran readily admits is "frightening," hopefully convinces them they should give up the habit, partly by scaring them and partly by conditioning them to believe the needle—a central part of their addiction—is a bad thing. If they ever try to go back to the needle, says Dr. Dorran, they remember how bad the "dying" experience was and, hopefully, put the needle down.

The drug used, succinylcholine, paralyzes the addicts so they can't even move their eyeballs, although they can still see and hear. And while they're desperately trying to breathe, medical personnel tell them they are experiencing what it's like to die.

"They feel the sensation of dying," Dr. Dorran told the *Journal*. "When they tell you it's scary, it really is."

This lasts about 20 to 30 seconds. The addicts are given oxygen as necessary during paralysis to prevent brain damage and other side affects. Meanwhile, the drug wears off by itself. The total experience lasts about one minute.

Addicts usually go through the "dying" experience 6 times over a period of 3 weeks, then go on to 8 to 12 months of intensive group psychotherapy with other addicts in the forensic unit. The unit is for people with medical and social problems that bring them in conflict with the law . . . .

What's it like to suffer the sensation of dying? Dr. Dorran couldn't give us the names of anyone who has gone through it but we were able to locate three addicts who have taken these treatments. They told us what it is like.

Addict A: "It's just like dying must be. You start getting paralyzed. After you shoot the stuff they lay you down and the air rushes out of your lungs. You can't talk, you can't breathe. Your mind screams out for air."

Addict B: "I think it's rotten. It does help, this experience, but it's rotten. It's hard to describe. It's really weird. If they didn't give you the oxygen you'd die."

Addict C: "You kind of get a tingling feeling. It starts in your feet. You're completely paralyzed. You can't move nothing. You can't even blink. You kinda start shaking. You're paralyzed for about 30 seconds but it seems like 2 hours. It's scary. I figured I could psyche myself out. I knew they were going to bring me out of it so I figured I could just lay back and let it ride. But you can't do it. You panic. All your thoughts are concentrated on breathing. All that was in my head was 'I gotta get some air. I gotta get some air, . . .' "

Dr. Dorran claims that as far as he knows the "dying" experience has been used in treatment only once before in the world—in England in the mid-60's.

He has been using the treatments at Oliver for about two years now. Forty addicts, mostly males, have taken them and the therapy, he says, and fifty-five to sixty per cent of them have succeeded in staying off hard drugs up to now. The first went back on the street about fourteen months ago.

Reprinted with permission of the Edmonton Journal.
Source: Edmonton Journal, *page 1, Saturday, March 2, 1974*

Most importantly, behavior modification works best with co-operative subjects, and, furthermore, legal and ethical principles rightly prohibit the application of these techniques among those who resist them. Among those who do cooperate, there is the additional problem of keeping subjects faithful to their therapies after leaving the treatment programme. In brief, subjects are often compliant in the controlled environment of the treatment institution, but quickly forgetful of these experiences when faced with the uncontrolled environment of the community. Lacking evidence of the long-range, large scale effectiveness of behavior modification programmes, then, many of us will remain doubtful of their widespread promise. This need not deny the usefulness of the more limited and non-coercive applications of behavior modification principles.

Where, then, does this short discussion of individualized treatment lead us? After reviewing 100 studies of this type, Logan (1972) concludes that none of them satisfy the standard criteria of adequate evaluation. Other reviews cynically, but accurately, point out that the *best evaluated* studies are characteristically shown to be the *least successful* (Hackler and Hagan, 1975; Hood and Sparks, 1970: Chapter 6; Weiss, 1970). Conclusions of this type prompted James Hackler (1974) to write a monograph titled *Why Delinquency Prevention Programmes in Canada Should NOT be Evaluated.* Hackler's argument against evaluation rests on three points: (1) it is extremely difficult to conduct an objective evaluation, (2) attempts to do so may actually defeat other important purposes, and (3) the pressure to evaluate from political and other forces can in fact make the situation even worse. Said differently,

> . . . a major danger from the Canadian perspective is that evaluation may in fact serve the purpose of damaging innovative and venturesome programmes while supporting traditional ones. The problem is that rigorous evaluation tends to show a minimum of impact. When . . . evaluators are able to operate independently utilizing rigorous techniques, and the programme is innovative and possibly struggling with other agencies, it is rather easy to show that the programme has had little impact. On the other hand, if one is attempting to evaluate well established agencies, they have the means to resist the impact of negative evaluation (55).*

Nonetheless, from all the gloom and expense of evaluation research one extremely important lesson does emerge. Several of these programmes demonstrate that *many offenders can continue to live in the community without an increase in recidivism.* Even more importantly, these experiments seem to suggest that expensive government programmes, regardless of their other benefits, are not necessary, or perhaps even useful, in decreasing the risk of reconviction. This possibility is suggested again by the more ambitious programmes of social reform we consider next.

PREVENTION THROUGH SOCIAL REFORM

Social reformist prevention programmes begin with the assumption that it is not the individual that must be changed, but rather the environmental influences of the peer group or community. The preferred tools of this approach are "detached workers" and "community organization."

The oldest of the social reform programmes is David McKay's and Clifford Shaw's Chicago Area Project (Kobrin, 1959). The primary component of this programme enlisted community membership and leadership in organizations through which welfare programmes were then developed and administered. Although this primary goal was achieved, the indirect effect of these efforts on the incidence of crime and delinquency is unclear. There is some evidence that rates of delinquency declined in areas served by the project,

Reprinted with permission of James Hackler.

and that the character of the communities themselves were altered; however, there are no means of separating these changes from those that occurred more generally in the Chicago area during the project's history.

A second programme, the Midcity Youth Project, again aimed its efforts at the total community, this time through the medium of detached street workers (Miller, 1962). Over a 3 year period, 7 street workers focused their efforts on some 400 members of 21 gangs. The best hopes of this project rested on the stabilizing influence of the street workers acting as middle class role models. The outcome: "All major measures of violative behavior—disapproved actions, illegal actions, during-contact court appearances, before-during-after appearances, and project-control group appearances—provide consistent support for a finding of 'negligible impact.'" (187.) A related effort, the Spring Street Project in Vancouver (Ratner, 1974), used social workers to work with youths in the community. Although a single police assessor of this project saw improvement in the participating boys, a collection of school teachers also included in the evaluation did not (cited in Hackler, 1975).

By far, however, the most expensive, dramatic, and disconcerting social reform programmes aimed at the prevention of crime and delinquency are described in Daniel Patrick Moynihan's (1969) book, *Maximum Feasible Misunderstanding*. This book chronicles the American "War on Poverty." Moynihan locates an influential source of North American poverty programmes in a New York-based delinquency prevention effort, the Mobilization for Youth Project (MFY). This project initially was oriented to the problem of juvenile delinquency, taking as its theoretical guide Cloward and Ohlin's differential opportunity theory of delinquency. Cloward and Ohlin argued that delinquents were resorting to desperately deviant and dangerous measures in order to conform to the routine success goals of the larger society. The theory seems to suggest that, "If . . . society wished . . . (lower class youths) to conform not only in their objectives but in their means for achieving them, it had only to provide the opportunity to do so." (Moynihan, 1969:51.)[1] Three priorities were thus established in the initial MFY project: (1) jobs for young people; (2) education for young people; and (3) community organization. The project was conceived as a social experiment: "From the outset it was understood that what came to pass in those 13 census tracts on the lower east side would have national significance." (Moynihan, 1969:59.)[2]

Much happened, however, between the initiation of the project and the appearance of its results. Juvenile delinquency became increasingly important to the Kennedy administration as it was linked to the problems of employment and race. Following Kennedy's death, Johnson continued the emphasis and replaced speculation with action. In advance of MFY's completion, much less evaluation, its translation of differential opportunity theory into social policy became a basis for national legislation. Differential opportunity theory *became* the War on Poverty. Importantly, community organization, or Community Action, was a residual part of the official legislation.

Four days before the War on Poverty was signed into law, the New York *Daily News* declared that the Mobilization For Youth Project had become "infested with subversives." Interestingly, it was not the employment or education programmes of MFY that drew the news fire; it was the community organization programme. Moynihan offers this analysis: "It (MFY) started out to create cooperative arrangements that would open the neighborhood opportunity structures to deviant or potentially deviant youth; in short order the opportunity structure was being defined as a power structure, and itself accused of deviance in the largest social sense of good and bad behavior . . . . Reform inched toward revolution. Right or wrong, MFY did not very long remain the carefully calibrated experiment it had set out to be." (107.)[3] Further, ". . . men such as Cloward moved fairly rapidly from the effort to integrate the poor into the system to an effort to use the poor to bring down the whole rotten structure." (112.)[4]

The same problems that plagued MFY proved soon to doom the War on Poverty. As in the Mobilization for Youth Project, education and job programmes soon took a back seat to community organization efforts guided through Community Action Programmes (CAPS). Moynihan suggests that a four-stage sequence characterized such programmes:

a period of organizing, with much publicity and great expectations;

the beginning of operations, with the onset of conflict between the agency and local government institutions, followed by even greater publicity;

a period of counter-attack from local government; and

victory for the established institutions, followed by the ultimate disappearance of the professional reformers.

It can be noted that a parallel sequence of events occurred in many Canadian communities, following similar activities of the Company of Young Canadians. *The lesson is that predicted by Saul Alinsky (1969): governments are unreliable instigators of their own social reforms.*

Moynihan provides a cryptic synopsis of this multi-national experience: "This is the essential fact: the government did not know what it was doing. It had a theory. Or, rather, a set of theories. Nothing more. The U.S. government at this time was no more in possession of confident knowledge as to how to prevent delinquency ... than it was the possessor of a dependable formula for motivating Vietnamese villagers to fight Communism." (170.)[5] A taxpayer's tragedy of this experience is that it was so expensive. Keeping this in mind, Hackler suggests one lesson of the experience: " ... in Canada we would probably learn as much by watching the experiments being conducted in places like the United States and Great Britain rather than launching such experiments ourselves. At present, we do not pay much attention to the basic work that has been done elsewhere, and, if we do, very few people seem to take such research seriously. Canada seems to persist in launching programmes that have been shown to be inadequate elsewhere." (1974:77-78.) Beyond this, we will argue that one additional thing the expensive American programmes suggest is that *we might be able to accomplish more in Canada by doing and spending less.* This principle may be of particular importance in the approach we consider next: police deployment.

POLICE DEPLOYMENT

If individual treatment and social reform do not produce desired results, then there may be a natural inclination to suggest that more policing will. Research by Lynn McDonald, reviewed in Chapter Four, argues against this view, suggesting that policing activities actually produce *more* crime. We noted that the assumption of causality in this research is open to further study and then offered the more modest conclusion that more policing is unlikely to *reduce* crime. In a recent review of police deployment programmes, James Q. Wilson similarly suggests that " ... there is ... some reason to believe that the number and deployment of the police has little or nothing to do with the crime rate." (1974:18.)[6]

Wilson bases his observation on a growing body of research that is concerned with evaluating the effectiveness of police allocation. These studies differ from McDonald's in focusing on selected communities or neighborhoods, for shorter periods of time. In other words, comprehensiveness is sacrificed in favor of detail. The first of these studies, "Operation 25," was carried out in 1954 in the East Harlem area of New York City. Police strength was more than doubled in the area for a period of more than four months. Although "street crimes" (e.g., muggings, auto theft, and burglaries) declined over this period, the design of the study left key questions unanswered. For example, only official crime reports were used in the evaluation and no attempt was made to determine if crime was simply displaced to surrounding precincts.

A second study conducted in 1965, in Great Britain, tested the effect of varying the number of foot patrol officers in an area. In four British cities, the number of patrol officers walking designated beats was varied from zero to four. After one year, the number of crimes reported decreased for beats where the number of officers varied from none to one; however, additional deployment of up to four officers produced minimal results. This finding assures us that *no* policework is *bad* policework, but it also suggests that the marginal gains of conventional expansion plans are not likely to be substantial.

In a more recent study, by Swimmer (1974), per capita expenditures on the police are related to crime rates in cities of over 100 000 population. Among the results it is found that, holding several socioeconomic variables constant, increases in police expenditures are significantly related to reductions in violent and property crime rates. However, the policy implications of this finding are unclear. Since the relationship established between police expenditure and reductions in crime is not large, it is not at all clear that the gains are worth the costs. In addition, since we do not know how the money was spent, the specific actions to be taken are not indicated. Finally, and most importantly, the use of official data, combined with very large aggregated units of analysis (i.e., whole cities, as opposed to precincts or beats), weakens the methodological base for the conclusions.

A singularly important advance in recent research on police deployment involves the use of victimization surveys to obtain a more accurate measure of actual variations in crime rates. Using a victimization survey as the dependent variable, George Kelling (1974) headed a research programme in Kansas City that produced important results. Fifteen police beats, matched for various community characteristics, were sorted into five groups of three. In each group, one beat was designated as a "control" and policed in conventional fashion. In the second beat, a strategy of "proactive patrol" was adopted: cars were assigned to patrol at two to three times the normal frequency. Finally, in the third beat, a pattern of "reactive patrol" was carried out: preventive patrol was eliminated, with service based entirely on citizen requests and radio dispatch. For the one year experimental period, no substantial differences were observed in criminal activity, the amount of reported crime, the rate of victimization, satisfaction with police work, or the level of citizen fear. In short, the type and level of police deployment seemed to make no significant difference. It should be added that the use of the victimization survey, of control groups, and of matching for background characteristics makes this the most reliable study available.

All of this does not mean, of course, that the police are of *no* importance, or that police work can be abandoned safely. Canada's own experience with the Montreal police strike (see Figure 6-2) makes such a conclusion clearly utopian (see Clark, 1975). However, the frequent suggestion to the taxpayer that *additional* deployment of police personnel will prevent crime also is shown to be dubious.

FIGURE 6-2

A NIGHT OF TERROR AS MONTREAL MOBS RUN RIOT

MONTREAL—Armed troops helped maintain a shaky peace today after an illegal one-day strike by police and firemen abandoned Montreal to a night of gunbattles, arson, and looting.

At the request of the Quebec government, federal authorities called in French-speaking soldiers of the Royal 22nd Regiment—the famed Van Doos—to protect strategic points in case mob violence erupted again.

A provincial policeman and a burglar were shot dead last night, 12 persons were wounded in a sniping battle between rival taxi and limousine drivers, and scores of downtown storefronts smashed and rifled by roaming gangs.

The rampage continued past midnight until police obeyed an emergency law passed by the National Assembly ordering them back under threat of jail terms, fines and loss of their unions.

But a senior provincial detective said city police operations were still in "total chaos" today and the soldiers were needed to guarantee order.

Underworld Had a Ball

As the law took a holiday the underworld had a ball. At least 25 banks were held up and others closed until someone could protect them again.

With nightfall, 300 militant taxi drivers took the opportunity to settle a long-standing grudge with Murray Hill Limousine Service, which has exclusive airport rights.

Limousines, including Rolls Royces, were overturned at the Murray Hill garage in a run-down part of the city's lower west end. Then they were set afire.

Molotiv cocktails were thrown inside parked buses. Rocks smashed windows of the two-storey building.

A few firemen arrived but did nothing. One was heard telling a cabby: "We're here to protect the neighboring buildings. Do what you like with Murray Hill. That's none of our business."

Then someone opened fire from the darkened upper storey of the garage.

The crowd outside—now swelled by hundreds of local thrill-seekers—retreated but came back with more gasoline bombs.

At least two men appeared with high-powered rifles and began returning fire from the garage.

Policeman Dead

Twelve persons were wounded and the provincial policeman fell dead.

Star reporter Mark Starowicz, who witnessed the Murray Hill siege, gave this account:

"I was standing on a roof

overlooking the shooting scene. I saw in the darkness below a man with a rifle and he was trying to shoot out spotlights on the roof across the street.

"I saw him get off about 12 shots at the snipers—who were on that roof. Then he screamed: 'If you're going to kill people, we'll get you, you bastards.'

"Another demonstrator shouted to the rifleman that he wasn't shooting straight enough. The rifleman shouted back: 'I was in the army. Don't tell me how to shoot.' "

Starowicz later was arrested in downtown Montreal, taken to a police station and questioned for several hours. No charges were laid against him and he was released early today.

Policemen Watch

A handful of other provincial policemen watched from the back of the crowd as the burning buses and gasoline fires in the street sent billows of smoke rising through a drizzle of rain.

They took no action against the mob until about 20 helmeted reinforcements arrived and ended the siege three hours after it began.

But then the cabbies headed for Dorval Airport to greet Mayor Drapeau as he flew back from a "Salute to Canada" week in St. Louis.

They never arrived at the airport, where RCMP and Dorval police had brought in cases of nightsticks to beat back a possible attack.

With the limousine service burned out, incoming passengers were forced to hitchhike into the city.

By this time anarchy reigned downtown.

A mob of separatists and leftists attacked the Queen Elizabeth Hotel, smashing ground floor windows and looting shops in the lobby.

Then they broke into Mayor Drapeau's newly opened restaurant Le Vaisseau d'Or, where they set fire to the drapes after smashing furniture.

The few customers were evacuated through a back door to the hotel lobby.

The demonstrators then continued their rampage toward the nearby Sheraton Mount Royal Hotel on Peel St. where the violence and looting were repeated.

Chanting separatists slogans and cheering the crash of broken glass, they rushed on to Ste. Catherine St. the city's main shopping thoroughfare.

They smashed windows of banks and stores, stopping occasionally to pluck a piece of merchandise out of a store display, upended potted trees and overturned garbage cans, strewing trash on the street.

At the corner of Ste. Catherine and Metcalfe, in the heart of the city, a handful of provincial police tried to disperse the crowd but were attacked. One policeman was seriously injured and taken to hospital.

The mob continued its march east, damaging the Simpson's, Eaton's, Birk's and Morgan's stores.

At Birk's, a jewelry store, security men inside fired warning shots through smashed windows when looters tried to get in.

Young demonstrators, hiding loot inside their jackets, began to leave the march and passed calmly through the hundreds of onlookers lining the streets.

Their next target was the Murray Hill transportation line office in the Sheraton Mount Royal Hotel on Peel St. which received the same treatment as other offices and stores.

The mob then moved up Metcalfe St. to McGill University, scene of a protest last March 28 calling for its conversion into a French-language institution.

They stormed onto the campus, wrecking a security guard's booth and smashing windows in several buildings before reaching the university administration building where they broke windows and shattered two glass doors.

A fire was set in a small building in the northeastern part of the building but was quickly extinguished by private security guards.

The demonstrators then broke up into a number of small groups which made their way separately south to Ste. Catherine St. for another window breaking and looting splurge.

There were about 200 in the gang that came down the hill from McGill University smashing windows and looting.

As they swung up Ste. Catherine St., then back down, Helmut Lorenzo saw them smashing up his store.

They were just kids, most of them, and in Helmut's radio and hi-fi store in the showplace Place des Artes they sounded as if they were having a lot of fun.

The big front windows were broken and the gang inside were helping themselves to radios when Helmut stepped through the window and pleaded with them.

He was just a little guy—did they really want to hurt the little guy? What was the sense of it all? And they seemed to listen. A couple of them set down the radios they were holding. Helmut walked over and took a couple of radios out of others' hands.

Then in the back someone shouted for them not to listen.

It was an angry voice: "Get him to (sic) hell out of the way."

And a big guy—no kid this one—came out of the crowd and smashed Helmut on the side of the head, knocking him down among the wrecked display tables and broken glass.

The crowd caught the fever and in a second they were grabbing everything in sight.

Helmut got trampled in the rush and received another long scrape over his eye. But he crawled outside.

He watched helplessly as someone backed a small truck up to his window and the crowd loaded in color television and big hi-fi sets, and took more away in cars.

Pretty soon it was all gone— about $40 000 worth—all but a few broken radios and some parts dumped out among the broken glass.

Source: Toronto Star, *October 8, 1969:1-3. Reprinted with permission of the* Toronto Star.

Innovations in deployment patterns may hold more promise. For example, the "crime attack" approach recommends placement of the police as close as possible to crime prone situations in ways that will enable them to apprehend criminals in action. Instrumental here is the use of the police as decoys, commonly assuming the disguises of preferred crime targets—the elderly, skidders, and unaccompanied women.

A second approach involves the concept of "team policing." Here officers try to integrate themselves into the target community, while also attempting to win neighborhood confidence and cooperation in prevention efforts. A recent Vancouver programme (Heywood, 1972) concerned with juvenile delinquency reports some success with this approach. More generally, however, the "attack" and "team policing" programmes remain without adequate evaluation (Sherman, Milton, and Kelly, 1973: Chapter 6). In addition, Wilson (1973) notes that communities may be divided in their support for the "team" and "attack" models. Thus, while some neighborhoods may welcome tough, vigorous policing as a way of keeping the streets safe and the "kids in their place," others may prefer a police force that is closely integrated with the community and perhaps even subject to its control. Wilson concludes that, "Indeed, it is likely that any given community will want both things at once—be tough and concerned, visible and invisible, enforcement-oriented and service-oriented." (1973:x.) For the moment, then, perhaps the best recommendation for either the attack or team programmes lies in the fact that both represent an innovative use of existing resources, rather than the recommendation of expensive new programmes. In addition, the team policing approach signals a new respect for the resources of the community. It is to this new interest in the community that we turn next.

RECENT TRENDS: REDISCOVERING THE COMMUNITY

Current approaches to crime prevention include a renewed emphasis on the community, and the efficient use of its resources. These new approaches include proposals for law reform, innovations in environmental design, and community corrections programmes. Each of these approaches promises not only less crime, but also a reduction in the cost of our response to crime. The price of these promises is the cooperation of the community. We will examine the content of each of the proposed programmes first, and the problem of community consent last. Needless to say, the issue of consent *is* "last but not least."

LAW REFORM

Radical Non-intervention. The most provocative of the prevention proposals argue that we could respond to crime best by doing least. These proposals fall generally under the concept of "diversion," a policy preference for minimizing contact at all stages of the criminal justice system—beginning with arrest, and continuing through conviction, sentencing, incarceration, and parole. The Law Reform

Commission of Canada (1975) identifies four important components of a diversion policy:

COMMUNITY ABSORPTION, individuals or particular interest groups dealing with trouble in their area, privately, outside of the police and courts;

SCREENING, police referring an incident to family or community, or simply dropping a case rather than laying criminal charges;

PRE-TRIAL DIVERSION, instead of proceeding with charges in the criminal court, referring a case at the pre-trial level to be dealt with by settlement or mediation procedures; and

ALTERNATIVES TO IMPRISONMENT, increasing the use of such alternatives as absolute or conditional discharge, restitution, fine, suspended sentence, probation, community service order, partial detention in a community based residence, or a parole release programme (4).*

Schur aptly summarizes the intent of this approach in the phrase "radical non-intervention": "Basically, radical non-intervention implies policies that accommodate society to the widest possible diversity of behaviors and attitudes, rather than forcing as many individuals as possible to 'adjust' to supposedly common societal standards." (1973:154.) Whenever possible, then, a diversion policy simply urges that we *leave the deviant alone.*

Obviously, a diversion response is not suitable for *all* acts currently called criminal. How, then, do we separate those acts that may merit diversion from those that call for conventional punishments? We can begin by reestablishing the distinction drawn between "conflict" and "consensual" crimes in Chapter One. Consensual crimes are distinguished by their perceived harmfulness, the widespread societal agreement about their normative status, and the associated severity of their statutory penalties. In short, consensual crimes are widely regarded as harmful, generally considered serious, and dealt with severely. In contrast, conflict crimes are a source of societal dispute, regarded as relatively harmless, and are handled with relative leniency. Although the distinction between consensual and conflict crimes is one of degree, we can give a more concrete impression of the differences by considering categories included in Canadian crime statistics for 1973.

Criminal non-traffic offences cleared by charge in 1973 are indicated in Table 6-1. Several of the categories listed represent consensus about what is widely considered criminal: murder and attempts at it, manslaughter, rape, wounding, and robbery.

Reprinted with permission of the Minister of Supply and Services Canada.

Table 6-I

CRIMES CLEARED BY CHARGE IN CANADA, 1973

Crime	Number of Crimes Cleared by Charge	Percentage of Total Crimes Cleared by Charge
Murder	346	<0.01
Attempted Murder	394	<0.01
Manslaughter	59	<0.01
Rape	675	<0.01
Other Sexual Offences	3 689	0.01
Wounding	1 061	<0.01
Assault	29 637	0.05
Robbery	3 777	0.01
Breaking and Entering	33 132	0.05
Theft—Motor Vehicle	13 212	0.02
Theft over $200	7 031	0.01
Theft $200 and under	58 744	0.09
Possessing Stolen Goods	12 148	0.02
Fraud	34 768	0.05
Prostitution	3 436	0.01
Gaming and Betting	2 578	<0.01
Possessing Offensive Weapons	6 340	0.01
Other Criminal Code	78 749	0.12
Federal Statutes	29 474	0.05
Possessing Addicting Opiates	2 995	<0.01
Possessing Cannabis (Marijuana)	34 201	0.05
Possessing Controlled Drugs	1 215	<0.01
Possessing Restricted Drugs	3 203	<0.01
Provincial Statutes	243 652	0.38
Municipal By-Laws	37 395	0.06

Reproduced with permission of the Minister of Supply and Service Canada.
Source: Criminal Statistics (1973)

However, the more dramatic figures in this table report charges filed for what many of us do *not* consider criminal. For example, 38 per cent of the offences cleared by charge, by far the largest grouping in the table, involve violations of provincial statutes. The author's own research (Hagan, 1975a) in the Crown Prosecutor's Office in the city of Edmonton indicates that up to 98 per cent of this figure (37 per cent) consists of violations of provincial liquor regulations. These regulations control the public sale, the possession, and, most frequently, the public consumption of alcohol. In brief, the largest part of these provincial regulations involves the use of the criminal justice system to control public drunkenness. In addition, another five per cent of the charges recorded in Table 6-1 involve the control of marijuana use. Combined, the attempt to control marijuana and alcohol abuse through criminal sanctions accounts for *up to 40 per cent* of the offences cleared by charge in Canada. Both of these offences are conflict crimes; neither of these offences, in the conventional sense, involves a victim.

Victimless Vice. A diversion approach can begin, then, by urging the removal of these offences from the criminal justice system. This does not mean that we condone marijuana and alcohol abuse; it simply means that the criminal justice system is not the place to demonstrate our sentiments of condemnation. In a book pragmatically titled *The Honest Politician's Guide to Crime Control*, Morris and Hawkins (1969) make this point forcefully: "For the criminal law at least, man has an inalienable right to go to hell in his own fashion, provided he does not directly injure the person or property of another on the way. The criminal law is an inefficient instrument for imposing the good life on others." (2.) This argument applies, of course, not only to marijuana and alcohol abuse, but also to prostitution, gambling, and other legally disreputable (but victimless) pleasures.

An important virtue of the diversion argument is that it would free the police and courts to improve their focus on *consensual* crimes. Monitoring victimless vice is an expensive, ineffective, and time-consuming task. Administrative and licensing violations can be handled more efficiently by civil regulatory agencies (Law Reform Commission, 1974a:7). Minimal care for alcoholics can be provided less expensively by subsidizing existing community groups like the Salvation Army. The latter group long ago learned that treatment cannot be forced. Where treatment *is* desired, however, it too can be subsidized. Meanwhile, the criminal justice system could be reserved for more serious matters.

Pre-Trial Diversion. There are additional opportunities for diversion. Much of the remaining crime reported in Table 6-1 consists of minor crimes against property and person. For example, two of the largest categories involve theft of property valued at two hundred dollars and under (nine per cent of the offences cleared by charge) and assault (five per cent of the offences cleared by charge). In a study for the Law Reform Commission, John Hogarth (1974) observed the relationships between offenders and victims of person and property crimes in East York. Among his findings, Hogarth reports that in

OTTAWA TO EASE UP ON MARIJUANA LAWS

Reprinted with permission of Aislin and the Montreal Gazette.

55.2 per cent of the person and property offences, the offender and victim had a pre-existing relationship of some kind. It is suggested that in many (most?) of these cases the complainant is not intent upon having criminal sanctions applied to the offender, but instead is summoning the police to contain a situation temporarily out of control. Hogarth presents some persuasive evidence for this conclusion.

First, an inverse relationship was observed between the intensity of the prior relationship and the use of charging options. Thus, the frequency of criminal charges declined as one moved from "strangers" to "commercial" to "other friends and relatives" to "neighbors" to "family." Hogarth notes, "That the criminal conflict generated within family relationships could be defused at the police level without laying criminal charges suggests that the motivation for seeking police intervention was to secure the assistance of an authoritative third party for interpersonal conflict resolution and, moreover, that that end was achieved without the need for further penetration into the criminal justice system." (19.) The implication, of course, is that with skill and determination this process of conflict resolution could be extended outside the family to successively further removed offender-victim relationships. Unfortunately, police and court personnel are not trained for this sort of task, and our legal process is not designed to encourage it.

Further evidence for this conclusion is provided by Hogarth. Here it is noted that when the initiative for prosecution resided with private complainants (as in cases of common assault), they tended to proceed to prosecution less often that when the decision to prosecute was primarily within police control (as in property offences and offences against the person other than common assaults). Again, the point is that the judicial process is unsuited for diverting from final adjudication many of the cases that it might. Obviously, the next question is "why?"

Part of the answer to this question lies in the fact that the Anglo-Canadian system of criminal justice is designed to determine guilt and innocence through the adversary process, with the threat of punishment hanging in the balance. However, this strategy may be inappropriate in those circumstances where the offender and victim can resolve the conflict themselves, out of court, without punishment, and therefore without a determination of legal responsibility.

There are several other factors that work against out-of-court settlements. First, police forces are commonly judged by comparing the number of offences reported to them with the number of offences cleared by charge. Most departments get little credit for otherwise resolving a case. In addition, the police often are paid overtime for their court appearances, and promotions are frequently based on the quantity, rather than the quality, of case resolution. Hopefully, these practices can be changed. How, then, would the new approach to conflict resolution proceed?

The Law Reform Commission of Canada, in its working paper on diversion (1975), suggests five preliminary criteria for deciding that a charge *not* be laid.

- The offence is not so serious that the public interest demands a trial.
- The resources necessary to deal with the case if it is screened out are reasonably available in the community.
- Alternative means of dealing with the incident would likely be effective in preventing further incidents by the offender in the light of his or her record and other evidence.
- The impact of arrest or prosecution on the accused or the family of the accused is likely to be excessive in relation to the harm done.

• There was a pre-existing relationship between the victim and offender and both are agreeable to a settlement (7).*

These conditions met, interest turns next to the grounds for settlement. The Commission is not rigid on this matter, suggesting that, "The agreement by the offender in such cases may be to make restitution, to undergo counseling, treatment or take up training, education or work programmes for a stated period." (9.) Restitution in particular is a neglected aspect of our Anglo-Canadian legal heritage (see Figure 6-3) and seems to represent an attractive way of resolving criminal as well as civil conflicts. There is, however, the problem of the inevitable failures. Here the Commission suggests that, " . . . the option of resuming criminal proceedings in the event of a wilful breach of a pre-trial settlement order would probably be desirable." (19.)

FIGURE 6-3

THE ROOTS OF RESTITUTION

In Anglo-Saxon England there was no criminal law as we know it. Disputes were dealt with by a process greatly resembling our civil law. When an individual felt that he had suffered damage because of another's wrongful conduct he was permitted either to settle the matter by agreement or to proceed before a tribunal. Restitution was the order of the day and other sanctions, including imprisonment, were rarely used.

As the common law developed, criminal law became a distinct branch of law. Numerous antisocial acts were seen to be "offences against the state" or "crimes" rather than personal wrongs or torts. This tendency to characterize some wrongs as "crimes" was encouraged by the practice under which the lands and property of convicted persons were forfeited to the king or feudal lord; fines, as well, became payable to feudal lords and not to the victim. The natural practice of compensating the victim or his relatives was discouraged by making it an offence to conceal the commission of a felony or convert the crime into a source of profit. In time, fines and property that would have gone in satisfaction of the victim's claims were diverted to the state. Compounding an offence (that is, accepting an economic benefit in satisfaction of the wrong done without the consent of the court or in a manner that is contrary

Reprinted with permission of the Minister of Supply and Service.

to the public interest) still remains a crime under the Canadian Criminal Code and discourages private settlement or restitution.

It would now seem that historical developments, however well intentioned, effectively removed the victim from sentencing policy and obscured the view that crime was social conflict.

Source: Law Reform Commission of Canada (1974b). Reprinted by permission of the Minister of Supply and Services.

The Day-Fine Programme. Obviously, there will be many offences that, although non-serious, are still unavailable for pre-trial diversion. In many of these instances, the offender and victim simply will not be agreeable. Here too, however, a diversion policy can be followed.

The use of fines is the fastest growing sentencing option in Canada (Hogarth, 1971). Fining (fines are paid about 80 per cent of the time) often represents a means of punishing offenders without isolating them from the community. In other words, the use of fines can be a diversion procedure. The problem, of course, occurs among those who cannot, or do not, comply. A recent study reviewed in the previous chapter indicates that up to 50 per cent of the admissions to provincial institutions in Canada are for default of fine payments (Hagan, 1974b). This is particularly a problem for poor and native offenders. The study reveals that nearly 66 per cent of the native offenders incarcerated over a 2 month period were institutionalized in default of fine payment. One solution to this problem, recommended by the Law Reform Commission (1974a) and used in Sweden, is a day-fine system.

Under the day-fine system, the amount of fine is determined by the income of the offender. In Sweden, for example, a day-fine is equivalent to 0.001 of the yearly gross income of the offender. Thus, a person with a gross income of 5000 dollars, and sentenced to 20 day-fines, would be required to pay 100 dollars. A second person, with a gross income of 50 000 dollars, would pay 1000 dollars. In Sweden, the introduction of the day-fine system led to a reduction by half in the number of defaulters imprisoned (Law Reform Commission, 1974c:47). The Law Reform Commission raises the possibility of going even further by excluding incarceration from all but the most intractable cases. Here it is suggested that fines be imposed without the threat of imprisonment. Instead, every means possible would be used to collect the fine, including extending the time period, the use of instalment payments, and even attaching the worker's earnings. Where all else fails, and where the offender *does* have means of payment, a judge would have the option of resentencing the offender to prison.

The Consequences of Diversion. The promise of diversion is not so much that it will prevent crime in a direct and traditional sense (it may or may not), but rather that it could reduce the costs of criminalization both to the taxpayer and the offender, while also freeing the criminal justice system to concentrate its resources on the more serious consensual crimes. Some of the potential social and economic benefits of various diversion policies can be estimated.

Current estimates of the costs of imprisonment begin at 30 dollars a day. Although it is more difficult to quantify the social and economic costs to the offender, the differential impact of these costs on various groups can be indicated. For example, laws controlling alcohol abuse, and the current fine system, have a disproportionately heavy impact on native and poor offenders. Using base data gathered in the Alberta study discussed earlier, it is possible to provide some estimates of the potential consequences of decriminalizing alcohol abuse and implementing the day-fine programme. The base data consists of all offenders (N=996) incarcerated in Alberta over a 2 month period, from February 15 to April 15, 1973.

Table 6-2

ESTIMATED PERCENTAGE OF NATIVE AND WHITE OFFENDERS INCARCERATED IN DEFAULT OF FINE PAYMENTS UNDER FOUR SETS OF LEGAL PROCEDURES

	1 *Current Procedures*	*2* *Liquor Offences Removed*	*3* *Day-Fine Programme*	*4* *Liquor Offences Removed and Day-Fine Programme*
White	34%(600)	32%(572)	20%(494)	19%(480)
Native	64%(396)	46%(251)	48%(269)	30%(193)
Total	46%(996)	37%(823)	30%(763)	22%(673)

Reprinted with permission of the Canadian Forum.
Source: Hagan (1975f:18)

Column One of Table 6-2 indicates the proportion of native and white offenders incarcerated under present procedures *in default of fine payments.* Thirty per cent more native than white offenders go to jail in lieu of fine payment. In Column Two, the consequences of removing liquor offences from the criminal justice system are esti-mated by removing from the sample all offenders incarcerated for such offences. Here the disparity between the 2 groups declines to 14 per cent. In Column Three, the consequences of a Swedish type day-fine system are projected, using the Swedish 50 per cent "success rate" as the prediction factor. Both groups benefit nearly equally from this approach, leaving a disparity of 28 per cent. Column Four, however, brings the best results, reflecting the combined consequences of decriminalizing liquor offences *and* introducing a day-fine pro-gramme. The estimated result of this combined programme is a disparity of 11 per cent. One possible means of further reducing this disparity would be to follow the Law Reform Commission's tentative recommendation to remove the imprisonment provision from fine sentences. However, since there is no known basis for estimating the frequency with which this approach would lead to *re*sentencing offenders to prison at a later date, we have not attempted to project the results of this approach. In this sense, then, our projections are built on a conservative foundation. It is very possible that the im-provement might even exceed our estimates.

Table 6-3

ESTIMATED PERCENTAGE OF NATIVE AND WHITE OFFENDERS DECARCERATED UNDER THREE SETS OF REFORMED LEGAL PROCEDURES

	1 Base Incarceration Figures from Current Data	2 Liquor Offences Removed	3 Day-Fine Programme	4 Liquor Offences Removed and Day-Fine Programme
White	600	5%	18%	20%
Native	396	37%	32%	51%
Total	996	17%	23%	32%

Reprinted with permission of the Canadian Forum.
Source: Hagan (1975f:18)

Table 6-3 presents a broader picture of the estimated gains in *decarceration* that might result from the three reform programmes. Overall, this table indicates that the number of persons incarcerated (directly *or* in default of fine) could be reduced by nearly 32 per cent if liquor offences were decriminalized and a day-fine programme introduced. Even more impressive is the improvement these reforms would bring for Native People. *The combined liquor and fine reforms could result in an estimated 51 per cent reduction in the number of Native Persons incarcerated.* Again, it needs to be emphasized that these figures are projections based on the Swedish experience. Perhaps we can do even better; it is possible we would do worse. Nevertheless, the possibility that nearly one out of every two Native Persons currently going to jail could be freed by such reforms seems at *least* to recommend strongly an experimental test.

If, on the other hand, there is a weak link in the various law reform proposals, it may involve the programmes for pre-trial reconciliation. The potential for offender-victim reconciliation, through restitution and other means, may be class-linked. In other words, it seems probable that middle and upper class offenders might be more capable of, and agreeable to, pre-trial reconciliation. The negotiation process leading to reconciliation would seem likely to follow many of the same patterns currently found in plea bargaining. The evidence available here does not suggest that all offenders are equally adept at accomplishing desired goals. For example, in a study of plea bargaining discussed in the previous chapter, Wynne and Hartnagel (1975b) report that native offenders fare unfavorably. An experimental demonstration project would seem a useful way of determining whether the same pattern would apply in the pre-trial negotiations leading to reconciliation.

It should be noted that the Law Reform Commission sometimes takes a rather light view of the potential for social disparities. At one point it is suggested that, "If the resulting inequality is not gross it may be worthwhile to put up with it in order to secure other desirable objectives." (1975:10.) A similar attitude shows through in a discussion of a possible role of community members in sentencing:

> Citizen participation in sentencing, particularly where citizens have the power to out-vote the judge, may raise a problem of increasing disparities in sentences, or bias, or even prejudice in sentencing unpopular offenders. If there are two citizens to assist each judge they may out-vote him but it is more likely that lay persons would seek an accommodation of views with the judge .... Studies of sentencing by juries as compared with judges do not support fears of undue bias or prejudice among lay members. Moreover, abuses of discretion can be guarded against ... by a statement of purposes, criteria, and standards

in a sentencing guide and through provision for review of sentences on appeal (29-30).*

The Commission seems too optimistic on these points. First, there *are* a variety of studies that strongly suggest the biasing influence of lay persons in sentencing (see Hagan, 1974a). Indeed, there is good reason to believe that jurors are the primary source of disparities in the use of capital punishment in the United States. Here too, appeal procedures have not been effective in correcting these injustices. Sentencing, then, may be the one place where the community might best be kept out of the courtroom. This does not deny, of course, the more general wisdom of the Commission's recommendations.

Law reform offers the hope of reducing the amount of officially recorded crime. In a literal, although not conventional sense, this constitutes prevention. In a more practical perspective, law reform offers the hope of reducing the costs of responding to non-serious forms of deviance. Learning to live with deviance in this sense may allow us to concentrate our efforts more efficiently on the more serious form of deviation we have called consensual crimes. It might also free resources for new types of prevention programmes. Our attention turns next to one of the more innovative of these potential programmes.

ENVIRONMENTAL DESIGN

Criminologists of the past focused their efforts on reforming the individual or society. One new approach argues that we instead should concentrate on changing the physical design of our communities. C. Ray Jeffery states this argument in its strong form: "The way we design our urban environment determines the crime rate and type of crime to a great extent, and yet to my knowledge we have never considered crime prevention an integral part of urban planning. We have finally gotten around to considering education, transportation, recreation, pollution, and shopping as variables with which any city planner must cope, but security of person and property is not yet an item taken into consideration when we design and build cities." (1971:216.)

The outline of a programme for "crime prevention through environmental design" is found in the work of Oscar Newman (1972). The basis of Newman's argument is the notion of "defensible space": the idea that individuals can be encouraged by architectural design to expand their feeling of responsibility for the care, protection,

Reprinted with permission of the Minister of Supply and Services Canada.

and security of surrounding social space. Newman argues that in the evolution of architecture over the past 1000 years, almost every culture developed devices to define the territorial realm of their dwellings. However, with the rush of new building techniques, urbanization, and the population explosion, the architectural traditions of modern western culture were neglected. In short, we have lost control of our living space.

Newman suggests four elements of environmental design that can be used in regaining control of our urban life space. These include the following.

Territoriality. The subdivision of buildings and grounds into zones which users begin to think of as their property.

— In the past, many North Americans were able to mark off their territory by the lots containing their single detached homes. However, with the pressures of population and declining resources, more and more urban dwellers now are forced to redefine their territory in terms of the floor space of high-rise apartment units. In the modern high-rise building, the grounds, corridors, lobbies, and elevators become a public "no man's land." Newman argues that we can reestablish a sense of territory held in common through the use of court-yards, low-rise building design, fences, open stairways, and other devices. For example, the illustration in Figure 6-4 of two North Toronto high-rises indicates how external fencing and the location of parking lots can influence the territorial character of a building. In the case of the second building, a person entering from the outside is given the impression that he is coming into a private area where he will be observed and perhaps even questioned. This possibility is made even more likely in Figure 6-5, where an L-shaped building design replaces the standard block effect, and increases the sense of enclosure. Within these confines, a sense of community can be reestablished.

Surveillance. The design of buildings to allow the easy observation of territorial areas.

— There is considerable evidence that most crime occurs in semi-public areas: lobbies, halls, elevators, and fire stairs. This situation is aggravated by the fact that apartment buildings frequently are designed so that their lobbies and elevators face away from the street. Entry is commonly from secluded pathways or access roads. The protective surveillance of these areas by tenants and persons passing by can be increased by facing the lobby and elevators to the street and by replacing walls with windows. In addition, apartments can be located so as to look onto these areas.

FIGURE 6-4

Parking is largely in view of residents and the lobby is clearly visible on two sides from the entrance driveway, with a clear view from one side to the other.

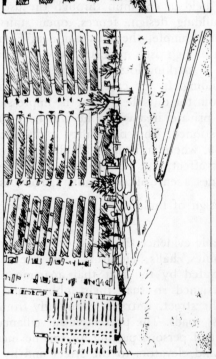

There is no division between public and private areas, lighting is poor, parking is too far from the building, and the lobby cannot be seen from the street.

FIGURE 6-5

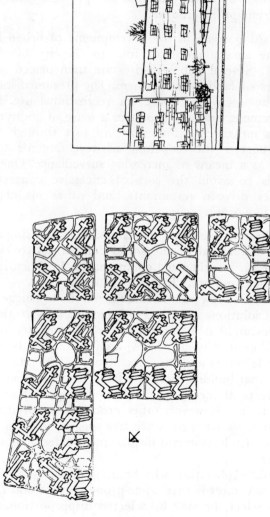

Site plan of Breukelen Houses, Brooklyn, New York

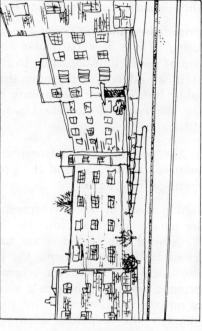

Street view of Breukelen Houses

Reprinted with permission of Macmillan Publishing Co., Inc., New York, and the Architectural Press, Ltd. London.
Source: Newman (1972:54-55)

Image. The design of public housing to avoid the easy identification as such, and the stigmatic results that may follow.

— Much high-rise living, and the crime associated with it, involves public housing. There is a particular concern that the easy identification of public housing serves to *attract* crime. Newman argues that it would cost little more than is currently spent to make public housing look like private housing, and that the reduction in the costs of vandalism would likely more than repay the difference.

Environment. The goal in relation to environment is to ensure an adequate amount of activity around the project, without excessive exposure to crime-prone groups.

— One standard pattern in the development of urban high-rises involves the amalgamation of four to six city blocks into a super-block. Several slab high-rises are then placed with large open spaces of land between them. The presumed intent is to conserve the open land space for recreational use. However, this arrangement typically produces a sense of anonymity that discourages movement of almost any sort through the area. Newman suggests the reopening of developments to limited traffic use as a means of increasing surveillance. One caution, however, is to avoid the sort of excessive congestion that accompanies drive-in restaurants, and other magnets of potentially crime-prone groups.

In all of these suggestions, the emphasis is on using architecture to encourage a renewal of the social control networks that often seem to disappear in urbanized communities. In short, it is a means of designing the community back into our cities.

One response to Newman's arguments is to suggest that the problems and solutions described are relevant only to the American condition. Research in Toronto (Mayor's Committee on Violence, 1974) and Edmonton (Gillis, 1974) argues that this is not the case. In fact, the latter study provides some of the most convincing evidence yet that building type is related to delinquency rates even when the effects of income and ethnic background are taken into account. There are, however, other problems involved in the interpretation and application of Newman's suggestions. These problems involve issues of selection and displacement effects, as well as community consent.

One possible explanation why building design is related to crime and delinquency rates is that crime-prone persons and families may be forced to select, or may be selected disproportionately out of, certain types of housing. Thus, the Edmonton study by Gillis reports a strong relationship between building type and social allowance rates. Families on social allowance may "choose" multiple dwellings for financial reasons, and the police may over-patrol such dwellings. In addition, this type of building design may make parental super-vision difficult and function as an indirect cause of delinquency. Thus, Gillis concludes that, "Building type may indeed encourage delinquency through the control problem discussed earlier, or attract delinquency-prone families, or both." (1974:312.) Further research utilizing measures of police surveillance, parental supervision, and length of exposure to building conditions will be required to resolve the issue of selection. This type of research may also have the poten-tial of helping us to match types of people to kinds of buildings more efficiently. In any event, resolution of this issue is an important prior step to large-scale investment in environmental design.

A second concern about environmental research is that improved building design may not prevent crime, but instead simply displace it onto surrounding communities. If this were the case, building "the perfect housing development" might simply aggravate the problems of a surrounding neighborhood. One major reason why environmental research seldom addresses this problem is because it is based on *area rates* rather than *individual behaviors*. What is required is more detailed information based on self-report responses of the individuals involved. Using such data, we could begin to determine whether individuals actually respond affirmatively to their architectural surroundings, or whether instead they simply shift their old behaviors to new locations. Again, this question is essential in determining the full promise of environmental design.

Finally, there is the issue of community consent. To engage in environmental design in a meaningful fashion, the community at large must indicate its willingness to change the character of public housing. This is not simply an issue of increased short-term expendi-tures. In fact, Newman argues that most of his suggested innovations can be implemented without increased costs. He adds that in the long run such alterations would reduce some of the high costs of crime anyway. A more fundamental issue is whether Canadians are willing to design away the identifying characteristics of public housing. To make public housing look more like private housing may offend valued conceptions about the rightful distribution of rewards in society. It may amount to the question of whether we are willing to subsidize governmentally the achievement of status symbols that others feel they have "earned." Weighed in the balance may be the high social and economic costs of crime. It can safely be predicted that this will be a source of conflict among Canadians.

Unfortunately, we can provide no resolution to this issue; it will require the public's consideration.

COMMUNITY CORRECTIONS

Where primary prevention and diversion fail, some form of punishment will follow. The issue becomes, what type of punishment? We in Canada cannot be accused of being unimaginative in our penal practices. In addition to imprisonment, the pillory, stocks, branding, and banishment have had their periods of popularity. Newfoundland deserves special recognition here for a rather unique policy: "Convicted persons were simply put on an outgoing boat, and eventually found themselves in Prince Edward Island, Nova Scotia, or New York State, there to fend for themselves." (Edminson, 1965:283.) A tightening of immigration laws spelled an end to this practice in 1902.

In many ways, the current use of incarceration is a means of perpetuating the early policies of banishment. Today's prisons typically are located at some distance from surrounding communities, with relatively little movement between prison and community. There are, however, current efforts to alter these arrangements. These efforts take the form of the "community corrections movement."

The vision of community corrections is described aptly as follows: "The development of an entirely new kind of correctional institution located close to a population centre, maintaining close relations with schools, employers, and universities, housing as few as 50 in each; serving as a centre for various kinds of community programmes and as a port of entry to the community for those offenders who have been exiled for a time to a penitentiary." (Moeller, 1974:897.)[7] Ericson (1973) extends this vision a step further with a rhetorical question: "Why not employ this type of centre in the first place without the period of imprisonment? If a person can still succeed in this setting after a lengthy period of confinement in a penitentiary, might he not also be at least as successful if he spent his entire sentence in one of these community based centres?" (4.)

The early community corrections programmes began in Canada in the late fifties. They were privately funded, and included the Beverely Lodge and the Elizabeth Fry Society House in Toronto, as well as Sancta Maria in Vancouver. In 1972, a task force headed by William Outerbridge (1973) completed a report on community-based residential centres (CRC's). This report identified 156 active CRC's in Canada, with a capacity to house up to 5700 persons. The only safe word for describing the programmes included in this report

FIGURE 6-6
THEY COME OUT FROM BEHIND BARS TO SERVE SENTENCES IN COMMUNITY

By BOB PENNINGTON
Star staff writer

Bob Sweezy has had his problems and doesn't mind talking about them.

"I was a disturber," he admits, "one of those guys who bucked prison authority and was always in trouble.

"Coming here was a new world for me. Got myself straightened out and now I know exactly where I'm going. The difference was being given a chance to live in a family atmosphere and work in a community instead of being locked away in an institution."

"Here" is Gerrard House, 562 Gerrard St. E., in the shadow of Toronto (Don) Jail, a large and stately edifice that was once the residence of its governors.

The official title of this white-painted, commodious confirmation of man's humanity to man is community resource centre.

Its residents are men serving sentences of less than two years in Ontario Correctional Institutions.

"They are men who are showing what can be achieved through rehabilitation rather than incarceration," says the centre's executive director, Rudy English.

"Without a centre like this, they would be just more prison inmates, shut out of society and largely unproductive.

Family support

"At Gerrard House they are part of a community, holding jobs, helping to support their families and paying taxes instead of being a burden to the taxpayer."

Individual financial responsibility is the very cornerstone of the Gerrard House philosophy as conceived by its joint creators, the John Howard Society of Ontario and the Ontario Ministry of Correctional Services.

"Financial difficulties and mismanagement of funds are among the major reasons so many guys end up in institutions," says 43-year-old English.

"Our residents are charged $4 a day for room and board. They are shown how to budget and encouraged to save. They meet their obligations."

It would be wrong to suggest that shopkeepers and residents in the neighborhood of Gerrard House were enthused or optimistic when this resource centre opened its doors in February.

Theoretically, it might be the very opposite of all the Don has represented over the years.

In fact, men who had been behind bars were now outside, mingling freely in the community, men with a record; men whose crimes had warranted punishment that was now being replaced by trust.

Rudy English was aware of this antipathy and sympathetic as to its causes. He was also confident in the program Gerrard House represented.

"Sunday is our official opening day, but already there is a lot to look back on with pride. Our total number of residents to date is 20, of whom 13 have been discharged, either on parole, or because their sentences expired, or they were returned to institutions."

The failure rate is two out of 20.

Reprinted with permission of the Toronto Star.
Source: *The* Toronto Star, *Friday, October 17, 1975*

is diversity: "A survey of contemporary residential centres through-out Canada provides a bewildering picture of residences offering everything from overnight accommodation to relatively permanent 'counter cultures' where residents make a long-term commitment to the programme and the ideology which underlies it." (x.)[8] One is not surprised to learn, then, that, "A review of evaluative studies of CRC's reveals no commonly accepted and adequate standards of evaluation." (9.)[9] This does not mean, however, that we know nothing about the consequences of such programmes.

First, the current cost of community programmes is comparable to their institutional counterparts, largely because the community programmes combine expensive support and training components with subsistence services. Second, several recent reviews of the correctional literature (Bailey, 1966; Martinson, 1974; Magid, 1972) reveal that community programmes are no more successful in pre-venting recidivism among adult criminals than were such programmes with juveniles (see the section on individual treatment). At the same time, our earlier positive finding again holds true: community programmes do not *increase* the risk of recidivism—at least on an individual probability level. However, such programmes may increase slightly the absolute *number* of individual occurrences. In other words, even if the *rates* of reconviction are equal for similar types of offenders in both types of programme, simply having a larger number of ex-offenders free in the community over a longer period of time may mean an increase in the *number* of violations that occur.

The research discussed suggests three things. One, that the expen-sive support and training programmes associated with the CRC's might possibly be dropped with little risk of reducing effectiveness. Two, that the community itself will want to weigh the costs and benefits of the new programmes before giving consent and support to their expanded use. Three, that new standards of evaluation will be needed to inform the public adequately about the success of such programmes. It is the last of these problems that is most immediate.

In the original task force report, Robert Hann and Richard Sullivan (Appendix A) proposed a sophisticated cost-benefit approach for evaluating community residential centres. Included in the design were 48 suggested indicators of the costs and benefits of alternative programmes. Unfortunately, this carefully conceived design proved to be ahead of its subject matter; the target programmes are simply not structured in a form definite enough to make such evaluation meaningful. In compensation, Burrel and Magid (1974) have recently proposed a methodology for the self-evaluation of CRC programmes. The goal is to encourage agencies to specify their own goals, and then participate in the measurement of their fulfillment. The challenge, of course, is to keep the agencies honest in their self-assessments. This accomplished, the research should provide important new information for the public evaluation of these programmes.

In the end, the success of the community corrections movement depends on the willingness of the community to provide cooperation and support. The whole thrust of this movement is to reintegrate the ex-offender into the community, a task that cannot be accomplished by the participants alone.

CONCLUSIONS

Past efforts at crime prevention focused on individual treatment, social reform, and police deployment. None of these approaches brought measurable success. However, from the individual treatment programmes we learned that many juvenile offenders can continue to live in the community without an increase in their likelihood of reoffending. Next, we learned from the expensive social reform programmes that governments are unreliable agents of their own change. Finally, the review of policing research indicated the dubious nature of the assumption that additional deployment of police personnel will reduce crime markedly.

Current approaches to crime prevention provide an expanded role for the community through law reform, environmental design, and community corrections programmes. The law reform approach focuses on the diversion of those convicted of conflict crimes and minor consensual crimes into the community. The environmental design perspective encourages the innovative use of architecture to stimulate a renewal of the social control networks that often seem lacking in urbanized communities. The community corrections movement attempts to reintegrate the ex-offender into the community by providing a connection between institutional programmes and community resources. None of these three approaches can succeed without the cooperation and support of the community: potential and immediate victims in the community must agree to law reform measures; involved and surrounding community members must accept architectural innovation; and representatives of the community must volunteer to participate in, and live alongside, community residential centres. However, given a cooperative community, these programmes promise a more humane and efficient response to crime.

Central to our argument is the assumption that diverting those convicted of conflict crimes into the community will free new resources for a more certain and expeditious response to the consensual crimes. We have already noted in the preceding chapter that, relative to that of other nations, the Canadian response to crime has been severe. In the remainder of this discussion, we will argue that this severity is a misguided means of attempting to reduce crime.

Conventional efforts to reduce crime through criminal sanctions are usually based on a three part assumption that *swift, certain*, and *severe* punishments deter involvement in crime. Policies of this sort are concerned with deterring crime on both an *individual* and more *general* level. "Individual deterrence" is concerned with the preventative effects of punishments on the persons who receive them. "General deterrence," on the other hand, is concerned with the preventative effects of these same punishments as they are experienced vicariously by others (i.e., society at large). There is now considerable research indicating that individual and general deterrent effects are more dependent on the certainty that some punishment will occur, than on the severity of the punishment that is finally selected.[10]

Research on individual deterrence indicates that as an adolescent's perception of the *certainty* of punishment increases, involvement in delinquency decreases; furthermore, as adolescents become older they are more likely to be aware that much crime goes unpunished (Jensen, 1969). On the other hand, there is little evidence that the *severity* of individual punishments deters crime (e.g., Wilkens, 1958). Thus, when Waller (1974) compares offenders released early on parole in Ontario with offenders who served their full sentences, he is able to find no evidence that the severity of sentence is causally related (either positively or negatively) to the success of outcome. In short, certainty but not severity of punishment seems to make a difference for the individuals involved.

Research on general deterrence reveals similar conclusions. Thus, although some of this research reports a modest general deterrent effect for severity of punishment (Gibbs, 1968; Gray and Martin, 1969), certainty of punishment has a stronger and more consistent effect (Tittle, 1969; Chiricos and Waldo, 1970; Bailey, Martin, and Gray, 1972). Canadian research on this issue is particularly significant in encouraging that capital punishment be abolished (Fattah, 1972). Teevan (1972) is able to conclude that in Canada, as in the United States, " . . . certainty but not the severity of punishment . . . appears to be related to variations in crime rates." (79.)

This presumably is one reason why in 1976 the government of Canada abolished the death penalty for murder. However, this same legislation replaced a prior distinction between capital and non-capital murder with a new division between first and second degree murder that increased the scope of this most severely punished crime. Thus, where capital murder previously consisted only of the murder of a police officer or a permanent employee of a prison, first degree murder is now expanded to include:

- all planned and deliberate murders;
- contracted murder;
- murder of police officers, prison employees, and other persons authorized to work in a prison from time to time; and
- murder while committing or attempting to commit rape, indecent assault on a male or female, kidnapping and forcible confinement, or hijacking.

Furthermore, while previously a person convicted of capital murder was eligible for parole after ten years imprisonment, a person convicted of first degree murder under the new legislation must serve an absolute term of twenty-five years imprisonment without the possibility of parole. Thus, it is unclear whether we are entering a period in Canada where the severity of punishment is increasing or decreasing.

The message of this chapter is that the severity of our penal response to deviance in Canada could be reduced without a substantial risk of increasing the level of crime. At the same time, we have also argued that law reforms diverting minor "conflict offenders" from the criminal justice system would free new resources for increasing the speed and certainty of the response to serious "consensual crimes." In addition, community correction programmes and efforts at environmental design promise new and productive responses to our crime problems, without requiring large new levels of resource commitment. In sum, we can learn to live with much of the deviance we experience in Canada, while at the same time making our society more humane, and probably also more efficient. We are learning to live with deviance, but we are learning slowly.

1. From Daniel P. Moynihan, *Maximum Feasible Misunderstanding.* © 1969 Free Press. Reprinted with permission of Macmillan Publishing Co., Inc.

2. Ibid.

3. Ibid.

4. Ibid.

5. Ibid.

6. © 1974 by the New York Times Company. Reprinted with permission.

7. From H.G. Moeller, "Community-Based Correctional Services," in Daniel Glaser (Ed.), *Handbook of Criminology,* 1974. Reprinted with permission of Rand McNally.

8. From William Outerbridge, *Report of the Task Force on Community-Based Residential Centres.* 1973 Solicitor General of Canada. Reprinted with permission of the Minister of Supply and Services Canada.

9. Ibid.

10. There is little research on the effect of the "celerity," or speed of punishment, on its outcome; nevertheless, an expeditious response is usually thought to be essential (Bailey, Martin, and Gray, 1974).

Epilogue: Putting the Pieces Together

We began our discussion with a series of questions: Why are some pleasures considered acceptable, and others disreputable? By whom, and how often, are the disreputable pleasures experienced? How do we explain deviance and disrepute sociologically? What are the pains and pleasures of a disreputable lifestyle? How do we, and how should we, respond to deviance and disrepute in Canada? We can now summarize our answers to these questions.

What is called deviant or disreputable varies by social location. For example, many of the acts Euro-Canadians held criminal, Native Canadian cultures did not. To accommodate this variation, we suggested a continuum definition of deviance that ranges from the most to the least serious violations of societal norms. According to this definition, the most serious acts of deviance involve high public agreement about what the norm is, widespread agreement about the harmfulness of the act, and a severe social response. Moving from the most to the least serious acts on this continuum, we encounter first the criminal forms of deviance—the consensus and then the conflict crimes, followed by the non-criminal forms of deviance—the social deviations and finally the social diversions.

A major sociological concern is to determine why in any given society some of these acts of deviance are considered criminal. Consideration of Canadian laws dealing with vagrancy, narcotics, and juvenile delinquency reveals that interest groups frequently mobilize cultural themes for the purpose of designating particular acts as criminally and non-criminally deviant. We noted that the influence of such groups varies, but that their impact is greatest when public opinion is dormant or divided.

Having defined our subject matter, we turned next to its measurement. We noted that all statistics of deviance contain two components. The first component is made up of actual behaviors and their authors, while the second component is an error term, representing either the over- or under-reporting of the events and persons involved.

We argued that the best statistics on deviance are informed by comparisons of alternative measures, drawn from a variety of sources, including: (1) official agencies of social control, (2) non-official agencies, (3) first person accounts, (4) victimization surveys, and (5) observational studies.

Using available measures, and focusing on problems of crime and delinquency, mental illness, alcoholism, and other forms of drug abuse, we suggested several necessarily tentative conclusions:

actual levels of deviation are higher than most of our official measures indicate;

in recent years, several measures of deviance, particularly the consensus crimes, have shown some increase in Canada;

although official records frequently overrepresent the link between social class and rates of deviant behavior, the underclasses disproportionately experience those forms of deviance currently considered serious; and

to date, those forms of deviance widely seen as most serious by the public (e.g., violent crime and "hard" drug abuse) are more common in the United States than in Canada.

Two types of explanations are offered for these and other findings: the consensus theories of deviance, and the conflict theories of disrepute. Various versions of these theories were considered, and the groups of explanations were then pooled to offer alternative explanations of the "facts of deviance" reported above. These alternative explanations were presented in response to four "fact-based" questions.

Why is there so much more deviance than appears in the official records of agencies of social control?

The consensus theories argue that by publicly responding to *some* forms of deviance, we *selectively* demonstrate our symbolic disapproval of those acts that threaten important norms and values. The important point here is that not *all* acts, even if they could be, need be punished. Each society punishes deviance in a way that seems best suited to insure the maintenance of the system in its desired form. It can be added that one of the measures of the "freeness" of a society is the

The conflict theories argue that deviance is more a matter of public evaluation and official response than actual behavior. It is argued that our impressions of how much deviant behavior occurs are manipulated by the interest groups in society that control the media portrayal of deviance. Two results are said to follow: (a) deviant behavior common to powerful interest group members is ignored, while (b) the levels of deviant behavior among less powerful groups are extent to which many forms of deviance are exempted from punishment and control.

exaggerated. From this viewpoint, the issue of "how much deviance," is one of *whose* definition is being applied to *what* sector of society.

Why are rates of deviance increasing?

The consensus theories suggest that rates of deviance will increase (a) when the gap between perceived goals and means widens for many people, and (b) when the social bond is weakened further by a reduction in the influence of the family and community. In the context of rapid urbanization, attachments, involvement, and commitment to the family and community are all seen as declining. Combined with an increasing sense of economic deprivation, these conditions provoke a feeling of "having little to lose," and much to gain through deviant involvements. In other words, deviant options become attractive, and rates of deviance increase.

The conflict theories argue that official rates of deviance will increase as the interest groups powerful in defining deviance increase the resources they have available for control purposes. For example, as economic resources grow, police forces expand in size and expenditures, and official rates of deviance follow. Added to this is the possibility that as unemployment rates grow, financial interests perceive a greater need for *protection* from the disadvantaged, and thus further intensify efforts at control.

Why is there a relationship between class background and rates of deviant behavior?

The consensus theories emphasize that the lower classes are systematically denied opportunities. As these class-linked differences in life-chances are experienced, individuals' conceptions of their stakes in conformity diminish. In addition, economic hardships are assumed to produce a disorganization of family and community life that weakens the control mechanisms restricting involvement in deviance.

The conflict theories answer this question in two ways. They argue first that agencies of social control discriminate in the handling of economic and ethnic minorities, and second that the laws themselves apply unequally to these groups. The latter argument is seen as more important, noting that many of our laws define as criminal acts that are more common among minorities, while defining more leniently those

Finally, in the face of poverty, the victimless crimes, alcohol and drug abuse, theft, and even violence can be seen as pleasurable, satisfying, and in this context rational, lifestyles.

acts more common among majorities.

Why is there less deviance in Canada than in the United States?

The consensus theories argue that Canadians and Americans differ in their values, particularly in their relative respect for law and order, and that these differences produce a cross-national disparity in the incidence of the more serious forms of deviance. Two factors, one environmental and the other political, are said to explain these differences: (1) the early tradition of strict legal control initiated in the development of Canada's northern and western frontier, and (2) the "Imperial Connection" linking Canada to the elite-based traditions of Great Britain. Together with a more conservative set of national values, these factors are offered in explanation of Canadian-American differences in the incidence of the more serious forms of deviance.

The conflict theories argue that the disparity between Canadian and American rates of deviance are a consequence of "cultural lag." It is then suggested that as the "Imperial Connection" diminishes, and the "American Connection" increases, that patterns of deviance in the two countries will become more and more alike. More specifically, as American investment continues, and the Canadian economy expands, new resources will become available for increases in police force size and expenditures. These factors are said to result in increasing rates of deviance, both in the United States and Canada.[1]

We did not attempt to impose a premature closure on the conflict-consensus debate. Instead, we suggested that the consensus theories work best in explaining the most serious forms of deviance, the consensus crimes, while the conflict theories serve best in explaining the societal response to those forms of deviance about which little consensus exists. We also noted that the consensual theories are more interested in explaining *behaviors*, while the conflict theories are particularly concerned with the disreputable *status* of these behaviors, as well as the manner in which consensual evaluations of behaviors sometimes emerge. We then turned to a discussion of the societal response to deviance. Following a review of this discussion, we will argue that both the consensus and conflict theories can be used to recommend important changes in the Canadian response to deviance.

Studies of the societal response to deviance suggest on the one hand that the various agencies of social control fit together in similar ways in Canada and the United States, but that particularly in the area of *crime*, Canadian policies and procedures have been more repressive. Thus, both in Canada and the United States there is evidence that *social resources* have some influence on the application of disreputable labels. Thus, when relevant behavioral variables are taken into account, some research on police and court operations indicates that criminal and delinquent labels are applied somewhat more frequently to the socially disadvantaged, while alcoholic and psychiatric labels are reserved somewhat more frequently for those who *take* social advantage. In explanation of these findings, it was suggested that when in a position that leads to being labelled deviant, middle and upper class persons are more likely to be labelled alcoholic or psychiatric cases. The other side of this coin is that socially disadvantaged persons more frequently are labelled criminals or delinquents. It is in this context that the existence of different types of deviance and agencies of social control becomes understandable. These observations seem as applicable in Canada as in the United States.

There does, however, seem to be evidence that Canada's criminal justice system has been more repressive than is the case in the United States and other western nations. Evidence was presented indicating that in the *past* Canada may have used incarceration more than the United States, that procedural safeguards spelled out in the Canadian Bill of Rights were late in coming and limited in application, and that penal reforms began much later in Canada than in the United States and Great Britain. These findings led us to consider possible changes in the response to crime in Canada.

Past efforts to prevent crime have focused on individual treatment, social reform, and police deployment. None of these approaches brought measurable success. More recent approaches to crime prevention provide an expanded role for the community—through law reform, environmental design, and community corrections programmes. Emphasized in many of these programmes is the diversion of minor offenders into the community. For example, it was demonstrated that by instituting a more equitable fine system and decriminalizing the public consumption of alcohol, as many as half of all native offenders in Canada could be decarcerated. It was then argued that by diverting minor offenders into the community, new resources could be devoted to a more certain and expeditious response to the serious consensual crimes. Finally, evidence was presented indicating that it is the certainty of punishment, rather than its severity, that deters crime most effectively. In sum, it was argued that we can reduce the severity of criminal punishments in Canada without risking a causally significant increase in our crime rates.

FIGURE 7-1

WHY ARE CRIME RATES LOWER IN CANADA THAN IN THE UNITED STATES?

A Consensus Explanation   *A Conflict Explanation*

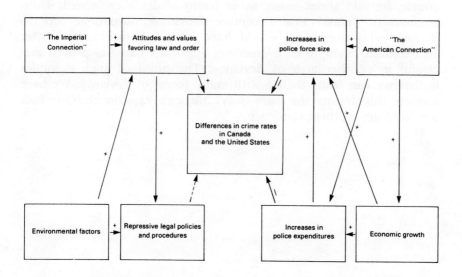

Much of our discussion, particularly as it relates to Canada and the United States, is summarized in Figure 7-1. This figure represents conflict and consensus explanations, as they relate to comparative crime rates in these two countries. The conflict theories to the right of this diagram suggest that differences in the two nations' rates of crime will be diminished by increases in police force size and expenditures in Canada. In short, the conflict theories argue that the differences in crime rates are largely an artifact of enforcement practices.

On the other hand, the consensus theories to the left of this diagram insist that the behavioral differences are real, and that they are caused by national differences in attitudes and values. The consensus theories go on to argue that such values are also causally related to repressive legal policies and procedures in Canada. Most importantly, however, it can be argued consistently with a consensus viewpoint that the relationship between these repressive practices and Canada's lower crime rates is *spurious*. According to this viewpoint, more conservative Canadian values are said to cause both repressive legal practices *and* lower crime rates, but the latter two variables are related to each other only by virtue of their causal relationship to the first. Thus, we have represented the non-causal link between these two variables with a dotted line. The finding that the severity of punishments is causally unimportant to crime rates reinforces this hypothesis. Our conclusion, then, is that both the consensus and conflict theories are consistent with a more moderate response to crime in Canada.

What has been said about criminal forms of deviance can, of course, be said about many other forms of deviance as well. Thus, community mental health centres providing outpatient care to persons who previously would have been institutionalized offer an excellent example of a diversion approach that has proved successful in another area of deviance. The point of such examples is that we can learn to live with many forms of deviance. We have learned this lesson the hard way: through experience. Our task now is to act on this experience.

1. It deserves mention that *neither* the consensus nor the conflict theories have focused on ethnic differences and governmental policies toward ethnic minorities in explaining differences in Canadian and American crime rates. By default, then, this remains an area for further research.

BIBLIOGRAPHY

Akman, D. D., A. Normandeau, and S. Turner
1967   "The Measurement of Delinquency in Canada." *Journal of Criminal Law, Criminology, and Police Science* 58 (September):330-337.

Alinsky, Saul
1969   *Reveille for Radicals.* New York: Vintage Books.

Archibald, D.
1907   *Report on the Treatment of Neglected Children in Toronto.* Toronto: Arcade.

Bailey, M. B., B. W. Haberman, and H. Alksne
1965   "The Epidemiology of Alcoholism in an Urban Residential Area." *Quarterly Journal of Studies on Alcohol* 26:19-40.

Bailey, W. C.
1966   "Correctional Outcome: An Evaluation of 100 Reports." *Journal of Criminal Law, Criminology, and Police Science* 57:153-160.

Bailey, Walter, J. David Martin, and Louis N. Gray
1972   "On 'Punishment and Crime' (Chiricos and Waldo): Some Methodological Commentary." *Social Problems* 19 (Fall):284-289.

Banfield, Edward
1968   *The Unheavenly City.* Boston: Little, Brown and Company.

Barter, James T., George Mizner, and Paul Werme
1970   "Patterns of Drug Use Among College Students: An Epidemiological and Demographic Survey of Student Attitudes and Practices." Department of Psychiatry, University of Colorado Medical School, Unpublished.

Becker, Howard
1963   *Outsiders: Studies in the Sociology of Deviance.* New York: Free Press of Glencoe.
1964   *The Other Side: Perspectives on Deviance.* New York: Free Press of Glencoe.

Becker, Theodore M.
1974   "The Place of Private Police in Society: An Area of Research for the Social Sciences." *Social Problems* 21(3):438-455.

Bédard, Théodore and James McLaughlin
1970   "Time Series Analysis and Projections of Crime Rates, Canada 1949-1971." Ottawa: The Queen's Printer.

Berg, D. F.
1970   "The Non-Medical Use of Dangerous Drugs in the United States: A Comprehensive View." *International Journal of Addictions* 5 (4):777-834.

Berton, Pierre
1976   "It's the Cops! The Terrifying Power of our Police." *Quest* 5 (2):8-14.

Biderman, A. D. *et al.*
1967   *Report of a Pilot Study in the District of Columbia on Victimization and Attitudes Toward Law Enforcement.* Washington: U.S. Government Printing Office.

Bienvenue, Rita M. and A. H. Latif
1974   "Arrests, Dispositions and Recidivism: A Comparison of Indians and Whites." *Canadian Journal of Criminology and Corrections* 16:105-116.

Birket-Smith, Kaj
    1959   *The Eskimos.* London: Methuen and Company, Ltd.
Bittner, E.
    1967a   "The Police on Skid Row: A Study of Peace Keeping." *American Sociological Review* 32 (October): 699-715.
    1967b   "Police Discretion in Emergency Apprehension of Mentally Ill Persons." *Social Problems* 14 (Winter): 278-292.
Black, Donald J. and Albert J. Reiss, Jr.
    1967   "Patterns of Behavior in Police-Citizen Transactions." *Studies in Crime and Law Enforcement in Major Metropolitan Areas,* Field Surveys III, Vol. 2, President's Commission on Law Enforcement in Major Metropolitan Areas. Washington, D.C.: U.S. Government Printing Office.
    1970   "Police Control of Juveniles." *American Sociological Review* 35 (February): 63-77.
Blum, Richard H.
    1969   *Students and Drugs.* San Francisco: Jossey-Bass, Inc.
Blumberg, Abraham S.
    1967a   "The Practice of Law as a Confidence Game." *Law and Society Review* 1 (January): 15-39.
    1967b   *Criminal Justice.* Chicago: Quadrangle Books.
Bodine, George E.
    1964   "Factors Related to Police Dispositions of Juvenile Offenders." Syracuse: University Youth Development Center.
Boorstin, Daniel J.
    1973   *The Americans: The Democratic Experience.* New York: Random House.
Bordua, David
    1961   "Delinquent Subcultures: Sociological Interpretations of Gang Delinquency." *The Annals of the American Academy of Political and Social Science* 338 (November): 119-136.
    1969   "Recent Trends: Deviant Behavior and Social Control." *The Annals of the American Academy of Political and Social Science* 369 (January): 149-163.

Boydell, Craig, Carl Grindstaff, and Paul Whitehead
    1972   *Deviant Behavior and Societal Reaction.* Toronto: Holt, Rinehart, and Winston of Canada, Ltd.
    1975   *The Administration of Criminal Justice in Canada.* Toronto: Holt, Rinehart, and Winston of Canada, Ltd.
Brenner, B.
    1967   "Alcoholism and Fatal Accidents." *Quarterly Journal of Studies on Alcohol* 28:517-526.
Brown, Lorne and Caroline Brown
    1973   *An Unauthorized History of the R.C.M.P.* Toronto: Lewis and Samuel.
Bruton, Paul W.
    1962   "The Canadian Bill of Rights: Some American Observations." *McGill Law Journal* 8:106-120.
Buckner, H. Taylor
    1970   "Transformations of Reality in the Legal Process." *Social Research* 37 (Spring): 88-101.

1974 "Police Culture." Paper presented at the Canadian Sociology and Anthropology Association Meetings, August, Toronto.

Bullock, Henry A.
1961 "Significance of the Racial Factor in the Length of Prison Sentences." *Journal of Criminal Law, Criminology, and Police Science* 52:411-417.

Burrell, Terrence and Simmie Magid
1974 "Toward the Evaluation of Community-Based Residential Centres: The Development of a Methodology for Self-Evaluation." A research proposal prepared under the direction of Robert Hann, Toronto: SDL Institute.

Burton, S. J.
1974 "The New Biotechnology and the Role of Legal Intervention." *American Journal of Orthopsychiatry* 44 (5):688-696.

Cahalan, Don
1970 *Problem Drinkers.* San Francisco: Jossey-Bass Inc.

Cameron, Mary Owen
1964 *The Booster and the Snitch.* New York: Free Press of Glencoe.

Campbell, D. T. and D. W. Fiske
1959 "Convergent and Discriminate Validation by the Multitrait-Multimethod Matrix." *Psychological Bulletin* 56 (2):81-105.

Canadian Civil Liberties Educational Trust
1971 *Due Process Safeguards and Canadian Criminal Justice: A One Month Inquiry.* Toronto.

Canadian Corrections Association
1967 *Indians and the Law.* Ottawa: The Queen's Printer.

Carter, Robert M. and Leslie T. Wilkins
1967 "Some Factors in Sentencing Policy." *Journal of Criminal Law, Criminology, and Police Science* 58 (4):503-514.

Cassidy, R. G. and R. George Hopkinson
1974 *Information and Statistics on the Canadian Criminal Justice System: Problems and Recommendations.* Ministry of the Solicitor General, Statistics Division.

Cavan, Ruth
1968 *Delinquency and Crime: Cross Cultural Perspectives.* Philadelphia: J. B. Lippincott Company.

Chambliss, William J.
1964 "A Sociological Analysis of the Law of Vagrancy." *Social Problems* 12 (1):67-77.

Chambliss, William J. and R. H. Nagasawa
1969 "On the Validity of Official Statistics: A Comparative Study of White, Black, and Japanese High-School Boys." *Journal of Research in Crime and Delinquency* 6 (January): 71-77.

Chambliss, William J. and Robert B. Seidman
1971 *Law, Order, and Power.* Reading, Massachusetts: Addison-Wesley Publishing Company.

Chein, Isidor
1966 "Narcotics Use Among Juveniles." in John O'Donnell and John Ball (Eds.), *Narcotic Addiction.* New York: Harper and Row.

Chiricos, Theodore and Gordon Waldo
1970 "Punishment and Crime: An Examination of Some Empirical Evidence." *Social Problems* 18 (Fall): 200-217.

1975   "Socioeconomic Status and Criminal Sentencing: An Empirical
          Assessment of a Conflict Proposition." *American Sociological
          Review* 40:753-772.

Chute, Charles L. and Marjorie Bell
1956   *Crime, Courts, and Probation.* New York: The Macmillan Com-
          pany.

Cicourel, Aaron
1968   *The Social Organization of Juvenile Justice.* New York: John
          Wiley and Sons.

Clairmont, Donald H.
1963   *Deviance among Indians and Eskimos in Aklavik, N.W.T.* Ottawa,
          Ontario: Northern Coordination and Research Centre, Depart-
          ment of Northern Affairs and National Resources.
1974   "The Development of a Deviance Service Centre." In Jack Haas
          and Bill Shaffir (Eds.), *Decency and Deviance.* Toronto:
          McClelland and Stewart, Ltd.

Clark, Gerald
1975   "What Happens When the Police Strike." In William Chambliss
          (Ed.), *Criminal Law in Action.* Santa Barbara, California:
          Hamilton Publishing Company.

Clark, John and Richard Sykes
1974   "Some Determinants of Police Organization and Practice in a
          Modern Industrial Bureaucracy" in Daniel Glaser (Ed.), *Hand-
          book of Criminology*, Chicago: Rand McNally.

Clark, Lorenne
1976   "The Offence of Rape and the Concept of Harm." Unpublished
          manuscript, University of Toronto.

Clark, Lorenne and Debra Lewis
1977   *Rape: The Price of Coercive Sexuality.* Toronto: The Canadian
          Women's Educational Press (forthcoming).

Clark, S. D.
1942   *The Social Development of Canada.* Toronto: The University of
          Toronto Press.
1962   *The Developing Canadian Community.* Toronto: The University
          of Toronto Press.
1976   *Canadian Society in Historical Perspective.* Toronto: McGraw-Hill
          Ryerson, Ltd.

Clausen, J. A.
1971   "Mental Disorders." in R. K. Merton and R. Nisbet (Eds.),
          Contemporary Social Problems. New York: Harcourt Brace
          Jovanovich.

Cloward, Richard A.
1959   "Illegitimate Means, Anomie, and Deviant Behavior." *American
          Sociological Review* 24:164-176.

Cloward, Richard and Lloyd Ohlin
1960   *Delinquency and Opportunity: A Theory of Delinquent Gangs.*
          New York: Free Press of Glencoe.

Coates, D. C. *et al.*
1969   "The Yorklea Study of Urban Mental Health: Symptoms, Prob-
          lems, and Life Events." *Canadian Journal of Public Health*
          60 (12): 471-481.

Cohen, Albert
1955   *Delinquent Boys.* New York: Free Press of Glencoe.
Cook, Shirley
1969   "Canadian Narcotics Legislation, 1908-1923: A Conflict Model Interpretation." *Canadian Review of Sociology and Anthropology* 6 (1):36-46.
1970   *Variations in Response to Illegal Drug Use.* Unpublished manuscript, Toronto: Alcoholism and Drug Addiction Research Foundation.
Costello, James
1972   "Behavior Modification and Corrections: Current Status and Future Potential." Santa Barbara, California: Institute for Applied Behavioral Science.
Courtis, M. C.
1970   *Attitudes to Crime and the Police in Toronto: A Report on Some Survey Findings.* Toronto: Centre of Criminology, University of Toronto.
Cousineau, D. F. and J. E. Veevers
1972a   "Incarceration as a Response to Crime: The Utilization of Canadian Prisons." *Canadian Journal of Criminology and Corrections* 14 (January): 10-31.
1972b   "Juvenile Justice: An Analysis of the Canadian Young Offenders Act." In C. Boydell *et al.* (Eds.), *Deviant Behavior and Societal Reaction.* Toronto: Holt, Rinehart, and Winston of Canada Ltd.
Cressey, Donald
1953   *Other People's Money: A Study of the Social Psychology of*
(1971)   *Embezzlement.* Glencoe, Illinois: Free Press of Glencoe.
1965   "The Respectable Criminal: Why Some of Our Best Friends are Crooks." *Transaction* 2 (March-April): 12-15.
Crime in Eight American Cities
1974   National Criminal Justice Information and Statistics Service. Washington, D.C.: Law Enforcement Assistance Administration.
Crysdale, S. and C. Beattie
1973   *Sociology Canada.* Toronto: Butterworth and Company (Canada), Ltd.
Cumming, Elaine, Ian Cumming, and Laura Edell
1965   "Policeman as Philosopher, Guide and Friend." *Social Problems* 12 (Winter): 276-286.

Davis, Arthur K.
1944   "Veblen's Study of Modern Germany." *American Sociological Review* 9:603-609.
1965   *Edging into Mainstream: Urban Indians in Saskatchewan.* Calgary.
1971   "Canadian Society as Hinterland Versus Metropolis." in Richard J. Ossenberg (Ed.), *Canadian Society: Pluralism, Change, and Conflict.* Scarborough, Ontario: Prentice-Hall of Canada, Ltd.
Davis, F. James
1952   "Crime News in Colorado Newspapers." *American Journal of Sociology* 57 (January): 325-330.

de Fleur, L. B.
1967   "Delinquent Gangs in Cross-Cultural Perspective: The Case of Cordoba." *Journal of Research in Crime and Delinquency* 4:132-141.

de Lint, Jan and Wolfgang Schmidt
1971   "Consumption Averages and Alcoholism Prevalence: A Brief Review of Epidemiological Investigations." *British Journal of Addiction* 66:97-107.

Decore, John V.
1964   "Criminal Sentencing: The Role of the Canadian Courts of Appeal and the Concept of Uniformity." *The Criminal Law Quarterly* 6 (February): 324-380.

Diana, Lewis
1960   "What is Probation?" *Journal of Criminal Law, Criminology, and Police Science* 51 (July-August): 189-208.

Dinitz, Simon, Frank R. Scarpitti, and Walter C. Reckless
1962   "Delinquency Vulnerability: A Cross Group and Longitudinal Analysis." *American Sociological Review* 27 (August): 515-517.

Dohrenwend, Bruce P. and Barbara S. Dohrenwend
1969   *Social Status and Psychological Disorder.* New York: John Wiley and Sons.

1974   "Social and Cultural Influences on Psychopathology." *Annual Review of Psychology* 25:417-452.

1975   "Sociocultural and Social-Psychological Factors in the Genesis of Mental Disorders." *Journal of Health and Social Behavior* 16 (4):365-392.

Downes, D. M.
1966   *The Delinquent Solution: A Study in Subcultural Theory.* London: Routledge and Kegan Paul.

Durkheim, Emile
1950   *The Rules of the Sociological Method.* Translated and edited by
(1895)   Sarah A. Solovay and John H. Mueller. Edited by G.E.G. Catlin. Glencoe, Illinois: Free Press of Glencoe.

1951   *Suicide.* Translation by John A. Spaulding and George Simpson.
(1897)   Glencoe, Illinois: Free Press of Glencoe.

Edminson, J. Alex
1965   "Some Aspects of Nineteenth Century Canadian Prisons." in W. T. McGrath (Ed.), *Crime and its Treatment in Canada.* Toronto: The MacMillan Company of Canada, Ltd.

Empey, LeMar and Maynard Erickson
1972   *The Provo Experiment.* Lexington, Massachusetts: Lexington Books.

Empey, LeMar and Steven Lubeck
1971   *The Silverlake Experiment.* Chicago: Aldine Inc.

Engstad, Peter
1975   "Environmental Opportunities and the Ecology of Crime." in Robert Silverman and James T. Teevan (Eds.), *Crime in Canadian Society.* Toronto: Butterworth and Company (Canada) Ltd.

Ennis, P. H.
1967   *Criminal Victimization in the United States: A Report of a National Survey.* Washington, D.C.: U.S. Government Printing Office.

Ericson, Richard V.
   1973   "Turning the Inside Out: On Limiting the Use of Imprisonment."
            Community Education Series 1 (3). John Howard Society of
            Ontario.
   1974   "British Criminology: A New Subject or Old Politics?" *Canadian
            Journal of Criminology and Corrections* 16: 352-360.
   1975a   *Criminal Reactions: The Labelling Perspective.* Westmead,
            England: Lexington Books.
   1975b   *Young Offenders and their Social Work.* Westmead, England:
            Lexington Books.
Erikson, Kai
   1962   "Notes on the Sociology of Deviance." *Social Problems* 9 (Spr-
            ing): 307-314.
Evans, Robert
   1973   *Developing Policies for Public Security and Criminal Justice.*
            Ottawa: Economic Council of Canada.
Eysenck, Hans
   1964   *Crime and Personality.* Boston: Houghton and Miflin.
Fattah, Ezzat Abdel
   1972   *A Study of the Deterrent Effect of Capital Punishment with
            Special Reference to the Canadian Situation.* Ottawa: Informa-
            tion Canada.
Ferdinand, Theodore
   1967   "The Criminal Patterns of Boston since 1849." *American Journal
            of Sociology* 73:84-99.
   1972   "Politics, the Police, and Arresting Practices in Salem, Massachu-
            setts since the Civil War." *Social Problems* 19:572-588.
Ferdinand, Theodore and Elmer Luchterhand
   1970   "Inner-City Youth, the Police, the Juvenile Court, and Justice."
            Social Problems 17 (Spring): 510-527.
Finestone, Harold
   1966   "Narcotics and Criminality." In John O'Donnell and John Ball
            (Eds.), *Narcotic Addiction.* New York: Harper and Row.
Fisher, Sethard
   1972   "Stigma and Deviant Careers in Schools." *Social Problems* 20
            (Summer): 78-83.
Fisher, Sethard and B. V. Paranjape
   1969   "Stigma and Deviant Careers in School: Part I." In B.Y. Card
            (Ed.), *Perspectives on Regions and Regionalism.* Edmonton:
            University of Alberta Press.
Fox, Richard and Patricia Erickson
   1972   *Apparently Suffering from Mental Disorder.* Toronto: Centre of
            Criminology, University of Toronto.
Francis, John and David Patch
   1969   "Student Attitudes toward Drug Programs at the University of
            Michigan." University of Michigan: University Committee on
            Drug Education.
Frankel, Marvin
   1972   *Criminal Sentences.* New York: Hill and Wang.
Frease, Dean E.
   1973   "Delinquency, Social Class, and the Schools." *Sociology and
            Social Research* 57 (July): 443-459.

Gandy, John M.
    1970   "The Exercise of Discretion by the Police as a Decision-Making Process in the Disposition of Juvenile Offenders." *Osgoode Hall Law Journal* 8 (November): 329-344.

Garfinkel, Harold
    1956   "Conditions of Successful Degradation Ceremonies." *American Journal of Sociology* 61:420-424.

Gibbons, Don C. and Manzer J. Griswold
    1957   "Sex Differences among Juvenile Court Referrals." *Sociology and Social Research* 42 (December): 106-110.

Gibbs, Jack P.
    1968   "Crime, Punishment and Deterrence." *Social Science Quarterly* 48 (March): 515-530.

Giffen, P. J.
    1965   "Rates of Crime and Delinquency." In W. T. McGrath (Ed.), *Crime and Its Treatment in Canada*, Toronto: The Macmillan Company of Canada, Ltd.
    1966   "The Revolving Door: A Functional Interpretation." *Canadian Review of Sociology and Anthropology* 3 (3): 154-166.
    1976   "Official Rates of Crime and Delinquency." In W. T. McGrath (Ed.), *Crime and Its Treatment in Canada*, Toronto: The Macmillan Co. of Canada, Ltd.

Gillis, A. R.
    1974   "Population Density and Social Pathology: The Case of Building Type, Social Allowance, and Juvenile Delinquency." *Social Forces* 53 (2): 306-314.

Goffman, Erving
    1952   "Cooling The Mark Out: Some Aspects of Adaptation to Failure." *Psychiatry* 15:451-463.
    1961   *Asylums*. Chicago: Aldine-Atherton, Inc.
    1963   *Stigma: Notes on the Management of Spoiled Identity*. Englewood Cliffs, N.J.: Prentice-Hall.
    1964   *Behavior in Public Places*. New York: Free Press of Glencoe.

Goldman, Nathan
    1963   *The Differential Selection of Offenders for Court Appearance*. New York: National Council on Crime and Delinquency.

Gove, Walter
    1975   "Labelling and Mental Illness: A Critique." in Walter Gove (Ed.), *The Labelling of Deviance: Evaluating a Perspective*. New York: Halsted Press.

Gove, Walter and Patrick Howell
    1975   "Individual Resources and Mental Hospitalization: A Comparison and Evaluation of the Societal Reaction and Psychiatric Perspectives." *American Sociological Review* 39 (1): 86-100.

Gray, Louis N. and J. David Martin
    1969   "Punishment and Deterrence: Another Analysis of Gibbs' Data." *Social Science Quarterly* 49 (September): 289-295.

Green, Edward
    1961   *Judicial Attitudes in Sentencing*. London: The Macmillan Company.
    1964   "Inter- and Intra-Racial Crime Relative to Sentencing." *Journal of Criminal Law, Criminology, and Police Science* 55 (3): 348-358.

1970   "Race, Social Status, and Criminal Arrest." *American Socio-logical Review* 35:476-490.

Grindstaff, Carl F. and Craig L. Boydell
1974   "Public Attitudes and Court Dispositions: A Comparative Analysis." *Sociology and Social Research* 58 (4): 417-426.

Grosman, Brian A.
1969   *The Prosecutor.* Toronto: The University of Toronto Press.

Haas, Jack and Bill Shafir
1974   *Decency and Deviance: Studies in Deviant Behavior.* Toronto: McClelland and Stewart, Ltd.

Hackler, James
1966   "Boys, Blisters, and Behavior—the Impact of a Work Programme in an Urban Central Area." *Journal of Research in Crime and Delinquency* 3 (July): 155-164.
1971   "A Developmental Theory of Delinquency." *Canadian Review of Sociology and Anthropology* 8 (2): 61-75.
1974   *Why Delinquency Prevention Programmes in Canada Should NOT Be Evaluated.* Edmonton: University of Alberta.

Hackler, James and John Hagan
1975   "Work and Teaching Machines as Delinquency Prevention Tools: A Four-Year Follow-Up." *Social Service Review* 49 (1): 92-106.

Hagan, John
1972   "The Labelling Perspective, the Delinquent, and the Police." *Canadian Journal of Criminology and Corrections* 14 (April): 150-165.
1973a   "Conceptual Deficiencies of an Interactionist Perspective in Deviance." *Criminology* 11 (3): 383-404.
1973b   "Labelling and Deviance: A Case Study in the 'Sociology of the Interesting.' " *Social Problems* 20 (4): 448-458.
1974a   "Extra-Legal Attributes and Criminal Sentencing: An Assessment of a Sociological Viewpoint." *Law and Society Review* 8 (3): 357-383.
1974b   "Criminal Justice and Native People: A Study of Incarceration in a Canadian Province." *Canadian Review of Sociology and Anthropology* Special Issue (August): 220-236.
1975a   "Parameters of Criminal Prosecution: An Application of Path Analysis to a Problem of Criminal Justice." *Journal of Criminal Law, Criminology, and Police Science* 65 (4): 536-544.
1975b   "The Social and Legal Construction of Criminal Justice: A Study of the Pre-Sentencing Process." *Social Problems* 22 (5): 620-637.
1975c   "Law, Order and Sentencing: A Study of Attitude in Action." *Sociometry* 38:374-384.
1975d   "Setting the Record Straight: Toward the Reformulation of an Interactionist Perspective in Deviance." *Criminology* 13 (3): 421-423.
1975e   "Explaining Watergate: Toward a Control Theory of Upperworld Crime." Paper presented at the American Society of Criminology Meetings, October, Toronto.
1975f   "Locking Up the Indians: A Case for Law Reform." *Canadian Forum* 55 (658): 16-18.

1976a   "Finding Discrimination: A Question of Meaning." *Ethnicity* forthcoming.
1976b   "Criminal Justice in Rural and Urban Communities: A Study of the Bureaucratization of Justice." *Social Forces* forthcoming.
1977   "Rethinking the Societal Response: A Review Essay on the Labelling of Deviance." In journal submission.

Hagan, John and Jeffrey Leon
1977   "Rediscovering Delinquency: Social History, Political Ideology, and the Sociology of Law." *American Sociological Review* forthcoming.

Hagan, John and John Simpson
1976   "Ties that Bind: Conformity and the Social Control of Student Discontent." *Sociology and Social Research* forthcoming.

Hammer, Muriel
1963-64 "Influence of Small Social Networks on Factors of Mental Hospital Admission." *Human Organization* 22 (Winter): 243-251.

Hanly, Charles
1970   *Mental Health in Ontario: A Study for the Committee on the Healing Arts.* Toronto: The Queen's Printer.

Harris, L.
1968   *The Public Looks at Crime and Corrections.* Washington, D.C.: Joint Commission on Correctional Manpower and Training.

Hartnagel, T. F. and Derek Wynne
1975   "Plea Negotiation in Canada." *Canadian Journal of Criminology and Corrections* 17 (1): 45-56.

Hayduk, Leslie
1976   "Formulations in Police Work: Some Observations and Related Theoretical Concerns." *Canadian Journal of Sociology* forthcoming.

Henshel, Richard L. and Robert A. Silverman
1975   *Perception in Criminology.* Toronto: Methuen Publications.

Heywood, R. M.
1972   "Community Policing." in K. C. Woorsworth (Ed.), *Report on an Advanced Seminar in Criminology,* University of British Columbia: Centre of Criminology.

Hindelang, M. J.
1970   "Learning Theory Analysis of the Correctional Process." *Issues in Criminology* 5 (1): 43-58.
1973   "Causes of Delinquency: A Partial Replication and Extension." *Social Problems* 20 (4): 471-487.
1974   "The Uniform Crime Reports Revisited." *Journal of Criminal Justice* 2 (1): 1-17.

Hirschi, Travis
1969   *Causes of Delinquency.* Berkeley: University of California Press.
1973   "Procedural Rules and the Study of Deviant Behavior." *Social Problems* 21 (Fall): 159-173.
1975   "Labelling Theory and Juvenile Delinquency." in Walter R. Gove (Ed.), *The Labelling of Deviance: Evaluating a Perspective.* New York: Halsted Press.

Hogarth, John
1971   *Sentencing as a Human Process.* Toronto: The University of Toronto Press.

1974 *East York Community Law Reform Project.—Studies on Diversion.* Law Reform Commission of Canada.

Hogg, P. W.
1974 "Equality Before the Law." *Canadian Bar Review* 52:263-280.

Honingmann, John J. and Irma Honingmann
1965 "How Baffin Island Eskimos Have Learned to Use Alcohol." *Social Forces* 44 (September): 73-83.

Hood, Roger and Richard Sparks
1970 *Key Issues in Criminology.* New York: McGraw-Hill.

Hopkins, Andrew
1975 "On the Sociology of Criminal Law." *Social Problems* 22 (5): 608-619.

Horning, Donald N.
1970 "Blue-Collar Theft: Conceptions of Property, Attitudes Toward Pilfering, and Work Group Norms in a Modern Industrial Plant." in Erwin O. Smigel and H. Laurence Ross (Eds.), *Crimes Against Bureaucracy.* New York: Van Nostrand Reinhold Company.

Horowitz, Irving Louis
1973 "The Hemispheric Connection: A Critique and Corrective to the Entrepreneurial Thesis of Development with Special Emphasis on the Canadian Case." *Queen's Quarterly* 80 (3): 327-359.

Horowitz, Irving Louis and Lee Rainwater
1970 "Journalistic Moralizers." *Transaction* 7 (7):5.

Household Survey of Victims of Crime
1970 Demographic Surveys Division, Washington, D.C.: Bureau of the Census.

Hughes, Everett C.
1951 "Work and the Self." in John H. Rohrer and M. Sherif (Eds.), *Social Psychology at the Crossroads,* New York: Harper and Brothers.
1958 *Men and their Work.* Glencoe: Free Press of Glencoe.
1962 "Good People and Dirty Work." *Social Problems* 10 (Summer): 3-11.

Humphreys, Laud
1970 *Tearoom Trade.* Chicago: Aldine Publishing Company.

Inciardi, James
1975 *Careers in Crime.* Chicago: Rand McNally.

Ingraham, Barton and Gerald Smith
1972 "The Use of Electronics in the Observation and Control of Human Behavior and its Possible Use in Rehabilitation and Parole." *Issues in Criminology* 7(2):35-53.

Jaffary, S.
1963 *Sentencing of Adults in Canada.* Toronto: The University of Toronto Press.

Jamieson, Stuart
1971 *Times of Trouble: Labour Unrest and Industrial Conflict in Canada, 1900-66.* Task Force on Labour Relations Study No. 22, Ottawa: Information Canada.

Jaspan, Norman and Hillel Black
1960 *The Thief in the White Collar.* Philadelphia: J. B. Lippincott Company.

Jeffery, C. R.
1971   *Crime Prevention Through Environmental Design.* Beverly Hills:
         Russell Sage Publications.

Jeffries, Fern
1973   *Private Policing and Security in Canada: Report of Proceedings.*
         Toronto: Centre of Criminology, University of Toronto.

Jensen, Gary
1969   " 'Crime Doesn't Pay': Correlates of Shared Misunderstanding."
         Social Problems 17 (Fall): 189-201.

Kalven, Harry and Hans Zeisel
1966   *The American Jury.* Boston: Little, Brown.

Kelling, George *et al.*
1974   *The Kansas City Preventive Patrol Experiment: A Summary
         Report.* Washington: Police Foundation.

Kelly, Delos H.
1974   "Track Position and Delinquent Involvement: A Preliminary
         Analysis." *Sociology and Social Research* 58:380-386.

Kennedy, Mark
1970   "Beyond Incrimination: Some Neglected Facets in The Theory
         of Punishment." *Catalyst* 5 (Summer): 1-37.

Kirkham, George L.
1974   "What a Professor Learned When He Became a 'Cop.' " *U.S. News
         and World Report* 76 (April 22): 70-72.

Kirkham, James, Sheldon Levy, and William Crotty
1970   *Assassination and Political Violence.* Washington: Government
         Printing Office.

Kitsuse, John I. and A. V. Cicourel
1963   "A Note on the Uses of Official Statistics." *Social Problems*
         11:131-139.

Kitsuse, John I. and David Dietrick
1959   "Delinquent Boys: A Critique." *American Sociological Review*
         24 (April): 208-215.

Klein, John and Arthur Montague
1975   "Cheque Writing as a Way of Life." In Robert Silverman and
         James Teevan (Eds.) *Crime in Canadian Society.* Toronto:
         Butterworth and Company (Canada), Ltd.

Klein, Malcolm and L. Y. Crawford
1967   "Groups, Gangs and Cohesiveness." *Journal of Research in Crime
         and Delinquency* 4:63-75.

Kobrin, Solomon
1951   "The Conflict of Values in Delinquency Areas." *American
         Sociological Review* 16 (October): 657-662.
1959   "The Chicago Area Project—A 25-Year Assessment." *The Annals
         of the American Academy of Political and Social Science*
         322 (March): 19-29.

Koenig, Daniel J.
1975   "Police Perceptions of Public Respect and Extra-Legal Use of
         Force: A Reconsideration of Folk Wisdom and Pluralistic
         Ignorance." *Canadian Journal of Sociology* 1 (3): 313-324.
1976   "Correlates of Self-Reported Victimization and Perceptions of
         Neighborhood Safety." In D. Brusegard and L. Hewitt (Eds.),

Social Indicators in Canada. Edmonton: Government of Alberta (forthcoming).

Krisberg, Barry
1972   Review of *Tearoom Trade. Issues in Criminology* 7 (Winter): 126-127.

Law Reform Commission of Canada
1974a   "The Principles of Sentencing and Dispositions." Working Paper No. 3.
1974b   "Restitution and Compensation." Working Paper No. 5.
1974c   "Fines." Working Paper No. 6.
1975   "Diversion." Working Paper No. 7.

Le Blanc, Marc
1969   *Inadaptation Et Classes Sociales A Montréal.* Montreal: Les Presses de l'Université de Montréal.
1975   "Middle Class Delinquency." in Robert Silverman and James Teevan (Eds.), *Crime in Canadian Society.* Toronto: Butterworth and Company (Canada) Ltd.

Leighton, Dorthea C. *et al.*
1963   *The Character of Danger.* New York: Basic Books.

Lemert, Edwin
1951   *Social Pathology.* New York: McGraw-Hill.
1962   "Paranoia and the Dynamics of Exclusion." *Sociometry* 25 (March): 2-20.
1967   *Human Deviance, Social Problems and Social Control.* Englewood Cliffs, N.J.: Prentice-Hall.

Leon, Jeffrey
1974   *The Oshawa Drug Study: Frequency and Patterns of Drug Use Among the Young People of Oshawa.* Toronto: Addiction Research Foundation.
1975   *Drug Related Deaths in Metropolitan Toronto.* Toronto: Addiction Research Foundation.

Lerman, Paul
1968   "Evaluative Studies of Institutions for Delinquents: Implications for Research and Social Policy." *Social Work* 13:55-64.

Letkemann, Peter
1973   *Crime as Work.* Englewood Cliffs, New Jersey: Prentice-Hall.

Leznoff, Maurice and William Westley
1956   "The Homosexual Community." *Social Problems* 3 (4): 257-263.

Linden, Eric
1976   "Religiosity and Drug Use: A Test of Social Control Theory." Paper presented at Canadian Sociology and Anthropology Association Meetings, May, Quebec City.
1977   "An Integration of Control Theory and Differential Association Theory." In journal submission.

Linden, Eric and James Hackler
1973   "Affective Ties and Delinquency." *Pacific Sociological Review* 16:27-46.

Lindesmith, Alfred
1947   *Opiate Addiction.* Bloomington, Indiana: Principia Press.

Lipscomb, W.
1959   "Mortality Among Treated Alcoholics: A Three Year Follow-Up Study." *Quarterly Journal of Studies on Alcohol* 20:596-603.

Lipset, Seymour Martin
1963   "The Value Patterns of Democracy: A Case Study in Comparative Analysis." *American Sociological Review* 28:515-531.
1964   "Canada and the United States: A Comparative View." *Canadian Review of Sociology and Anthropology* 1:173-192.
1968   *Revolution and Counterrevolution: Change and Persistence in Social Structures.* New York: Basic Books.

Logan, C. H.
1972   "Evaluation Research in Crime and Delinquency: A Reappraisal." *Journal of Criminal Law, Criminology, and Police Science* 63:378-387.

Lowe, George D. and H. Eugene Hodges
1972   "Race and Treatment of Alcoholism in a Southern State." *Social Problems* (Fall): 240-252.

Macleod, R. C.
1976   *The North-West Mounted Police and Law Enforcement 1873-1905.* Toronto: The University of Toronto Press.

Madley, John
1965   "Probation." in W. T. McGrath (Ed.), *Crime and its Treatment in Canada,* Toronto: The Macmillan Company of Canada, Ltd.

Magid, Simmie
1972   "The Evaluation of Community-Based Residential Centres." a paper prepared for the Task Force on Community-Based Residential Centres, under the supervision of Irwin Waller, Centre of Criminology, University of Toronto.

Mann, William Edward
1968   *Deviant Behaviour in Canada.* Toronto: Social Science Publishers.
1971   *Social Deviance in Canada.* Vancouver: Copp Clark.

Manzer, Ronald
1974   *Canada: A Socio-Political Report.* Toronto: McGraw-Hill Ryerson, Ltd.

Marshall, Victor and David Hughes
1974   " 'Nothing Else But Mad': Canadian Legislative Trends in the Light of Models of Mental Illness and Their Implication for Civil Liberties." in Jack Haas and Bill Shaffir (Eds.), *Decency and Deviance.* Toronto: McClelland and Stewart, Ltd.

Marshall, W. L.
1973   "The Modification of Sexual Fantasies: A Combined Treatment Approach to the Reduction of Deviant Sexual Behavior." *Behavior Research and Therapy* 11:557-564.

Martin, John
1955   *The Criminal Code of Canada.* Toronto: Cartwright.

Martin, John, Alan Mewett, and Ian Cartwright
1972   *Martin's Annual Criminal Code: 1972.* Agincourt, Ontario:
1974'   Canada Law Book Company.

Martinson, Robert
1974   "What Works?—Questions and Answers About Prison Reform." *The Public Interest* 35:22-54.

Masters, D. C.
   1950   *The Winnipeg General Strike.* Toronto: The University of Tor-
             onto Press.
Mathews, A. R.
   1970   "Observations on Police Policy and Procedures for Emergency
             Detention of the Mentally Ill." *Journal of Criminal Law,
             Criminology, and Police Science* 61:283-295.
Matthews, Victor
   1972   "Social-Legal Statistics in Alberta: A Review of their Availability
             and Significance." Edmonton, Alberta: Human Resources
             Research Council.
Matza, David
   1964   *Delinquency and Drift.* New York: John Wiley and Sons.
Mayor's Committee on Violence
   1974   *Environmental Factors Relating to Violence.* Report No. 2,
             Borough of North York.

McAuliffe, William E.
   1975   "Beyond Secondary Deviance: Negative Labelling and Its Effect
             on the Heroin Addict." In Walter Gove (Ed.), *The Labelling
             of Deviance: Evaluating a Perspective.* New York: Halsted
             Press.
McCall, George J. and J. L. Simmons
   1969   *Issues in Participant Observation: A Text and Reader.* Reading,
             Massachusetts: Addison-Wesley Publishing Company.
McCord, William, Joan McCord, and Irving Zola
   1959   *Origins of Crime.* New York: Columbia University Press.
McDonald, Lynn
   1969a   *Social Class and Delinquency.* London: Faber.
   1969b   "Crime and Punishment in Canada: A Statistical Test of the
             'Conventional Wisdom.' " *Canadian Review of Sociology and
             Anthropology* 6 (4): 212-236.
   1976   *The Sociology of Law and Order.* London: Faber.
McEachern, A. W. and Riva Bauzer
   1967   "Factors Related to Disposition in Juvenile Police Contacts." in
             Malcolm W. Klein (Ed.), *Juvenile Gangs in Context: Research,
             Theory, and Action.* Englewood Cliffs, New Jersey: Prentice-
             Hall.
McGrath, William Thomas
   1965   *Crime and its Treatment in Canada.* Toronto: The Macmillan
   (1976)   Company of Canada, Ltd.
McInnis, Edgar W.
   1942   *The Unguarded Frontier.* Garden City: Doubleday.
Merton, Robert
   1938   "Social Structure and Anomie." *American Sociological Review*
             3 (October): 672-682.
   1957   *Social Theory and Social Structure.* Glencoe: Free Press of
             Glencoe.
   1959   "Social Conformity, Deviation, and Opportunity Structures: A
             Comment on the Contributions of Dubin and Cloward."
             American Sociological Review 24:177-189.

Miller, Walter
1958   "Lower Class Culture as a Generating Milieu of Gang Delin-
        quency." *Journal of Social Issues* 14 (3): 5-19.
1962   "The Impact of a 'Total Community' Delinquency Control
        Project." *Social Problems* 10 (Fall): 168-191.

Moeller, H. G.
1974   "Community-Based Correctional Services." in Daniel Glaser
        (ed.), *Handbook of Criminology*, Chicago: Rand McNally.

Morand, Justice Donald
1976   *The Royal Commission into Metropolitan Toronto Police Prac-
        tices.* Province of Ontario.

Morris, Norval and Gordon Hawkins
1969   *The Honest Politician's Guide to Crime Control.* Chicago: Univer-
        sity of Chicago Press.

Moyihan, Daniel P.
1969   *Maximum Feasible Misunderstanding.* New York: Free Press of
        Glencoe.

Murphy, Emily F.
1920   "The Grave Drug Menace." *Maclean's Magazine* 33 (3): 1.
1922   *The Black Candle.* Toronto: Thomas Allen.

Murphy, R. J.
1969   "Stratification and Mental Illness: Issues and Strategies for
        Research." in S. C. Plog and R. B. Edgerton (Eds.), *Changing
        Perspectives in Mental Illness.* San Francisco: Holt, Rinehart
        and Winston.

Nagel, Stuart
1969   *The Legal Process from a Behavioral Perspective.* Homewood,
        Illinois: The Dorsey Press.

Nettler, Gwynn
1973   *Explaining Crime.* New York: McGraw-Hill.
1974a   "Embezzlement Without Problems." *British Journal of Crimin-
        ology* 14 (1): 70-77.
1974b   "On Telling Who's Crazy." *American Sociological Review* 39 (6):
        893-894.

Newman, Donald J.
1956   "Pleading Guilty for Considerations: A Study of Bargain Justice."
        Journal of Criminal Law, Criminology, and Police Science
        46:780-790.
1966   *Conviction: The Determination of Guilt or Innocence without
        Trial.* Boston: American Bar Association.

Newman, Oscar
1972   *Defensible Space: Crime Prevention through Urban Design.*
        New York: The MacMillan Company.

Nisbit, Robert A.
1953   *The Quest for Community: A Study in the Ethics of Order and
        Freedom.* New York: Oxford University Press.

Nye, F. Ivan
1958   *Family Relationships and Delinquent Behavior.* New York:
        John Wiley and Sons.

Nye, F. Ivan and James F. Short
1957   "Scaling Delinquent Behavior." *American Sociological Review*
        22 (June): 326-332.

Outerbridge, W. R.
1973   *Report of the Task Force on Community-Based Residential Centres.* Ottawa: Solicitor-General of Canada.

Parsons, Talcott
1951   *The Social System.* Glencoe: Free Press of Glencoe.
Piliavin, Irving and Scott Briar
1964   "Police Encounters with Juveniles." *American Journal of Sociology* 70 (September): 206-214.
Platt, Anthony M.
1969   *The Child Savers: The Invention of Delinquency.* Chicago: University of Chicago Press.
Playboy Advisor
1975   "The Alka-Seltzer Screw." *Playboy* 22 (February): 35.
Polsky, Ned
1969   *Hustlers, Beats, and Others.* New York: Anchor Books.
Popham, R. E.
1956   "The Jellinek Alcoholism Estimation Formula and its Application to Canadian Data." *Quarterly Journal of Studies on Alcohol* 17:559-593.
Porter, John
1965   *The Vertical Mosaic.* Toronto: The University of Toronto Press.
Porterfield, Austin
1943   "Delinquency and its Outcome in Court and College." *American Journal of Sociology* 49 (November): 199-208.
Powers, Edwin and Helen Witmer
1951   *An Experiment in the Prevention of Delinquency.* New York: Columbia University Press.
Price, J. E.
1966   "A Test of the Accuracy of Crime Statistics." *Social Problems* 14:214-221.

Quinney, Richard
1970   *The Social Reality of Crime.* New York: Little, Brown and Company.

Ratner, Robert
1974   Final Evaluation of the Spring Street Project. Mimeo.
Reasons, Charles
1974   "The Politics of Drugs: An Inquiry in the Sociology of Social Problems." *Sociological Quarterly* 15(3): 381-404.
Reckless, Walter C.
1961   "A New Theory of Delinquency and Crime." *Federal Probation* 25:42-46.
Reiss, Albert
1951   "Delinquency as the Failure of Personal and Social Controls." *American Sociological Review* 16:196-207.
1967a   *Measurement of the Nature and Amount of Crime.* Washington, D.C.: U.S. Government Printing Office.
1967b   *Public Perceptions and Reflections about Crime, Law Enforcement, and Criminal Justice.* Washington, D.C.: U.S. Government Printing Office.

1968   "How Common is Police Brutality?" *Transaction* July/August: 10-19.

1971a   "Systematic Observation of Natural Social Phenomena." in Hebert Costner (Ed.), *Sociological Methodology 1971.* San Francisco: Jossey-Bass Inc.

1971b   *The Police and the Public.* New Haven, Connecticut: Yale University Press.

Reiss, Albert J. and David J. Bordua
1967   "Organization and Environment: A Perspective on the Municipal Police." in David J. Bordua (Ed.), *The Police: Six Sociological Essays.* New York: John Wiley and Sons.

Reiss, Albert J. and Albert Rhodes
1961   "The Distribution of Juvenile Delinquency in the Social Class Structure." *American Sociological Review* 26 (October): 720-732.

Robins, Lee and George Murphy
1967   "Drug Use in a Normal Population of Young Negro Men." *American Journal of Public Health* 57 (September): 1580-1596.

Rock, Ronald, Marcus Jacobson, and Richard Janopaul
1968   *Hospitalization and Discharge of the Mentally Ill.* Chicago: University of Chicago Press.

Roman, Paul M. and H. M. Trice
1967   *Schizophrenia and the Poor.* Ithaca: Cayuga Press.

Rosenhan, D. L.
1973   "On Being Sane in Insane Places." *Science* 179 (19 January): 250-258.

Rossi, Peter *et al.*
1974   "The Seriousness of Crimes: Normative Structure and Individual Differences." *American Sociological Review* 39 (April): 224-237.

Rubington, Earl and Martin Weinberg
1973   *Deviance: The Interactionist Perspective.* New York: The Macmillan Company.

Sagarin, Edward
1973   "The Research Setting and the Right Not to be Researched." *Social Problems* 21(1): 52-64.

Sawchuk, Peter
1974   "Becoming a Homosexual." in Jack Haas and Bill Shaffir (Eds.), *Decency and Deviance.* Toronto: McClelland and Stewart, Ltd.

Scheff, Thomas
1966   *Being Mentally Ill: A Sociological Theory.* Chicago: Aldine Publishing Company.

Schmeiser, Douglas
1972   "Indians, Eskimos and the Law." Unpublished manuscript, Saskatoon: University of Saskatoon, University of Saskatchewan.

Schmidt, Wolfgang
1971   "The Prevalence of Alcoholism in Canada." in Craig Boydell, Carl Grindstaff, and Paul Whitehead (Eds.), *Critical Issues in Canadian Society.* Toronto: Holt, Rinehart, and Winston of Canada, Ltd.

Schmidt, Wolfgang and J. de Lint
    1969   "Mortality Experiences of Male and Female Alcoholic Patients."
               Quarterly Journal of Studies on Alcohol 30:112-118.

Schmidt, Wolfgang, Reginald Smart, and Maria Moss
    1968   *Social Class and the Treatment of Alcoholism.* Toronto: The
               University of Toronto, Addiction Research Foundation
               Monograph No. 7.

Schur, Edwin
    1973   *Radical Non-Intervention: Rethinking the Delinquency Problem.*
               Englewood Cliffs, New Jersey: Prentice-Hall.

Schwartz, Richard and Jerome Skolnick
    1964   "Two Studies of Legal Stigma." in Howard Becker (Ed.), *The
               Other Side: Perspectives on Deviance.* New York: Free Press
               of Glencoe.

Schwendinger, Herman and Julia Schwendinger
    1967   "Delinquent Stereotypes of Probable Victims." In M. W. Klein
               and B. Meyerhoff (Eds.), *Juvenile Gangs in Context.* Engle-
               wood Cliffs, New Jersey: Prentice-Hall.

Schwitzgelel, Ralph K.
    1971   *Development and Legal Regulation of Coercive Behavior Modifi-
               cation Techniques with Offenders.* Washington: U.S. Govern-
               ment Printing Office.

Scott, P. D.
    1956   "Gangs and Delinquent Groups in London." *British Journal of
               Delinquency* 7:4-26.

Seeley, John, with R. A. Sim, and E. W. Loosley
    1956   *Crestwood Heights.* Toronto: The University of Toronto Press.

Sellin, Thorsten
    1937   *Research Memorandum on Crime in the Depression.* New York:
               Social Science Research Council, Bulletin 27.
    1938   *Culture Conflict and Crime.* New York: Social Science Research
               Council.

Shallo, J. P.
    1933   "Private Police." Philadelphia: The American Academy of Polit-
               ical and Social Science.

Shearing, Clifford
    1973   "Dial-A-Cop: A Study of Police Mobilization." Toronto: Centre
               of Criminology, University of Toronto.

Shearing, Clifford and Jeffery Leon
    1974   "The Police Image." Paper presented at the Canadian Sociology
               and Anthropology Association Meetings, August, Toronto.

Sherman, Lawrence, Catherine Milton, and Thomas Kelly
    1973   *Team Policing: Seven Case Studies.* Washington: Police Founda-
               tion.

Short, James, Ramon Rivera and Ray Tennyson
    1965   "Perceived Opportunities, Gang Membership, and Delinquency."
               American Sociological Review (February): 56-67.

Short, James and Fred Strodtbeck
    1965   *Group Process and Gang Delinquency.* Chicago: University of
               Chicago Press.

Silverman, Robert and James Teevan
    1975   *Crime in Canadian Society.* Toronto: Butterworth and Company
            (Canada), Ltd.

Simmons, J. L.
    1969   *Deviants.* Berkeley: Glendessary.

Skogan, Wesley
    1975   "Measurement Problems in Official and Survey Crime Rates."
            Journal of Criminal Justice 3:17-32.

Skolnick, Jerome
    1966   *Justice Without Trial: Law Enforcement in a Democratic Society.*
            New York: John Wiley and Sons.

Smart, R. G. and D. Fejer
    1971   "The Extent of Illicit Drug Use in Canada: A Review of Current
            Epidemiology." in Craig Boydell, Carl Grindstaff, and Paul
            Whitehead (Eds.), *Critical Issues in Canadian Society.* Toron-
            to: Holt, Rinehart, and Winston of Canada, Ltd.

Smart, R. G., D. Fejer, and J. White
    1970   "The Extent of Drug Abuse in Metropolitan Toronto Schools:
            A Study of Changes from 1968 to 1970." Toronto: Addiction
            Research Foundation.

Smart, R. G. and D. Jackson
    1969   "A Preliminary Report on the Attitudes and Behavior of Toronto
            Students in Relation to Drugs." Toronto: Addiction Research
            Foundation.

Smigel, Erwin and H. Laurence Ross
    1970   *Crimes Against Bureaucracy.* New York: Van Nostrand Reinhold
            Co.

Smith, Kathleen, Muriel Pumphrey, and Julian Hall
    1963   "The 'Last Straw': The Decisive Incident Resulting in the Re-
            quest for Hospitalization in 100 Schizophrenic Patients."
            American Journal of Psychiatry 120 (September): 228-232.

Smith, Michael D.
    1975   "The Legitimation of Violence: Hockey Players' Perceptions of
            their Reference Groups' Sanctions for Assault." *Canadian
            Review of Sociology and Anthropology* 12 (1):72-80.

Snider, Laureen
    1976   "Corporate Crime in Canada: A Preliminary Report." Paper
            presented at the Canadian Sociology and Anthropology
            Association Meetings, Quebec City.

Snow, Frances L.
    1901   *Snow's Annotated Criminal Code of Canada.* Montreal: Snow
            Law Publishing Company.

Stanley, George F.
    1961   *Louis Riel: Patriot or Rebel?* Ottawa: Canadian Historical Associ-
            ation.

Stebbins, Robert A. and Colin Flynn
    1974   "Police Definitions of the Situation: Evaluation of a Diploma
            Program in Law Enforcement and Community Relations."
            Paper presented at the Canadian Sociology and Anthropology
            Association Meetings, August, Toronto.

Stinchcombe, Arthur
   1963   "Institutions of Privacy in the Determination of Police Administrative Practice." *American Journal of Sociology* 69 (2): 150-160.
   1964   *Rebellion in a High School.* Chicago: Quadrangle Books.

Suchman, Edward A.
   1968   "The Hang-Loose Ethic and the Spirit of Drug Use." *Journal of Health and Social Behavior* 9 (2): 146-155.

Sudnow, David
   1965   "Normal Crimes: Sociological Features of the Penal Code in a Public Defender Office." *Social Problems* (Winter): 255-276.

Sutherland, Edwin
   1924   *Criminology.* Philadelphia: J. B. Lippincott Company.
   1945   "Is 'White Collar Crime' Crime?" *American Sociological Review* 10:132-139.
   1961   *White Collar Crime.* New York: Dryden.
   (1949)

Swimmer, Gene
   1974   "The Relationship of Police and Crime: Some Methodological and Empirical Results." *Criminology* 12 (3): 293-314.

Sykes, Gresham and David Matza
   1957   "Techniques of Neutralization: A Theory of Delinquency." *American Sociological Review* 22:664-670.
   1961   "Juvenile Delinquency and Subterranean Values." *American Sociological Review* 26:712-719.

Tannenbaum, Frank
   1938   *Crime and the Community.* Boston: Ginn.

Tappan, Paul W.
   1947   "Who is the Criminal?" *American Sociological Review* 12 (February): 96-102.
   1960   *Crime, Justice and Correction.* New York: McGraw-Hill.

Tarnopolsky, W. S.
   1971   "The Canadian Bill of Rights from Diefenbaker to Drybones." *McGill Law Journal* 17:437-475.
   1975   "The Canadian Bill of Rights and the Supreme Court Decisions in *Lavell* and *Burnshine:* A Retreat from *Drybones* to *Dicey?*" *Ottawa Law Review* 7 (1): 1-33.

Taylor, Ian, Paul Walton, and Jock Young
   1973   *The New Criminology: For a Social Theory of Deviance.* London: Routledge and Kegan Paul.

Teevan, James
   1972   "The Deterrent Effects of Punishment: The Canadian Case." *Canadian Journal of Criminology and Corrections.* 14 (1): 68-82.

Tepperman, Lorne
   1977   *Crime Control: The Urge Toward Authority.* Toronto: McGraw-Hill Ryerson, Ltd.

Terry, Robert M.
   1965   *The Screening of Juvenile Offenders: A Study in the Societal Response to Deviant Behavior.* University of Wisconsin: Unpublished Ph.D. dissertation.

Thornberry, Terrence P.
  1973   "Race, Socioeconomic Status and Sentencing in the Juvenile
            Justice System." *Journal of Criminal Law and Criminology*
            64:90-98.
Thornton, Leonard M.
  1975   "People and the Police: An Analysis of Factors Associated With
            Police Evaluation and Support." *Canadian Journal of Soci-
            ology* 1 (3): 325-342.
Thraser, Frederic M.
  1937   *The Gang.* Chicago: University of Chicago Press.
Timasheff, Nicholas S.
  1949   *Probation in the Light of Criminal Statistics.* New York: D. X.
            McMullen Co.
Time
  1968   "The Thin Blue Line." 92 (19 July): 39.
Tittle, Charles R.
  1969   "Crime Rates and Legal Sanctions." *Social Problems* 16 (Spring):
            409-423.
  1975   "Deterrents or Labelling?" *Social Forces* 53 (3): 399-419.

Toby, Jackson
  1957a   "Social Disorganization and Stake in Conformity: Complemen-
            tary Factors in the Predatory Behavior of Young Hoodlums."
            Journal of Criminal Law, Criminology and Police Science
            48 (May-June): 12-17.
  1957b   "The Differential Impact of Family Disorganization." *American
            Sociological Review* 22 (October): 505-512.
  1974   "The Socialization and Control of Deviant Motivation." in Daniel
            Glaser (Ed.), *Handbook of Criminology.* Chicago: Rand-
            McNally.
Toronto Star
  1974   "Evel Knievel: The $6 Million Man." *Toronto Star* (7 September):
            A7.
Towle, Charlotte
  1973   *Common Human Needs.* London: Allen and Unwin.
Transcripts
  1974   *The Presidential Transcripts.* New York: Dell.
Trasler, Gordon
  1962   *The Explanation of Criminality.* London: Routledge and Kegan
            Paul.
Tribble, Stephen
  1972   "Socio-Economic Status and Self-Reported Juvenile Delin-
            quency." *Canadian Journal of Criminology and Corrections*
            14:409-415.
Turk, Austin T.
  1969   *Criminality and the Legal Order.* Chicago: Rand McNally.
  1976   "Law, Conflict, and Order: From Theorizing toward Theories."
            Canadian Review of Sociology and Anthropology 13(3):
            282-294.
  1977   *Political Criminality and Political Policing.* Unpublished manu-
            script.

U.S. Department of Justice
  1975   *Criminal Victimization Surveys in 13 American Cities.* U.S. Government Printing Office.
Urban Social Redevelopment Project
  1970   "Social and Mental Health Survey, Montreal, 1966 Summary Report." in W. E. Mann (Ed.), *Poverty and Social Policy in Canada.* Toronto: Copp Clark.
Vallee, F. G.
  1962   *Kabloona and Eskimo in the Central Keewatin.* Ottawa, Ontario: Northern Coordination and Research Centre, Department of Northern Affairs and National Resources.
van den Steenhoven, Geert
  1957   *Legal Concepts among the Netsilik Eskimos of Pelly Bay, N.W.T.* Canada: Department of Northern Affairs and National Resources, Northern Co-ordination and Research Centre.
Vaz, Edward
  1962   "Juvenile Gang Delinquency in Paris." *Social Problems* 10:23-31.
  1965   "Middle-Class Adolescents: Self-Reported Delinquency and Youth Culture Activities." *Canadian Review of Sociology and Anthropology* 2 (1): 52-70.
  1966   "Self-Reported Delinquency and Socio-Economic Status." *Canadian Journal of Criminology and Corrections* 8:20-27.
  1967   *Middle Class Juvenile Delinquency.* New York: Harper and Row.
  1976   *Aspects of Deviance.* Scarborough: Prentice-Hall of Canada, Ltd.
Veblen, Thorsten
  1967   *The Theory of the Leisure Class.* New York: Viking Press.
  (1899)
Vold, George
  1958   *Theoretical Criminology.* New York: Oxford University Press.
Von Hoffman, Nicholas
  1970   "Sociological Snoopers." *Transaction* 7 (7): 4.
Wahl, Albert and Daniel Glaser
  1963   "Pilot Time Study of the Federal Probation Officer's Job." *Federal Probation* 27 (September): 20-25.
Wallace, John A.
  1974   "Probation Administration." in Daniel Glaser (Ed.), *Handbook of Criminology,* Chicago: Rand McNally.
Waller, Irvin
  1974   *Men Released from Prison.* Toronto: The University of Toronto Press.
Waller, Irvin and Janet Chan
  1975   "Prison Use: A Canadian and International Comparison." *Criminal Law Quarterly* 47-71.
Wallerstein, James S. and Clement Wyle
  1947   "Our Law-Abiding Lawbreakers." *Probation* 25 (April): 107-118.
Weeks, H. Ashley
  1958   *Youthful Offenders at Highfields.* Ann Arbor: University of Michigan Press.
Weiss, Carol H.
  1970   "The Politicization of Evaluation Research." *Journal of Social Issues* 26:57-68.

Westley, William
    1953   "Violence and the Police." *American Journal of Sociology* 59 (July): 34-41.

Wheeler, Stanton, Edna Bonacich, Richard Cramer, and Irving K. Zola
    1968   "Agents of Delinquency Control." in Stanton Wheeler (Ed.), *Controlling Delinquents*. New York: John Wiley and Sons.

Whitehead, Paul and Reginald Smart
    1972   "Validity and Reliability of Self-Reported Drug Use." *Canadian Journal of Criminology and Corrections* 14 (1): 83-89.

Wilkins, James L.
    1972   "Due Process Safeguards and Canadian Criminal Justice." *Criminal Law Quarterly* 14(2): 220-235.

    1975   *Legal Aid in the Criminal Courts*. Toronto: the University of Toronto.

Wilkins, Leslie T.
    1958   "A Small Comparative Study of the Results of Probation." *British Journal of Delinquency* 8:201-209.

    1964   *Social Deviance*. London: Tavistock Publications.

Wilkinson, Karen
    1974   "The Broken Family and Juvenile Delinquency: Scientific Explanation or Ideology." *Social Problems* 21 (5): 726-739.

Williams, J. Ivan, Kathryn Kopinak, and W. David Moynagh
    1972   "Mental Health and Illness in Canada." in Craig Boydell, Carl Grindstaff and Paul Whitehead (Eds.), *Deviant Behavior and Societal Reaction*. Toronto: Holt, Rinehart, and Winston of Canada, Ltd.

Wilson, James Q.
    1968a   "The Police and the Delinquent in Two Cities." in Stanton Wheeler (Ed.), *Controlling Delinquents*. New York: John Wiley and Sons.

    1968b   *Varieties of Police Behavior*. Cambridge: Harvard University Press.

    1973   "Foreword." in Lawrence Sherman, Catherine Milton, and Thomas Kelly (eds.), *Team Policing*. Washington: Police Foundation.

    1974   "Do the Police Prevent Crime?" *New York Magazine*, October 6:18.

    1975   *Thinking About Crime*. New York: Basic Books.

Wolfgang, Marvin
    1958   *Patterns of Criminal Homicide*. Philadelphia: University of Pennsylvania Press.

Wolfgang, Marvin and Franco Ferracuti
    1967   *The Subculture of Violence*. London: Tavistock Publications.

Wolfgang, Marvin and Marc Riedel
    1973   "Race, Judicial Discretion, and the Death Penalty." *The Annals of the American Academy of Political and Social Science* 407 (May): 119-133.

Wynne, Derek and Tim Hartnagel
    1975a   "Plea Negotiation in Canada." *Canadian Journal of Criminology and Corrections* 17 (1): 45-56.

1975b   "Race and Plea Negotiation: An Analysis of Some Canadian Data." *Canadian Journal of Sociology* 1 (2): 147-155.

Yablonsky, Lewis
1959   *The Violent Gang.* New York: The Macmillan Company.

Yinger, J. M.
1960   "Contraculture and Subculture." *American Sociological Review* 25:625-635.

Zay, Nicolas
1963   "Gaps in Available Statistics in Crime and Delinquency in Canada." *Canadian Journal of Economics and Political Science* 29 (February): 75-89.

Znaniecki, Florian
1934   *The Method of Sociology.* New York: Rinehart and Company, Inc.

INDEX